Walking the Way Together

So thankful that our paths have crossed!

Walking the Way Together

How Families Connect on the Camino de Santiago

KATHLEEN E. JENKINS

OXFORD
UNIVERSITY PRESS

OXFORD
UNIVERSITY PRESS

Oxford University Press is a department of the University of Oxford. It furthers the University's objective of excellence in research, scholarship, and education by publishing worldwide. Oxford is a registered trade mark of Oxford University Press in the UK and certain other countries.

Published in the United States of America by Oxford University Press
198 Madison Avenue, New York, NY 10016, United States of America.

Library of Congress Control Number: 2020047727

ISBN 978-0-19-755305-3 (pbk.)
ISBN 978-0-19-755304-6 (hbk.)

DOI: 10.1093/oso/9780197553046.001.0001

1 3 5 7 9 8 6 4 2

Paperback printed by Marquis, Canada
Hardback printed by Bridgeport National Bindery, Inc., United States of America

Contents

Acknowledgments

I am forever grateful for the pilgrims who welcomed me into their Camino journeys and who shared and trusted me with their family stories. This book would not have been possible without their voices. *Walking the Way Together* was also shaped in large part by people who have dedicated many years to helping pilgrims: Stephen Shields, John Rafferty, Rebekah Scott, and Nancy Frey, all of whom welcomed me into their homes and shared sacred practices. The efforts of these volunteers, pilgrim guides, and friends inspired my exploration of the nature of spiritualities in pilgrimage experience. Maria Loureiro and Ivar Rekve provided friendship, listened to my research plans, gave advice, and helped me to find spaces to work and write in Santiago. Thank you to Maria Loureiro and her colleagues at the University of Santiago de Compostela who offered office space and faculty affiliation during the spring of 2017, and to Miguel Taín Guzmán at the University of Santiago for inviting me to speak at the annual summer conference dedicated to the study of the Way of Santiago as I was completing this book.

Support from my colleagues and funding from my home institution were critical in making this research possible. George Greenia introduced me to the Camino and pilgrimage studies and offered guidance, encouragement, and friendship throughout the process. My work was supported by a Plumeri Award and Arts & Sciences funds at William & Mary, monies that were essential in my ability to travel to Spain and complete this ethnography. I am especially grateful for my colleagues on the Leadership Committee of the Institute for Pilgrimage Studies at W&M: in particular, Ben Boone, James Barber, Brennan Harris, George Greenia, and Barbette Spaeth. I must also acknowledge the enormous influence of the scholars I have met over the years who have attended our Institute of Pilgrimage Studies yearly symposium, pointing me to new literature, perspective, and ways of understanding. Our scholarly community at the Institute represents the power of interdisciplinary approaches to research and teaching.

A number of individuals have been key in helping me write this book. Thank you to Cynthia Read and the anonymous reviewers at Oxford University Press for their editorial feedback and efforts. Emerson Ives and

Manon Murray, W&M undergraduate sociology majors, both worked as research assistants organizing and coding data. Ben Boone helped me make contacts with families in Santiago and collected informal interviews. Ken Chih-Yan Sun helped shape the analysis I present in Chapter 4. Gul Ozyegin carefully read and commented on each chapter and provided advice and inspiration in the final stages of this book. Several other colleagues and friends have read and commented on drafts and related articles, including George Greenia, Ben Boone, Nancy Frey, Kathleen Slevin, and Jennifer Bickham Mendez. Debra Osnowitz offered advice on a number of writing and editing issues and picked up the phone to answer my questions and listen whenever I needed grounding. Debbie Eck provided constant administrative support as I served as the chair of the Sociology Department, allowing me to carve out time to collect data and write. My family has been an integral part of this project: my daughter Kathryn Lerman, a recent W&M graduate ('19), worked with me on final versions of the text, organizing endnotes and references and reading through chapters with a careful editorial eye. My mother, Beverly Olsen, also a W&M graduate ('59), has read each chapter twice and offered valuable editorial feedback. My stepbrother, Erik Olsen, gave editing advice on the final manuscript. My son, Martin Katzoff, contributed the etchings and drawings that are represented throughout this text. My daughter Jackie Lerman offered culinary creations and music that comforted me throughout this process. Thank you to my husband, Mark Lerman, who walked with me in Spain, and cared for our family in the United States as I spent time away on Camino paths and volunteering and interviewing pilgrims in Santiago.

Prologue

On a warm night in June, Katy, her father, José, and I sat outside on a plaza in the medieval city of Santiago de Compostela, the capital of Galicia, an autonomous region of Spain. That evening, in the height of the tourist season, the city was full of pilgrims and local residents walking on stone streets lined with cafés, restaurants, hotels, and tourist shops. In the heart of the city stood the Cathedral of Santiago de Compostela and the crypt of St. James, the end point for many of these pilgrims who had walked for weeks on Camino de Santiago routes. The tables outside restaurants and cafés were full of people. We could hear children playing in a nearby town square as we sat with our gin and tonics, cured meats, bread, and olives. Three months earlier, Katy's mother had answered a call for participants that I had posted on the Camino Forum website. She put me in touch with her husband and daughter, who agreed to contact me when they finished walking the Camino de Santiago. As I answered their questions about my research, their attention turned to a young woman walking toward us. Katy explained that she had walked with them some of the way and they had gotten to know each other. They waved for her to come over and introduced me.

I hesitated, knowing that it would be polite to invite their pilgrim friend to join us at our table, and yet wanting to be alone with this father and daughter to focus on their Camino story. José and Katy, sensing the awkward moment, told me not to worry and that they would see her later. It seemed that they too wanted to talk without interruption.

"How did you learn about the Camino?" I asked.

José answered first. "I went first with my wife several years ago. We are a Catholic family, so we know about the Camino, but my wife is more Catholic than I am and went to every pilgrim Mass in the evenings and I went with her. My daughter went to Catholic school but . . ."

Katy added: "I'd say I'm a spiritual person, but not a religious person."

José continued:

> On my first Camino with my wife, I prayed for a miracle. I was praying for a miracle to happen to be reunited with my son. We had not talked in a long time and my ex-wife, it was a bad situation. So, I was praying on the trip for some miracle, and when I got back home, I asked my priest what I should do to reunite with my son and he said, "It begins with you." So, I called my younger son and asked if he would ask my older son, the one I hadn't seen, if he would come at Christmas to see us. And he did and the older said yes for Christmas and at that time we talked, and I asked him to walk the Camino with me. He said yes. And so, the Camino miracle, it doesn't happen so suddenly, because I had to come home and act, and he acted too. He was thirty-three by then and in walking the Camino, we became friends.

"You wanted to go with your daughter too?" I asked.

"This Camino is for her, she is my youngest, my baby. She would ride on my shoulders with me, go everywhere. She would go fishing with me and ride everywhere in the car with me to go places, run errands. So Katy, my baby, she is different. We are already close."

Katy offered another motivation: "I have anxiety, and so the Camino I was hoping could help me."

"Yes," José added, "anxiety runs in my family, so she gets it from me. Anxiety, you know, it is the fear of the unknown, and I think from her studying to be a doctor, she can see how vulnerable human bodies are, what germs can do."

The look on Katy's face suggested that she did not agree with her father's assessment, and she said nothing about her anxiety relating to her medical studies. Instead, she commented that her father was protective and careful to keep track of her while they were walking: "He wanted to protect me while we were walking so he always knew where I was if we weren't walking together."

José explained, "I didn't want her to walk alone. Mom made me promise to keep an eye on her."

"Well," Katy said, "there was that girl last year."

The three of us nodded in mournful recognition. A Spanish man had lured a young woman off the Camino with arrows pointing the wrong way and killed her. Pilgrims had been talking online about it and debating whether it was safe for women to walk alone.

José said, "You never know what can happen. You can break an ankle, or the weather could get in your way somehow. I always kept her in sight—even if I was walking behind."

Katy added, "He took care of me too. He had all the stuff to take care of my blisters: he carried the Compeed [gel plasters for healing blisters], and as a doctor, he would put it on my feet and helped other people too."

She lifted up a foot to show me evidence of her painful sores, and then we talked for a while about the experience of walking for hours each day with blisters.

Given that Katy said she was more spiritual than religious, I asked, "Did you find the Camino was a spiritual walk for you?"

She paused, and I quickly came to realize that I had asked a difficult question. Her eyes teared up.

"I was afraid I would cry about this. I really feel cheesy saying this, but . . ."

"You don't have to tell me if you don't want to."

"No, no, I want to," she assured me.

José leaned in toward the table, signifying he wanted to listen carefully to what his daughter had to say about spirituality. I sensed his deep affection for Katy in his loving and concerned gaze. We, father and interviewer, waiting patiently as she paused and prepared to speak. Katy then told us the story of what happened to her at the Hospital of the Soul, a Camino event that she told me was the most "spiritually" filled moment in her life.

> I had some energy left after walking all day, so I went out to see the town we were in. I saw this building with a bike outside of it and flowers and it

said, *Hospital of the Soul*. It had music playing, a nice backyard and a place to make tea, meditation pillows, and photos on the wall with quotes that I read. It said not to take pictures of anything. So I didn't.

I just sat on a pillow after looking around for a while. There was nobody there. I felt calm. So calm. I stayed there like that for about forty-five minutes and felt detached from things . . . and then had this [her eyes teared up again] . . . spiritual experience, not religious, it's hard to explain, but where you feel the presence of God. I was in this room where there was no talking and no phones and no picture taking, and it was the first time in my life where I felt like I was alone, where I felt peace.

It was so amazing I went back to find the friend we had been walking with for a few days; I wanted to show her the place. I found her and took her back, but it had changed. She brought her camera and phone and we were talking to each other and she wanted to take pictures. So, she took pictures and then I took pictures too. I took pictures of the quotes on walls.

[Katy showed us a photo of a black sign with white letters that read: El engaño fundamental de la humanidad es suponer que yo estoy acqui y tu estás alli afuera.

The fundamental mistake of humanity is to suppose that I am here and you are there.]

And the room was different. I didn't feel anything like before. Being by myself there, I think that was what made it spiritual.

When she finished telling her story, I asked Katy and her father broad questions about how technology impacted their Camino, as I did with every pilgrim I interviewed: What kind of technology did you bring? How did you use it? Katy began to talk about how disturbed she was by her attachment to her phone. She saw it as a source of her anxiety. She said, "I wish I hadn't brought my phone. I would have been talking with more people on the Camino." She went back and forth, voicing the pros and cons of having her phone with her and being able to access Wi-Fi in most cafés and lodging points along the French Way: "I was all over all the media—Instagram, Twitter, Facebook, I posted maybe seven times a photo to Instagram. I have to admit I like the likes. And the phone was good because it did actually help when I was homesick."

Katy and José showed me some of the pictures they had taken; Katy pointed out the ones she had shared on Instagram for her followers. She showed me her most recent post, an image of father and daughter with backpacks in front of the Cathedral of Santiago de Compostela.

José said, "I have to show you what happened one day!"

Katy moaned, "Are you going to show the video, Dad? Don't show the video." He did, and it was loud, but because people regularly shared videos and photos at café tables, our behavior did not stand out. It was a humorous video of cows walking through the street as Katy and José were trying to cross the road, and of bikers trying to make their way through the animals. We laughed—even Katy, who had tired of the visual memory.

Toward the end of our time together at the café, José, referring to Katy's experiences of feeling peace at the Hospital of the Soul and being truly alone with the presence of God, said, "That is why the Camino, it was worth every penny."

Katy said she was afraid that she would not be able to experience that feeling in her daily life, and added, "I wish I could feel that again. I don't know how. I don't know how to stay away from it [social media] and worrying about what people say. Do you know how to? What do you think?"

"I don't know," I replied. I could sense that she saw me as some kind of an expert who might have an answer. "I don't have any answers," I said. "I'm trying to understand more about how to manage it too." I did share with her, given that we were toward the end of our interview, that many of the pilgrims I had met talked about making a concentrated effort to have tech-free time, and that I tried to do that in my own life and gave the same advice to my three children and my students at William & Mary.

"What I learned walking," Katy said, is that "it's okay not knowing the answer, sometimes the Camino teaches you—over time. It develops, takes a while to happen, but you can learn to just be still. To be by yourself. I did feel peace one other time on the Camino. It was at one of the Pilgrims' Masses when the priest looked at each of us and blessed us, but he wasn't fast. It was like he really stopped and looked at each of us and took his time."

José reminded us both again how it had taken time for his first Camino with his wife to bring its purpose: much time passed before his son agreed to walk the Camino with him and they reconciled their differences. Maybe it would take the passing of time for Katy, he suggested, to learn how to recall that spiritual energy, to be able to claim ritual practices that would bring the kind of feeling of peace and being alone with God that she experienced at the Hospital of the Soul.

We spoke a little longer about what they would do in Santiago that evening and the next day. As our time together at the café ended, our phones buzzed on the table. Katy sent me photos, and she received texts and notifications from other pilgrim friends who were gathering to celebrate that evening in the city.

Introduction: Seeking Connection

My encounter with José and Katy captures the heart of *Walking the Way Together*: stories of families investing in the Camino de Santiago as a practice for building relational intimacy, and the social forces and spiritual encounters that supported and inhibited these goals. José and Katy's decision to walk was a commitment they hoped would bring them closer to understanding each other's emotional and religious/spiritual worlds, as well as providing them time to grow as individuals *together* and to experience meaningful relationships with other pilgrims. This commitment surfaced in my fieldwork with most of the families I met while on various Camino routes and in Santiago de Compostela. Their expectations were formed from Camino books, films, and online presentations suggesting that personal transformation and deep connection between pilgrims who walk together are inevitable rewards. José, like several family members I interviewed, also drew from previous memories of walking the Camino and the relational changes they understood as born from those experiences.

The family members I came to know brought a range of issues and concerns to their expectations of the Camino. Some walked with the hope of healing together from deep relational wounds, such as a death in the family or a divorce-related conflict. Others saw their Camino time as a rare

Walking the Way Together. Kathleen E. Jenkins, Oxford University Press (2021). © Oxford University Press.
DOI: 10.1093/oso/9780197553046.001.0001

opportunity to be with each other when parents were still physically able and young adults were not yet overcome by work and family responsibilities. Many desired to escape together from everyday attachments to technology and social media, to share a mystical experience uninterrupted by digital ties. Combined, their stories represent a range of understandings about spiritual experience in our contemporary world: spirituality as realized through close relationships, spirituality as caring for others, spiritual practice as engaging in the natural world, and for some, spiritual ritual as connection to a Divine force.

Researchers have suggested that sharing religious/spiritual practices and beliefs can build family intimacy, through acquiring deep personal understandings and developing relational bonds. Gaining such a window into family members' spiritual lives and identity may indeed have the potential to strengthen bonds with kin.[1] However, scant research has explored how families might experience such connection outside of the institutional walls of religion. Most of the scholarship that addresses families and shared practice in religious communities focuses on younger children and teens. We know little about how parents and young adult children might engage spirituality together, and how they might find meaning in memories of such shared mystical experience.[2]

This book offers a rare in-depth ethnographic perspective of the motivations, aspirations, and perceived successes and failures of families who traveled from North America, Western Europe, and other points across the globe to walk long distances together on Camino routes. It is my interpretation of the stories that parents and their sons and daughters (ages eighteen to twenty-eight) told me, individual and co-constructed accounts that illustrate the choices they faced in planning their journey and investing time and resources into the Camino's transformative promise. They are narratives of pleasant surprises, disappointments, lessons learned, and the far-reaching emotional power that the memory of ritual failures and successes can carry.

Walking the Way Together, however, is not exclusively about the Camino or extended walking pilgrimage. The family stories in this book reflect larger social, economic, and technological forces at work in early twenty-first-century family life in Western cultures. Parents and young adults in the first decades of the twenty-first century have experienced the rapid encroachment of digital worlds into their everyday lives, blurring the boundaries between family life and work as well as changing how family members share conversation and reflective thoughts.[3] Contemporary families in Western culture also feel the pressure of a therapeutic culture that values self-work and emotion-work in the service of intimate others. Parents feel the weight of expectations to help young adult children build emotional strength for future success in careers and relationships, and young adults hold fast to the idea that self-work in various forms will help them be competitive, retool, and build emotional fortitude in an economy with increasing employment insecurities and rising costs of living.[4] The majority of parents and young adults with whom I spoke embraced a set of beliefs about family relationships that see kin as strongest when they are both alone and together in these therapeutic pursuits: family members as ideally able to succeed in life as strong individuals, but who are also mutually supportive and deeply aware and present together.[5] They understood the Camino as a practice and sacred space that could help them achieve these therapeutic ideals.

The stories of parents and their young adult children in *Walking the Way Together* are those of families who had the resources and means to travel long distances to walk routes of the Camino de Santiago in search of family connection and individual growth. Most of them understood the exceptional nature of their travel to Spain and acknowledged their economic privilege in a world where some can pursue individual and family wellness and leisure with ease, yet most struggle to feed and house their families. In fact, many of the privileged parents and adult children with whom I spent time were drawn to the Camino, in part, for the shared experience of developing a sense of spiritual connection to humankind and a commitment to helping those less fortunate. They were passionately drawn to the Camino's promise of leveling social positions and roles. Such attempts to push aside difference led to new kinds of relationships with family members, as well as fresh bonds with new pilgrim friends, described by many as kin—their "Camino family." The Camino was a strategy for coming to know family members in a deeper way through challenging physical and emotional experiences and for sharing spiritual purpose through adopting together an ethical position of inclusivity and embracing difference—of forging deeper connections with the world and its people. Taken together, their stories provoke consideration of how walking pilgrimage may be understood as an engaged spiritual practice driven by hopes for bettering social relationships, local communities, and the world.

The Camino de Santiago

The Camino de Santiago, as with other Christian pilgrimages, can be traced to the Middle Ages as an enthusiastic practice for people across all levels of society. The most favored sites were Jerusalem, Rome, and Santiago de Compostela, all tomb cults in the ancient Mediterranean model—the grave sites of sacred figures thought by many to reach down and assist the living. The Church of the Holy Sepulcher in Jerusalem was held to be the site where Jesus rose from the dead. The burial places of the martyred apostles Peter and Paul dignified Rome, and at the opposite extreme of the known world stood Compostela and the tomb of James, the only other apostle of the New Testament whose burial site was in Europe. These premodern journeys could be short or long and were often motivated by a specific need. Sacred travelers sought a closer relationship to God, forgiveness for past sins, a cure for some disease, or perhaps a divine favor: "Can I be justified as a child of God? Will my leprosy be cleansed? Will we be granted a son or daughter?" Today the Camino de Santiago (in English, the Way of St. James, or just the Way), like many pilgrimages, may entail religious motivations, but it is widely understood in a broader way as a *spiritual* experience.[6]

Pilgrimage to Jerusalem and Rome persisted through the ages, at least in the form of site visitation, and millions still journey to those places in wonder and expectation, but there is a striking difference that marks the contemporary Camino de Santiago. Since the 1980s, the custom is to actually *walk* the ancient trails to get there. The trickle of travelers on foot who persisted after ancient times strengthened in the late nineteenth and twentieth centuries, first as random clusters and then modest droves. Numbers swelled toward the end of the last century, prompted by believers, scholars, adventurers, and cultural and religious tourism, and then exploded in the first two decades of this century, due in part to the growth of film, media, and digital technologies that fueled knowledge of the practice and the multiple options for lodging and assistance while walking.

Camino paths closed due to COVID-19 in the spring of 2020, but in 2019 347,578 people came to the official Pilgrim's Office, run by the Cathedral of Santiago, to claim a certificate of completion. In 2004, 179,944 pilgrims arrived in Santiago at the Pilgrim's Office. Of those, about 56 percent were men and 44 percent were women. The majority of pilgrims in 2004 were from Spain, with 2,028 from the United States and 1,090 from Canada. Most of these pilgrims walked on the popular Camino Francés (138,646). By 2016, the overall number of pilgrims checking in at the Pilgrim's Office had reached 277,854, with about 52 percent men and 48 percent women. Of these, 15,236 were from the United States and 4,354 from Canada. In 2017 the number of pilgrims rose to 301,036, and by 2018, 327,378 received documents of completion.[7] While these statistics represent a substantial increase, many skip this ceremonious gesture, with perhaps an additional 100,000 using portions of the public trails without arriving in the city of Santiago at all.

In the 1970s, Galician parish priest Elías Valiña Sampedro began mapping Camino routes with symbolic shells and yellow arrows that led to the growth of accommodations along the best-known marked path, the Camino Francés (French Way).[8] This route begins in St. Jean Pied-de-Port in France and ends about 780 km later in Santiago. Contemporary pilgrims can start anywhere on any Camino route, and many declare their true launch point as simply their front door, but those on foot must complete the 100 km into Santiago at minimum if they wish to receive the Compostela, the Catholic Church's document of welcome and blessing. Some pilgrims march on to the rocky promontory of Finisterre, which overlooks the boundless Atlantic, their pilgrimage halted in the face of the infinite. Finisterre has grown in popularity as both a second spiritual terminus of one's Camino journey and, like Santiago, a tourist destination.[9]

Camino discourse is shaped through local Spanish cultural and religious organizations, a growing Camino cinema, online forums, and published narratives, and it promotes an expectation of transformation through a spiritual experience. Many modern pilgrims to Santiago long for this spiritual journey, less scripted by a single church these days, but still potent. Katy was raised in a Catholic household, but like many of the families with whom I spoke, it was identification as a spiritual person that shaped her narrative of walking together with her father. Some, like Katy, described this expectation of a spiritual experience on the Camino using theistic language, an understanding of peace that came from feeling closer to God. For others, whether raised in a religious/spiritual tradition or not, spirituality and mystical encounter were more about connection to nature and people. Almost all of the pilgrims I encountered understood spiritual practice as an ethical call to care physically and emotionally for family and strangers. Walking Camino paths offered a structured way for the family members with whom I spoke to experience a variety of types of spiritual encounters together.

The Study

I was first introduced to the Camino in 2012 through a study-abroad program at William & Mary that I organized with my colleague George Greenia. George is an accomplished medievalist, a scholar of pilgrimage, and a dedicated pilgrim who has walked Camino routes on more than twenty occasions. I did not expect to study families on the Camino; instead, I saw the trip primarily as a way to teach students how to observe the social world using sociological methods. But during that first summer-abroad teaching experience with George, I worked closely with a student on a research project about mothers who walked the Camino. I began to think about the extensive emotional labor and family work that went into women taking young children on the Camino or leaving them at home. I also talked to parents walking with their young adult children and became interested in how they articulated the extraordinary nature of walking together, the challenges they faced, and at times the painful emotional conversations they shared. Many of these family members were marking graduation from high school or college; some had a desire to reconcile after years of separation, and others talked of healing from family dynamics of divorce; a few had started walking with a family member but along the way, for various reasons, had separated. I met a number of young adults who spoke of a lack of direction or purpose regarding educational or career goals, or of striving to overcome some form of anxiety or depression. My sociological imagination led me to want to know more about how family members came to walk with each other, how they found value in a shared commitment to the practice, and what meaning their memories of walking Camino paths held for them.

The following year, I began formally interviewing parents and their young adult children (ages eighteen to twenty-eight) who had walked Camino routes together for at least a week. I also continued talking with families informally about their experiences and taking detailed field notes while walking Camino routes and spending time in Santiago. I read more family blogs, making sure to get access, if possible, to the online journals and Facebook postings of the families I interviewed. I also began to read and think critically about the books that pilgrim families consulted before traveling to Spain, and the films they said were influential in their decision-making and planning. At the same time, I was intrigued by the research emerging from scholars across disciplines exploring this increasingly popular pilgrimage/cultural tourism practice, and the importance that spirituality and biography played in motivations for contemporary pilgrimage.[10] As I was designing a research plan and approach, I went back several times to Nancy Frey's 1998 book *Pilgrim Stories: On and Off the Road to Santiago*, an exemplary ethnography of thick description, a careful uncovering of the Camino's webs of meaning that illustrates how pilgrims were able to encounter and live in a structure that was removed from everyday time and relational responsibilities.[11] Comparing her account to what I observed, I was struck by how the contemporary Camino was deeply shaped by technology and by changes in social interactions and infrastructure over the last twenty years that appeared to have eroded opportunities for being, as Frey would put it, "out of time."

In the end, I collected more than one hundred informal field interviews, seventy-eight structured interviews from forty-one family cases, and ten Camino blogs and private family travel photo journals, primarily from those I formally interviewed. My formal interview sample was obtained through advertisements on Camino forum sites and nine months (across four years) interacting with pilgrims on the Camino and in Santiago. All of the people I interviewed gave informed consent, and the majority of interviews were in English. I have changed the names of the people involved, and in a few cases details of Camino interactions or background, to protect confidentiality.

Seven cases involved father/daughter pairs, fourteen were mother/daughter pairs, eight were father/son pairs, and four were mother/son pairs. The remaining cases involved larger family groups: three groups of a mother with two daughters; one group of a mother, daughter, and son; and one group of a mother and two sons. Three cases involved two parents walking with two or more young adult children. Twenty-two of these formal cases were from the United States, and nineteen from other countries: three from Australia, three from Canada, two from Spain, three from the Netherlands, three from Ireland, and single cases from the United Kingdom, Germany, Sweden, South Africa, and the Philippines. Most of the parents I interviewed were professionals or had the resources and time to travel; one parent from a lower socioeconomic status had saved for over two years to make the trip possible. Twenty-two identified as Catholics and as both religious and spiritual, sixteen as Protestants, one as Anglican, one as Pagan, one as Buddhist, thirty-four as spiritual, and three as not religious or spiritual. As I suggested earlier, regardless of religious/spiritual identification, almost all family members saw potential in the Camino to bring what they named as a spiritual experience.

I interviewed some parents and adult children together, at first out of necessity during field studies, but as I started to see how these co-authored family stories reflected the shaping of a spiritual intimacy between family members, I purposely gathered more parent-and-child interviews in Santiago. I wanted to know more about the construction of these shared memories and their purpose, and how families managed contradictions as they told me about their Camino experience. Katy, for example, asserts that she is a spiritual and not religious person, as elaboration on her father's naming of their family as Catholic. The importance of this more complex Catholic identity is revealed through her story of the Hospital of the Soul, a significant spiritual memory that emerges in their co-constructed narrative of Camino connection and purpose. Overall, the people I interviewed reflect diversity in how stories were told (as individuals or families recounting together), length of trip (anywhere from approximately one to five weeks), the Camino path they walked (e.g., French Way, English Way, Portuguese Way), when they told their story (on arrival in Santiago or after their return home), and family composition. Such diversity gave me distinct vantage points for coming to understand the different types of spiritual practices that families saw as impactful and the dynamics of ritual memory.

I formally interviewed families in the field as they finished the Camino, or via FaceTime/Skype or phone within approximately one year after return. With respondents' permission, I recorded and transcribed phone and FaceTime/Skype interviews. Phone interviews were approximately an hour, but when I spent time with families or individual family members in Santiago, as I did with Katy and José, we generally spent two hours or more talking over coffee, drinks, or a meal. I also kept a detailed field log of informal interviews and all encounters with pilgrims and the Camino culture. My identity in the field as both a pilgrim and a researcher helped in building trust and connection with pilgrims.

Like most ethnographies, there are strengths and limitations regarding claims based on the research. For the formal interviews, I spoke with those pilgrims who agreed to tell me their story, a group that likely consisted of people who felt they had stories about family experiences that were about connection. I was able, through participant observation walking Camino routes, spending time in Santiago, and working two summers as a volunteer at the Pilgrim's Office, to talk with pilgrims who agreed to participate in the research by telling me brief stories of walking with family members that were, to them, unsuccessful attempts to connect with each other. I also cannot say whether everything people told me actually happened to them on the Camino, nor can I make any concrete assessment of whether the family experiences they had have carried over into their everyday lives, but that is not my purpose. The ethnographic goal is to capture how they understood their journeys and the meaning they found in these experiences. In other words, what is important is how they made sense of and represented their Caminos and the sacred weight they gave to them.

I make sense of their stories using my sociological toolkit: in particular, a systematic inductive approach that seeks to produce new theory through empirical analysis informed by existing sociological theories.[12] Randall Collins's (2004) work provides concepts for my exploration of the social implications of ritual energy, memory, and spiritual connection. Sociologist Nancy Ammerman's (2013) research about discourses of spirituality has helped me articulate the multiple understandings of spirituality voiced by the pilgrims with whom I spent time. In addition to Nancy Frey's work, I use the work of pilgrimage scholars Daniel Olsen (2016), Ian McIntosh (2018), and others who have produced empirical studies that address the contradictions and demands of pilgrimage in a contemporary world deeply shaped by cultural tourism and digital technologies. Scholars, students of sociology and culture, and other readers wishing to engage more deeply with the theory and methods that shaped my analysis and interpretations may choose to read the endnotes and methods appendix, which offer a more in-depth description of my ethnographic method, methodology, and the analytical process that unfolded over six years.

The Book

In chapter 1, "Planning the Mysterious," I illustrate how parents and their young adult children approached making decisions about how they would walk the Camino together and the role that guidebooks, published pilgrims' narratives, and online sites played in their Camino expectations and design. I highlight the abundance of choices they faced regarding hospitality, travel, and digital products, and describe how, through familiar mechanisms of buying family leisure time, they pursued the Camino's call to be open to the unknown and its promise of sacred connection to others, nature, and mystical encounter.

In chapter 2, "Camino Promises," I interpret family members' expectations of the Camino as a spiritual practice that could bring miracles, life lessons, and individual and relational healing through spiritual encounter. I detail how they expected the Camino to be a pilgrimage space where they could develop the kind of shared bond between pilgrims that Victor Turner (1969) spoke of as *communitas*: the leveling of social relationships and expectations in a time and place away from the everyday that brought them into shared meaning with other pilgrims. This chapter illustrates the Camino promises they sought and how they are related to the multiple ways people talk about spirituality and its effects in our contemporary world.

In chapter 3, "Spiritual Intimacies," I illustrate how family members' expectations played out in their descriptions of the Camino experience. I underscore how their stories matched the self-searching, relational connection, and caring expectations found in larger cultural therapeutic understandings and expectations of family intimacy. While not all family members achieved their goals and expectations, almost all who agreed to talk with me told stories of shifting understandings of each other that involved connection and/or becoming individuals through practice together. In this way, their Camino stories demonstrate a larger archetype of travel for transformation: they were narratives of journeying through a space that brought change to their everyday relationships upon their return home. In this chapter, I also underscore the salience of gender as it relates to the type of spiritual intimacy parents described.

In chapter 4, "Intimacy and Disciplining Technology," I turn to families' stories of managing technology so that it did not undermine their Camino expectations, and also describe how they used technology to stay connected while traveling and become closer.[13] Many of the family members I interviewed negotiated and reflected, before and as they walked, on their use of smartphones, tablets, and computers. Family members described creating the time and space away from digital devices to self-reflect and come to know each other as spiritual co-practitioners. In this chapter, I demonstrate how the Camino presented, in compressed form, complicated relational and individual habits regarding digital technologies.

In chapter 5, "Connective Memories," I illustrate how families constructed recollections of spiritual intimacy that had the potential to shape new experiences of intimacy upon their return home from the Camino. Here I draw from Randall Collins's (2004) work on the character and function of the emotional energy at work in ritual life as I demonstrate how pilgrims talked about particular forms of ritual memories that held emotional weight—symbolic recollections of spiritual intimacy that brought change to how they understood and lived family identity.[14] I describe three types of distinct and at times overlapping connective memories family members talked about as significant: *quiet memories*, storied and sensory memories that are generally more private and shared with intimate others; *digital memories*, photographs and other media forms of constructed memory; and *material memories*, printed photographs, symbolic objects like jewelry, a pilgrim's stamped credentials, and Camino tattoos. I also discuss how types of memory can manifest in the form of *distancing memories*, negative ritual emotional memory with the potential to sever feelings of family/group identity and solidarity with others and nature.

In the Conclusion, "Engaged Spiritual Sensibilities," I argue that the stories in this book are about people working to strengthen family relationships, but that in many cases they also represent shared discovery of commitment to an ethic of care for those outside of their intimate circles. I stress how most parents and their adult children recognized their privilege and expressed a desire for their Camino experience to translate to daily interactions with distant others and contemplation of larger social problems. At the same time, I underscore how distancing memories demonstrated a potential to undermine such effects. I suggest that their stories, taken as a whole, push us to think more deeply about the social forces that stand in the way of positive outcomes related to engaging in practices such as the Camino. I identify how various institutions and individual actors have worked to promote inclusivity in opportunities for travel for transformation in North America. I pay attention as well to spiritual inequalities, highlighting differences in the United States regarding access to spiritual practices that may foster relational intimacy, and suggesting actions for building opportunities and promoting understanding of social inequities and injustices.

The choices these family members faced on their Camino journeys reflect options that many of us encounter in our everyday lives: how to balance self-focused spiritual consumption with efforts to help others and engage in critical reflection about social problems in local and global communities. My hope is that the stories I relate in this book can be a catalyst for readers from various backgrounds to consider how they might invest in creating time and structures that make travel for transformation opportunities more inclusive; such investment may open new spaces for families to move through the world in ways that encourage self-reflection and awareness of their relationship with others.

1
Planning the Mysterious

> Welcome the unknown, keep an open mind and heart, let go expectations and feel the freedom to be found along this ancient pilgrim path.
>
> —Brierley 2018: 7

I met Maia, a twenty-four-year-old woman from the United States, in the summer of 2013 as she was leaving the Pilgrim's Office in Santiago after walking for two weeks with her parents, who were in their early sixties, and her twenty-one-year-old younger brother. Maia had first walked the Camino with a study-abroad program in college. Her parents had been moved by their daughter's descriptions of her Camino, in particular how she had bonded with people from across the world and experienced the culture and natural landscape in Spain. As a Catholic family, they were also invested in the religious ritual of making a pilgrimage to Santiago de Compostela, and so they talked with their daughter about the possibility of the family walking together. Maia was excited to share the Camino practice with her parents and brother.

Maia noted that it was the ideal time for them to engage in such a long journey, as her father was just retiring as an executive and both of her parents

Walking the Way Together. Kathleen E. Jenkins, Oxford University Press (2021). © Oxford University Press.
DOI: 10.1093/oso/9780197553046.003.0001

were still physically able to walk several hours each day. In addition, Maia had just finished graduate school and her brother, who was twenty-one, had graduated from college earlier that May. It could be the last summer, she stressed, that she and her brother would be free from work obligations that could stand in the way of taking three weeks to travel together. She called their Camino "priceless time" and the "first time in ten years" that the family had had a vacation without other family or friends, a time when they could be "goofy" and "funny together" and not "hide from each other." When I interviewed her father, Kyle, he stressed this rare window of time as well: "Maia was just completing her master's degree and starting an internship. My son was finishing his senior year of college and we didn't know where he would be the next year, so we decided, 'Let's do this!' And we picked out sixteen days right after they got out of school."

Once all agreed that the family would walk together, Maia knew, based on her previous experience of walking the Camino, that she would need to make smart choices about how they should approach the journey. She talked about compromising her own opinions about the ideal way to walk in order to choose what was going to work for her family, and putting effort into planning how her parents and brother could interact to promote the most intimacy: "I sort of designed it, shifted who was walking with who so that we could all get to know each other better." Maia mapped out their approach with her father:

> We put together a plan of where we were going to stay because I knew I would have to compromise the traditional pilgrimage like I had before in the *albergues* [pilgrim's hostels]. Dad was really into the planning and we worked on the battle plan for the trip on a whiteboard. He is a type-A planner personality like me, likes to have everything planned out. The opposite of my mother.

Sally, Maia's mother, also recalled during her interview that her husband had been in charge of planning:

> He was our main planner. I mean, he had his nose in that guidebook the whole time. He had it charted. We had a big whiteboard in our dining room with red pins at the places we were going to stop each night, then all these pictures of the things we might see while there and different options, so for several months it was there. As time went along, we decided that we would

> divide it up and each person would pick stops and places to stay, so everybody got about three nights their way.

Kyle talked about how helpful the guidebook was for coming up with a plan: "We used the Brierley book to set up, stage by stage, the distance we would walk each day. We started hiking more and more to prepare and enjoyed it, and then we started buying all the paraphernalia."

Maia said that when they practiced their ten-mile walks together at home they filled their backpacks with carefully calculated weight for each person. Despite this effort, Maia sighed, her mother's backpack was "seven pounds heavier" when they left for Spain; it had "created matter!"

Kyle described the extensive efforts in sharing planning:

> Another cool thing we did, and it was my wife's idea, was that everybody invested in the planning for this. We had a couple of family meetings and said, all right, here's what we are thinking about hiking here and where we are going to stop each day. We said, okay, everybody gets three nights for where we want to stay and it's up to you to have a couple of places to stay in mind, where we're going to sleep, and figure out where we're going to eat and do the research on the little towns we will be in.

Even though they discussed how many hours they would walk each day, the towns they would stop in, and the kind of lodging they wanted to secure, they made sure not to be burdened in advance with reservations for lodging in order to leave room for the unexpected. Maia described a fortuitous encounter with hospitality early on their Camino that shaped their eventual approach:

> We tried to find a nice albergue the first night, but it was so full we had to go to our second-choice albergue, and there were only two beds for my parents, so I was like, yes! They didn't have to sleep outside. My mother was like, where are you guys going? We didn't sleep outside either; we ended up at Miguel's albergue, the guy folks talk about with the claw hand, and it was a bit out-there of an albergue. They had a communal meal and Mom and Dad came to have the communal meal. Miguel woke us up at six a.m. with a Gregorian chant and then nineties pop music. I was worried then that all the planning would fall apart, but it didn't, we made hotel reservations after that a day ahead. I was sweating it that night: is this plan we made really

going to work? But that night with Miguel and that communal dinner was one of our best nights on the Camino.

Making reservations "a day ahead" gave them some confidence in securing lodging, but also a level of freedom to adapt to what their Camino might bring. In fact, they did experience serious unexpected problems. Sally suffered a knee injury after walking for several days, and so the family worked together to adjust their plans for their route and how they would complete the Camino. Other pilgrims, the owners of the hostel where they were staying when Sally's injury grew unbearable, and a local cab driver made sure Maia's mom got the care she needed. As I discuss in the final chapter of this book, Kyle's memories of these unexpected encounters with selfless strangers were about profound shared family spiritual moments. Walking through a rural path in Galicia with his kids as his wife bused ahead to the next town, he was overcome by the beauty of the landscape and the people of Galicia, and how lucky he was to have his family. Maia said this was one of the few times in her life that she saw her father cry, standing with her in a state of awe as they gazed at the farmland and hills in the distance.

In planning for their Caminos, many of the parents and young adults with whom I spoke, like Maia's family, were doing the relational labor of connecting and thinking together about how they wanted to approach the walk, setting spiritual goals, and talking with each other about their expectations, fears, and desires. Most were familiar with John Brierley's popular Camino guidebook that calls for people to welcome the unknown and let go of expectations. Most of the family members I encountered also took this advice to heart, welcoming the spiritual, cultural, and physical encounters and challenges they might face. However, this did not keep them from spending time together planning walking routes, where to stay, and what they would carry on their backs. An abundance of online resources for purchasing Camino package plans, making advance reservations, and listening to advice posted on Camino websites made this relational work not so different from the strategies they used to plan other vacations and activities. They were families with resources and access to a flourishing spiritual marketplace with online assistance in designing individual and family trips to wellness spas, health retreats, amusement parks, and other historical, cultural, and spiritual/religious tourist locations.[1] The Camino was one opportunity for mystical transformation among a sea of others that encouraged careful forethought.

Sources of Inspiration and Design

> Once we decided to do it, I said okay, let's do it in two years, I saved money . . . then I started reading more about it and I got some books and started reading about it in books and we started doing some research about it and then we found the Forum [www.caminodesantiago.me/community], and that helped. It was nice for us to be able to ask questions and get answers on it. Any questions that we had.
>
> —Allie, mom from the United States

When I asked family members how they came to walk the Camino and if they did any kind of preparation, the majority told stories of serious efforts planning and gathering information. They did not have to look far for guidance: a wealth of online resources and printed texts helped them decide which route they would take, what items they should include in their backpack, goals for how much their backpack should weigh, whether to make reservations ahead for lodging, and even what kind of spiritual preparation they could do. Beginning their journey with some basic knowledge and strategy gave family members confidence that they would be ready to welcome the unexpected individual or relational discoveries that might lie ahead.

As Maia's story indicates, securing family time was an important first step in negotiating and designing their Camino. This was especially so for families outside of Western Europe who needed to set aside larger blocks of time for travel. Many of the parents with whom I spent time were professionals whose occupations offered flexible work hours and the ability to complete essential work online while traveling. Securing time away from other family and work obligations—and, for many of the young adults, time away from educational pursuits and/or new career opportunities—demanded forethought as well.

Securing time meant consideration of each family members' stage of work and educational life, obligations, opportunities, and time limitations. Parents generally paid for most of the trip. Only a handful of the young adults were at a point in their lives where they were supporting themselves. Most were in undergraduate or graduate school and so were still somewhat dependent on their parents. Parents and young adults told stories of seizing, as several put it, a "window of opportunity" where both parent(s) and adult children were free to travel. One mother advised that parents who want to do the Camino with their children should just "grab those moments." She explained: "When they're off in college they have vacation times and once they get out in the real world they don't—you know—they get a couple of weeks of vacation time and they are going to spend it with you? If they have a significant other, it's unlikely that you are going to get it, other than a holiday or something like that." Victoria (twenty-three), from Canada, who walked with her sister, McKenzie (twenty-two), and her mother, Lauren (fifty), planned their trip around a celebration of their graduations from graduate school: "We wanted to do this as a celebration for both of our graduations. . . . We started planning two years in advance and we set a date. . . . We aligned our schedules, which was challenging to do." Jan (fifty-eight), a lawyer from the Philippines who traveled with her husband, Marcus (late fifties), and their daughter Sue (twenty-eight), noted that they were able to walk the French Way from St. Jean to Santiago because she and Marcus both had breaks in their employment and Sue was "in between college graduation and the kind of work that she could want to do for the next stage of her life." In a few cases, to accommodate schedules, parents or young adult children would walk longer routes and their family member would join them for a week or two of walking.

Nancy Frey writes in her 1998 ethnography of the Camino that "pilgrims begin to shape their journeys well before they leave the front door" and that they do this in individual ways. Some "plan and prepare the journey for years," and "others may find themselves unexpectedly on their way to their starting point several days or a month after first hearing about it" (47–48). Pilgrims may prepare spiritually and physically, coordinate time to walk with vacation time, plan routes, and decide on what they will carry in their backpacks. Frey notes they may turn as well to friends who have walked, clergy, "Friends of the Camino" associations, or books and articles to make these preparations and decisions. Many of the Americans Frey met in the 1990s had been inspired by a Smithsonian article, "The Long, Sweet Road to Santiago de Compostela" (Winchester 1994), and others by Paul Coelho's ([1987] 1995) book *The Pilgrimage*. Writing later in 2017, Frey documents a rise in information available to pilgrims: "Since the mid- to late 1990s and especially from the year 2000 on, the amount of information available on every conceivable aspect of the Camino is remarkable" (9). Indeed, the family stories I heard reflect an abundance of guidebooks, resources, and inspirational fictional and nonfictional depictions of Camino experience. Several of the family members

I interviewed did reference Coelho's text, but in the early twenty-first century, it was Emilio Estevez's (2010) movie *The Way*; John Brierley's guidebook, *A Pilgrim's Guide to the Camino de Santiago: Camino Francés–St. Jean Roncesvalles* (first published in 2003 and in its sixteenth edition in 2019); and the Camino Forum (www.caminodesantiago.me/community/) that were dominant points of knowledge. In addition, families accessed a growing stream of online Camino websites and travel blogs, sifting through advice and following others' Camino journeys as they contemplated their own.

An evangelical Christian family from the United States talked of first learning about the Camino through watching the movie *The Way* as a family and being immediately taken by the idea that they should do the Camino. When I interviewed this family together in a café one morning over breakfast, the second day after they finished the Camino, the mother (fifty-one) said that, as Christians, they had high expectations of the Camino as a spiritual journey that would bring some kind of individual and family discovery. In planning the details of their trip, one daughter, Tammy (twenty), said that they read "lots of blogs and did a lot of research," and that they had extended discussions together about how long they should walk and which route they wanted to take. They developed a "spreadsheet" with weights on it (reminiscent of the battle plan that Maia and her father constructed) to determine how light they could make their backpacks. The father, Brad (fifty-two), bought four books and "circulated them" among the family: Kevin Codd's (2008) *To the Field of Stars: A Pilgrim's Journey to Santiago de Compostela*, Bill Walker's (2011) *The Best Way: El Camino de Santiago*, Brierley's updated guidebook, *A Pilgrim's Guide to the Camino de Santiago*, and the English version of the popular *Losing and Finding Myself on the Camino de Santiago*, by German author Hape Kerkeling (2009). Brad thought it was important for the family to read books about the Camino to prepare and take the journey seriously.

Families mentioned other texts as influential in inspiring a family Camino and directing their planning. Todd (sixty), a divorced father from Canada who walked with his son Richard (twenty-eight), talked of first becoming aware of the Camino while at his gym one "Saturday morning, listening to CBC radio," where he heard an interview with Julie Kirkpatrick, who wrote *The Camino Letters: 26 Tasks on the Way to Finisterre* (2010). Todd bought the book and said it "made complete sense as a means to walk and spend time with Richard." He then turned to "other books online, the Camino Forum, and people who had blogged." Todd identified as a "planner" who organized and orchestrated his time with his son: "I plan, and he [Richard] shows up on the day and says let's go. That's how he's always been in his life."

Natalie (fifty), a Catholic woman from the United States who walked with her daughter Nell (twenty-one), described conceiving and planning their trip as a religious and spiritual process. The "Holy Spirit," she said, is a force that pulls people together. She described being at a wedding where the priest, as he was speaking about love, held up a copy of *To the Field of Stars: A Pilgrim's Journey to Santiago de Compostela*, by the American Catholic priest Kevin Codd. He then talked about a pilgrimage practice that Nell and Natalie had "never heard of before." *To the Field of Stars* is one of many Camino travel narratives published at the turn of the century as the number of pilgrims walking increased dramatically and pilgrims began to publish more personal, reflective journals. The book follows Codd's journey and encounters with other pilgrims, describing challenges and lessons he learned. Natalie and Nell bought the book, read it, discussed it together, and decided to travel to Spain to walk the Camino. In fact, the book was so influential in their spiritual intent and planning that they brought it with them to Spain, carried it with them on their Camino, and read passages aloud to each other each night.

Books that inspired and shaped family members as they designed their Caminos fell into several categories: personal Camino narratives, spiritual and religious Camino literature, and travel guidebooks. These types are not mutually exclusive. John Brierley's *A Pilgrim's Guide to the Camino de Santiago: Camino Francés–St. Jean Roncesvalles*, frequently updated with new maps and photos to capture the changing landscape and help pilgrims plan routes, determine terrain for the day, and find hostels and other forms of accommodations available in each town, is also peppered with inspirational spiritual thoughts to help pilgrims as they prepare for the Camino and while they are walking. For example, Brierley titles sections "Mystical Path" and "Personal Reflection." Some families mentioned referencing and carrying other guidebooks as well, but the Brierley book was the most-used guidebook for the English-speaking pilgrim families I encountered while walking Camino routes and spending time in Santiago. Peter, a sixty-five-year-old father from Australia and repeat Camino pilgrim who had just walked with his twenty-three-year-old son Mike, demonstrates the popularity of Brierley as a Camino celebrity. Peter sent me a photo of the "John Brierley Room" in an albergue where Peter had slept during an earlier Camino: "I actually slept in that room. I slept in the room where John Brierly slept." The frequency with which family members mentioned the importance of this guidebook in planning, and the number of families who read and engaged his "Mystical Path" and "Personal Reflection" sections, speaks to the importance of Brierley's voice in their strategies and expectations of what the Camino could bring, which I address in more depth in chapter 2.

Family members also talked about learning from following online travel blogs. Camino Facebook pages offered numerous windows into other pilgrims' experiences. Brad's wife, Ellie, said that not only had she read other blogs as she conducted research for their trip for about a year before they left, but that she started blogging as well about how their family planning was taking shape. The rise of such digital journaling and its importance as representations of the Camino journey and as a source of advice in online space grew significantly from 2012 to 2017, as I was conducting my research. Cristina Ogden (2016), who studies Camino blogs, captures bloggers' intent to offer advice to those considering pilgrimage. She notes a 2013 entry where a blogger writes that "his entries about his various pilgrimages 'are aimed toward friends and family, but also future pilgrims who one day will travel these paths'" (82).

Victoria, the young woman from Canada who walked with her mother, Lauren, and her sister, McKenzie, on the northern Primitivo route, said that upon hearing about the Camino, she "immediately got online and purchased some books and watched the movie *The Way*." She added, "You must hear that a lot in your research," noting that pilgrims she met while walking talked with her about the movie's influence on their decision to do the Camino.

"Yes, I do," I told her.

Victoria added that her mother also "did her research" and shared her findings with her daughters about paths other than the French Way, that there were "many different ways you can walk."

When I interviewed Lauren, she told me that as they were planning, she would "send each of them [her daughters] something" when she found new information on sites like the Camino Forum. Her daughters were away at university while they planned and so much of the conversation about their pending trip happened via phone and online. The daughters immediately "jumped on board" when presented with the movie, *The Way*, but also stayed engaged with Lauren during the entire planning process.

Victoria said the three of them, after their initial research, "had a little conference and decided that, number one," they "were up for the physical challenge of doing the tougher route [Primitivo] and that it was much more beautiful and fewer people did it." After that point in their planning, she said, their Camino became a kind of "family dream."

Over half of all the family members I formally interviewed named the movie *The Way* as inspiration for walking, which is not surprising given the film's family-centered storyline: a father carries the ashes of his son who died attempting the Camino, spreading them as he walks the paths his son had planned to travel. The movie becomes not just about the father's journey of grieving but about a reconciliation of his strained relationship with his son, fueled by his own realization about what life can bring outside of his professional occupation and upper-middle-class lifestyle. The father, Martin Sheen's character, comes to the Camino with no preparation and is warned by officials at the beginning of his journey in France that he is not "prepared" to walk. But the father invites the unexpected. Armed with the backpack that his son had carefully assembled, he faces challenges with a Camino guidebook in hand and knowledge conveyed by characters he meets along the way. This film was the spark that first led Maia's father, Kyle, to the Camino, and his wife, Sally, had watched it and wanted them to do it together one day as a couple. One Methodist mother, Bess (fifty-one), from the United States, talked about the Camino and *The Way* in relation to a "God sighting": "Once I watched the movie and saw what it was about, I started checking for flights online. It was totally meant to be—my daughter had just graduated from college, so it was like a graduation gift to her, but the strange part about it was that, not that I struggle that much for money, but, flights are really expensive and I got online with my American account and I had enough miles that both of us could fly for free!" Mitch (fifty-one), a father from the United States who walked with his son William (twenty), told me he met Emilio Estevez in person, and that when he shared with Emilio how much he loved the movie, Emilio told him, "You should walk it!"

Young adults mentioned *The Way* as well as inspiration for walking, generally having watched it on recommendation from their parents. Jim (forty-seven), a stepfather from the United States who walked with his wife (forty-six), Sheri, and her daughter Anita (twenty-two), said he learned about the film while in an airport, "rummaging through Netflix." He watched it and then "presented it to the family." Ann (fifty), from California who walked with her daughter Hannah (twenty-three), said: "I watched the movie and decided that I wanted to do that walk. And then the most incredible thing happened. She [Hannah] watched it once with me and then watched it alone a couple of months later and was so moved and said, 'Mom, that's going to be your birthday present. I don't know when, but we are going to do it,' she said."

There were other films and documentaries that families named as influential in planning their Caminos as well. For example, some were motivated by a Dutch documentary television series. Sophie (twenty-two), from Amsterdam, who walked with her mother, Danielle (fifty), said she found a Dutch Camino documentary that encouraged her to walk and presented the Camino as a place that would bring her into conversation with "just people, no matter their age." One mother from Holland, Kirsten (forty-nine), who had walked once with her daughters, Amy (twenty-three) and Sarah (twenty-five), and another time with just her younger daughter, Sarah, said that she had watched a Dutch documentary series years ago, which marked the beginning of her catching what she called the Camino "virus." Families mentioned other documentaries as well that brought them to the Camino with their family member. Rene (fifty-three), a mother from Australia who walked with her son Tom (twenty-two), said she first learned about the Camino through the movie *The Way*, but invited her son to watch the 2014 documentary *Walking the Camino: Six Ways to Santiago* with her when it was showing in a local movie theater. After seeing this film, her son began to encourage their Camino.

How families planned their trip and who ultimately took charge of the organizing varied. At times a parent took control of most details; in other cases it was the young adult child who made most of the arrangements and decisions. In twenty-eight family cases, like Maia's story earlier, parents and children made joint efforts in planning and preparing. In most cases, both parents and young adults played some role, discussing together about how far they would walk each day, where they would stay, which routes they would walk, and what kind of weight they would carry. Several parents, like Natalie and Nell, talked about the planning for the trip as purposeful in itself. Sally said: "Now that we are back, and it is the fall, I am missing something. We spent so much time planning for it that it seems like an emptiness here now."

For those families who lived close to one another in everyday life, walking together to condition bodies before traveling to Spain became a part of their planning. Like Jan, many of these family members had read Brierley's advice about physical preparation before walking the Camino: "It is always advisable to put in some physical training before you go. I would be surprised if more than 10% of pilgrims actually act on this advice" (20). Jan's research involved Brierley and "nine other books" that encouraged family walks together at home before departure: "Six months before we began the Camino, I would walk more than nine kilometers two or three times a week—just city walking. My daughter doesn't like city walking, so she did not begin walking with us until a month and a half before the Camino. We did a seventeen-kilometer and a seven-kilometer uphill plus seven-kilometer return, all with loaded backpacks." Kyle, Maia's father, mentioned the Brierley book as helpful as well in encouraging an early walking practice: "We used the Brierley book to set up stage by stage the distance we would walk each day. So we started hiking more and more to prepare and enjoyed it."

Jan and Maia's family, like most of my respondents, also "joined forums on the Camino." The most popular one mentioned by family members was the English-language Camino website The Camino Forum, started by Ivar Rekve. The Forum invites questions and conversation among future and veteran Camino pilgrims and provides links to various resources and services. Given that I had placed an advertisement on this site for my study, it makes sense that many of those I interviewed had accessed this site for resources. But almost all English-speaking pilgrims I encountered on Camino routes and in Santiago had heard of and visited the Forum at some point before and/or during their trip. Pilgrims from the Netherlands and from Germany had also spent time on German or Dutch sites. Questions about whether one should walk the Camino without training, how not to get blisters and how to treat them if you do, how to plan daily routes and distances to walk, and the best time of the year to go are some of the dominant categories found on Rekve's Forum. Ellen, a sixty-two-year-old Catholic mother who walked with her sixty-year-old husband, twenty-year-old-son, and twenty-five-year-old daughter, talked about "lurking on the Forum to get information about which walks would be less populated," and then using Brierley's book to help plan exact routes that she fashioned on cards for the family to carry: "We walked differently and so I made them cards so we would know where we are going every night. The deal was you could walk with anybody you wanted, walk by yourself, go faster, slower, just end up every night, this is where we end up; and it turned out we were never out of sight of one another. We would walk sometimes in twos, sometimes in fours, you know, sometimes in ones."

As is true with most forms of contemporary leisure and hospitality, the planning and securing of a Camino experience—in particular, turning to online guides, engaging expert knowledge, and seeking advice from other travelers—were strategies that parents and their young adult children used in organizing meaningful family travel.[2] Tripadvisor, MapQuest, and other online platforms were somewhat routine digital tools that enabled families to search through the Camino marketplace with ease for accommodations and services that fit family budgets.

Engaging the Camino Marketplace

The Camino, other than the plane ticket to Europe for those in North America, was a fairly affordable vacation for most of the families I interviewed. Lodging and food, as many of them put it, were cheap. A Camino day could cost anywhere from approximately 25 euros for lodging and food to over 100 euros in towns with higher-end hotels and restaurants. The Camino is not alone in its commercialization of sites of pilgrimage. Religious/spiritual tourist sites across the globe offer a number of products, entertainment, and hospitality options.[3] For example, a simple google search reveals a number of travel services and options for the Islamic pilgrimage, the hajj, experiences that can range from modest accommodations to five-star hotels in Mecca. Few popular contemporary pilgrimage settings are untouched by socioeconomic status hierarchies that result from consumer choice and local business entrepreneurs marketing of the sacred. The stories I heard of families planning Camino journeys illustrate how Camino marketplace choices played a role in shaping their pilgrimage experiences.

Stuff

Pilgrims talk about shedding mental issues and concerns as part of their Camino preparation, but letting go of the everyday also included the material stuff of their everyday lives. At the same time, many of the books and resources that families read suggested a number of purchases for their Camino: backpacks, water bottles, pants, shorts or "shants" (pants that unzip at the knee), lightweight tops and undergarments that can be washed easily and will dry hanging overnight, trusted shoes or boots, a warm fleece top and in colder months a lightweight jacket, a foldable rain poncho that can cover the backpack, walking sticks or poles, a sleeping mat and sleeping bag or sheet bag (depending on if one stays in hotels/pensions or albergues), first-aid items, and a good sun hat, among other things. In addition, families formed their pilgrim identity together through purchasing symbolic objects such as a pilgrim's shell to attach to their backpacks and their pilgrim's passport (providing space for credentials to be stamped in each town to document their travel).

The stuff of the pilgrim backpack could be purchased in a number of ways and at a range of prices. Brierley sets the stage for pilgrims' purchasing in a way that represents the start of a journey that embraces caring for others: "Your pilgrimage starts at the planning stage. So start by invoking the highest intention for your journey and bring awareness to what you buy" (21). In his 2017 edition, he advises purchasing with political purpose: "There is so much exploitation of human and natural resources supported by our unconscious consumerism. Become informed and use your voice and money to support those companies who genuinely try to make a positive difference in the world. To walk a pilgrim path for peace in gear produced from exploitative business practices or oppressive regimes is not congruent—we must make every effort to *walk our talk*" (21). Almost half of the families I interviewed worked together to consider what to buy, whom to buy it from, and how to assemble their backpacks. Those who had read Brierley's text talked about making choices regarding gear for family members with such awareness in mind. Jan shared her "research about ponchos, umbrellas, raincoats, Gore-Tex jackets, and shoes" with her family, and told them they had to make their own decision about what they would use and how much weight they were going to carry. Over time, she said, "we put our kits together. Sue and I enjoyed looking at secondhand clothing stores for trekking shirts and pants as well as for merino wool tops." Danielle, who had walked the Camino several times before by herself, told a story about wanting her daughter Sophie to have strong boots and making the choice to give her daughter a pair of her sturdy broken-in boots from a previous Camino.

Brierley also advises pilgrims to deepen their experience by leaving behind "camera, watch, mobile phone" in order to "break the dependency and taste the freedom." Leaving these items behind, he suggests, helps the pilgrim to be "present to each passing moment," and that being "in the 'here and now' is to free the mind from constant connectivity with the digital universe and its web of distractions" (10). Most of the families did not follow this advice about technology. Rather, they engaged the Camino digital marketplace with fervor, buying overseas phone plans, electronic maps, guidebooks, and digital apps to help find their way, secure lodging, and communicate with each other and people at home. In fact, Brierley's book and maps ended up on these devices. Jan said: "I brought a small smartphone that doubled as my camera, watch, flashlight. My Brierley guidebook was a PDF file in the phone; so were other guides and material on the Camino, including an e-book with daily reflections for the Camino." Steven (sixty-eight), a father from South Africa who walked with his son Daniel (twenty-two), brought his tablet, which had on it a "very good Camino guide" that gave "a lot of history on where you are visiting." Ric (fifty), a father from the United States who walked with his son David (twenty-two), talked about how much he valued his "geo app." This presence of electronic stuff in most families' backpacks fell far from Brierley's advice. As I discuss in chapter 4, "Intimacy and Disciplining Technology," some family members did work together to manage technology use, but family members' digital worlds were so much a part of their everyday lives that no one questioned the need for at least one family member to pack a phone or small computer device and to secure mobile access in Spain.

Lodging and Support Services

Nancy Frey's 1998 ethnography captures the symbolic threads of Camino culture at a distinct point in time regarding hospitality, lodging, and pilgrims' options for traveling paths into Santiago. Frey's participant observation study took place just as the Camino's hospitality structure for accommodating large numbers of pilgrims was taking shape and Wi-Fi was not pervasive. In her analysis, Frey divides pilgrims into groups and subdivisions based on their choice of travel (by foot, on horseback, or by bicycle—noting some as "support-car pilgrims" and others as "non-motorized") by those who were "part-time," "week-end," and "full-time pilgrims" (the last of these groups made up the majority). Support-car pilgrims carried lighter packs and met up with their bags at the next town. On the contemporary Camino, these categories are still useful, but numerous groups have emerged within them. Support-car pilgrims are now aided by a number of Camino bag services, vans that carry larger packs or luggage to the next night's lodging, and additional routes have developed with reliable infrastructure. The Camino Ingles, for example, offers a week-long pilgrimage that meets the 100 km rule (walking 100 km in from Santiago) required to receive a Compostela.

Choices regarding lodging have grown extensively since Frey's ethnography, as has the number of types of refuge: public albergues, private albergues and hostels with single rooms and private baths, hotels, and a number of small pension-hotels designed to serve pilgrims are now found in towns on popular Camino routes. Writing about the Camino in the 1990s, Frey describes the "fundamental role" that the "pilgrims' refuge plays in the creation of connection among pilgrims." Group hostels, or albergues, were growing in number at the time: "In the early 1990s," she writes, "the refuge system barely existed; pilgrims slept in barns, abandoned schoolhouses, and churches and, more frequently, under the stars. Since then the refuges have developed into a vital pilgrimage institution." Refuges varied in type, but in general pilgrims could stay for one night and had "basic amenities: communal bathrooms with showers and sleeping quarters, a place to wash and hang laundry, often a common room for writing, resting, eating, or conversations, and occasionally a cooking facility" (94). On the contemporary Camino, multiple options exist that offer pilgrims refuge from the refuges—escape from shared bathrooms and crowded dorm rooms with snoring travelers in bunk beds. In 2016, I began seeing private albergues that installed pods, enclosed stacked bed units with their own plugs for charging digital devices. These pods are an alternative to paying for a private room, allowing pilgrims to separate themselves somewhat from others at the end of a long day. Families' stories almost always included some element of negotiation regarding how they planned to approach lodging and the number of options they had considered.

Maia's family talked about deciding that they would let each person "pick stops and places to stay so everybody got about three nights." The general openness with which they planned their trip allowed the kind of communal experience that Maia described at the beginning of this chapter as happening at Miguel's albergue. About half of the families I interviewed decided to make advance reservations, meaning at least one day before arrival in a town. When I walked routes, I would make reservations at least a day ahead as well through Tripadvisor on my tablet, or by calling on my phone. Only a couple of families planned to take the more "traditional" approach, embracing the unknown by trusting that the Camino would provide lodging when they arrived in a town each day.

Parents and their young adult children voiced preferences. Maia's father, Kyle, talked about how his vision of the Camino, as shaped through Brierley's book, informed his understanding of the value of albergues: "I understood the albergue thing and you know I could do a couple of those, but I wasn't necessarily interested in sleeping every night with forty of my new best friends." He also found hotels and bed-and-breakfasts named in the Brierley guidebook: "So I got on the internet and popped up some pictures and they had the magic words, 'private bathrooms.' I started thinking this might be doable." Other parents compromised with young adults who wanted the communal sleeping experience of the albergue. Ann, the mother from the United States who traveled with her daughter Hannah, talked about her need to have a private room, and the albergue-style communal character of some of the private hotels:

> I had made these reservations ahead, not in hostels, well they call them hotels, but you know they were, they were spartan, but we had our own bathroom and that was sort of my own thing. I just said, you know I have to get up at least a couple of times in the night to go to the bathroom. I don't want to waddle through a bunch of folks, you know, with not being able to take a shower perhaps if I wanted to. I wanted that little bit of luxury. At first Hannah was calling me a diva and we were joking about it. But it was funny because by the time we finished, I think she was really glad that we did the thing that we did because some of the hotels were like a hostel and we did stay at some of the hostels/albergues, she didn't like it at first, but she was thankful for it in the end.

Barbara, a fifty-five-year-old mom from Canada who traveled with her twenty-two-year-old-son Lance and twenty-year-old daughter Michelle, planned with her children not to stay in hotels because they wanted to experience communal meals on the Camino with those they met while walking. She said her kids "really encouraged that full experience and so I went with the intention of being a part of that. They pressed me harder to lean into that." But they also left open the possibility that they might need to stay in a hotel some nights and so did not make advance reservations. "Over the course of thirty-five days," Barbara said, "we had four nights in hotels. At the end in Santiago and in Leon and Burgos and two nights in Santiago." "At times," she said, "I just was cold and irritable and wanted a nice bed and bath but they [her kids] kept me steadfast on that endurance side."

As I discuss in chapter 3, the albergue communal experiences played a role in Barbara's story of growing closer to her children. However, it was not always the parents who wanted to steer clear of albergues. Steven, the father from South Africa, talked about leaving the choice of lodging open for each day and letting his son Daniel choose where they would stay:

> Once or twice we stayed in a private hostel. Look, I would have liked . . . my son is a bit of a private boy in some ways, and I kept giving him the option, albergue or private, and he was making the option to stay private. Which

> is a pity because by staying in the albergues, that is where you get the true feeling of companionship on the Camino. When you have to lie there and smell people's dirty socks and the snoring. So even when we did stay in the albergue we stayed in the private room.

Most family members feared they would miss the community brought through sharing meals with other pilgrims if they stayed in private accommodations, although as Ann noted, at times private establishments offered such practices at the end of the day to encourage strangers to come together. There still exist shared pilgrims' meals around large tables in a refuge or albergue, where people buy food and make a meal together, or where they are served a communal meal by *hospitaleros*, volunteers who help care for pilgrims in albergues. Private establishments on the contemporary Camino (albergues, pensions, hotels, and cafés) also at times offer meals at large tables with other pilgrims. More traditional pilgrim fare (e.g., a plate of potatoes, fish, or pork) is still common, but there are a growing number of pre-made food options for pilgrims on the more popular routes to work to replace the 4,000 or more calories pilgrims burn each day.

Families knew that their choices regarding lodging and hospitality had consequences. They were concerned about how to plan in ways that would welcome the unexpected stranger as friend and fellow pilgrim, and to find and build the *communitas*, the communal bonds established with other pilgrims, through lodging or a meal that many of the texts they had read presented as a core element of the Camino experience.[4] Concern for connecting with other pilgrims was important as well to those who bought Camino packages from online services or decided to send their luggage ahead each day and carry smaller day packs.

Prefabricated Camino Designs

> The word *real* has a certain tone of bravura about it because even now I know that I could never be a *real* pilgrim, not like those hundreds of thousands who walked their way to Santiago de Compostela in times past. At best, I now realize, most of us in these times can only be approximate pilgrims, for few of us can actually do what they did: step over the threshold of our kitchen door with almost nothing to sustain us and begin walking to a place we have never seen and

> which is hundreds if not thousands of kilometers away, endure no end of tribulations along the way, arrive, say our prayers, then walk all the way home again. Some still do that, but very few.
>
> —Codd, *To the Field of Stars*, 2008, xv

Several families used online services to design their Camino trip; in doing so, they took seriously Codd's suggestion that a contemporary Camino is something different from those accomplished by medieval travelers. Brierley talks about a "traditional pilgrim" way being "on foot, carrying all your 'worldly goods,'" which "allows the freedom to choose where to stop and tests your faith that there will be room in the inn!" (8). He encourages a different kind of freedom in the number of contemporary options he presents for accommodations, path, and understandings of the purpose in walking.

That a pilgrim's journey is an individual one, not to be labeled as authentic or inauthentic, but rather a personal practice based on choices made and motivations acted on, is pervasive in Camino travel narratives and guidebooks. Frey (1998: 137) notes of her Camino observations in the 1990s: "I began to see how endings and arrivals may or may not be place- or space-specific" and that "different internal endings or resolutions can come at any moment and may not be linked to the physical arrival in Santiago." She offers an example of this image from Paulo Coelho's ([1987] 1995) book, a text that several of my respondents mentioned as significant in their decision to walk and planning: Coelho "recounted that the Camino ended for him in Cebreiro when he found his sought-after spiritual enlightenment and the sword that would convert him into a *mago*, or magician. At that point his primary goal was reached, he found himself at peace with his mission, and he continued to Santiago by bus" (137).

The families I interviewed who used services to book hotels and meals in advance and/or those who used pack services saw themselves as crafting a legitimate individual Camino design. Each defended these choices not only as acceptable, but for some necessary and/or having advantages regarding the welcoming of unexpected Camino gifts.

In a handful of cases parents had serious physical injuries or limitations that kept them from carrying a backpack, and so they described online services as enabling them to even pursue the trip. Natalie, for example, had been afraid to walk the Camino, despite much enthusiasm after watching *The Way* and reading Codd's book. She had serious disk problems in her neck and thought she would "never be able to carry a backpack." Natalie described herself as not "much of a risk-taker" but that "technology" made her "brave": "I went online and quickly learned from Camino Facebook pages and websites that people didn't have to carry their bags." She found companies that would "transfer bags," and booked her trip through Camino Ways, which, she said, ultimately "made the walk more enjoyable and meaningful." Because they did not have to worry about getting to the next town fast enough to secure lodging and beat the crowds in the summer, she said, she and Nell could "stop and smell the roses." They could "stop and pray together," and linger at cafés for a rest. It brought, she expressed, a different kind of "spirituality to it." There were drawbacks—some labeling from other pilgrims, who gave them glances and whispered about day-packers as "cheating" or not "real pilgrims." I met a sixty-year-old mother from Ireland in Santiago who had booked a one-week trip from Sarria with her two young adult daughters. She said the booking company that carried their heavy bags made it physically possible for her to walk, and less "stressful" for the family. Her daughters seemed proud that they had been able to make arrangements so that their mother could relax and be free to enjoy the walk and meet new people.

Camino Ways is just one example of a number of online booking travel services used by families who wanted to walk together on Camino routes. Others mentioned in interviews were One Foot Abroad (Ireland) and Marly Camino. A quick look at these websites gives a picture of the various services and approach to marketing the Camino as an individual custom-crafted spiritual adventure. For example, Marly Camino claims that "for more than 12 years we have been curating exclusive routes along the French Way, Portuguese Camino, North Coast route and Andalusian Way. As well as other walking routes in Spain."[5] They boast that their "warm and friendly team of professionals and impeccable organization will bring all our Pilgrims the top support and highest personal attention." Camino Ways uses the popular contemporary leisure marketing concept of an "experience" to distinguish the mystical character of the Camino: "Today, more than a pilgrimage, the Camino is an unforgettable experience and unique journey."[6] Camino Ways offers a number of trips and tours, but also gives the customer the option of making their own individual plan, much in the spirit of the contemporary Camino. In this vein, the site presents a "Camino Planner" function that will help you: "Make it yours . . . select any Camino route and create the perfect tour." The Camino Planner assists you in planning your "starting & finishing point, stops in between depending on how many kilometers you'd like to walk each day, and other services."

Online Camino travel services such as Camino Ways, Marly Camino, and companies that specialize in carrying luggage made it possible for pilgrims to carry just a day pack, or a lighter pack that resembled a larger backpack to avoid being labeled by other pilgrims as "not authentic." I walked for two weeks once with a woman who carried a day pack that passed as a full pack. I did not learn until the end of the trip, when I booked a room in a hotel and witnessed her enormous suitcase arrive, that the backpack she carried each day represented a fraction of her belongings that traveled along the way (the mystery of her well-groomed hair and daily makeup finally explained!). Pack services helped several families I interviewed as they planned for individual members' physical needs. Ellen (sixty-two), who walked with her husband and two children, said the entire family chose to book hotels ahead, and that she was able to add the pack services just for her: "They [family] wanted to carry their earthly belongings. I was going to have mine sent from place to place. So, I had all of my things packed in a fairly small backpack that I was going to have carried around with me . . . they [the service] said they would pick it up and deliver it to the next place and so I gave them my duffle bag and it was like clockwork, that was fabulous to me."

Families who booked ahead or made use of pack services at times defended their decisions by arguing that such a choice could make their Camino more challenging. For example, Ed (sixty) from the United States, who walked with his daughter Julie (twenty-two), validated the choice to book ahead as one that pushed them to walk farther at times: "It's probably more difficult when you have everything reserved" because "if you are tired you have to keep walking." The guidebooks and online resources that families turned to in learning about what to bring with them and where to walk, sleep, and eat were great producers of meaning, determining in large part what they expected and thus how they told stories about their family Caminos. For Ed and Julie, like Natalie and Nell and many of the other families I interviewed, planning to embrace the mystical, the unknown, or the transformative nature of the Camino often entailed spiritual preparation.

Preparing Spiritually

> A majority of those setting out on the *Camino de Santiago* give a religious or spiritual reason for going, yet few appear to undertake any conscious inner preparation for the journey.
>
> —Brierley 2018: 36

> On a whim, in the summer of 2009, I decided to walk the Camino de Santiago with my seventeen-year-old-daughter.... I had almost no idea where the Camino was. And I definitely did not set out on a pilgrimage, although I knew that this was an ancient pilgrimage route. In my mind, I was simply going on a long walk with my daughter, and for this purpose I closed my law practice for a month and left my life behind.
>
> The very real experience of pilgrimage came to me only while walking. The act of putting one foot in front of the other, day after day, with only my tasks to answer to, led me on an interior journey that I was not prepared for and was not expecting.
>
> —Kirkpatrick 2010: 5

A dominant theme in published Camino narratives is the idea that the Camino is an experience with a promise of transformation, a vision of some undisclosed individual and relational change. Most of the people with whom I spoke named that transformative experience as "spiritual." Most recognized that some pilgrims prepare spiritually, and others do not. They believed that, as Julie Kirkpatrick's words just quoted suggest, a life-changing experience could come from simply putting one foot in front of the other. However, a significant part of many of their stories was that planning should involve some preparatory thought about spirituality to help foster Camino transformation. The guidebooks and resources they read named the Camino as an "inner journey," a "spiritual experience," or a "mystical path," all language that captured a Camino promise of travel that would bring some profound change. Some of the most popular texts—for example, Brierley's guidebook, suggested that they should prepare spiritually for this transformative journey—even if, as Brierley suggests, they do not want to call it spiritual:

> I urge you to find a spiritual purpose for taking this journey. If you have difficulty with this term, find one more meaningful to you, and check out your local bookstore – you'll find a wealth of literature on the subject. The words "significant journey" threw up 63 million suggestions on my web browser – so you get the idea! But attend to this promptly so that you have time to mull over your motivation *before* you travel. A core question arises: what turns a walking holiday into pilgrimage? When you receive an answer you may find a fundamental change in how you approach the journey—from intention down to what you put in your backpack.
>
> —Brierley 2018: 8

Brad, whom I spoke of earlier in this chapter, asked his son and two daughters to read Kevin Codd's book before they decided to walk with the family, as this text addresses young adults and spirituality in particular:

> Young people out here walking day after day belong to what is now called the "postmodern" era and are really quite secularized as far as institutional religion is concerned, there are nevertheless some kind of "receptors" within them that pull in spiritual signals. They are not closed to spiritual realities at all. . . . [T]he vagueness of their answers makes it clear to me that the real issue is that, unlike their forebears, they just don't have much in the way of vocabulary to describe what goes on spiritually within themselves. (Codd 2008: 72–73)

The Camino, as Brierley and Codd make clear, provides numerous kinds of mystical encounters with nature and other pilgrims that offer vocabulary and spiritual signals. Brierley writes: "When asked to describe a personal experience of the sacred, an overwhelming majority refer to a time alone in nature, 'A sunrise over the sea; animal tracks in fresh powder snow; a walk under the full moon.' " He continues, further clarifying the sacred: "It was not the sun or the moon that created any shift in perception but they acted as a reflection of a larger perspective, a distant memory of something holy—something bigger than, and yet part of, us. This is where the Camino can provide such a powerful reminder of the sacred in our lives and the desire to reclaim our spiritual inheritance" (36). Brierley provides as well "self-assessment" questions to ask in preparation for a Camino that will "encourage" pilgrims to "reflect" on their "life and its direction." Questions include: "How do you define spirituality – What does it mean to you? How is your spirituality expressed at home and at work," and "How aware are you . . . of your inner spiritual world?" (38)

Camino texts introduce expectations of this mystical quality. Codd talks of walking at the beginning of his Camino into "a world very distinct from that which I knew down below, a world somewhere between earth and heaven that feels like nowhere and everywhere." He continues with physical and religious descriptors: "Up here everything is close. . . . I feel myself enveloped, overtaken, absorbed into something quite unnamable. It is like being with Moses on top of old Sinai or with Jesus on Mount Tabor. This may be the closest I ever get in my life to a mystical experience. I am high" (14). He then encounters "mountain goats" and has a conversation with them:

> They bleat and I bleat back.
>
> I ask them: "Do you speak Spanish or French for if you speak French we can only nod to one another and offer the simplest of greetings but if you speak Spanish, we can discuss the universe and our place in it."
>
> They answer that either is fine with them so I ask them how they like life up here. They respond, "Enjoying life is not something we ponder; we just live. However, life here is good enough if you must have an answer. Both life's hardships and life's pleasures come to us as they will and we accept them; there is no other way for goats to live."
>
> I ask them if in their mountain wisdom they have any advice for one who is not yet so wise. They answer that of course they do: "Remain humble on this road or the road will humble you." (15)

For Natalie and her daughter Nell, reading Codd before they left in preparation, and then reading again to each other each day as they walked, they said, helped them to remember the goats' advice: "Stay humble in the walk." They also told stories about seeing trees and other parts of the landscape in ways that brought them together in a kind of spiritual intimacy, which I explore in more detail in chapter 3. Natalie and Nell both identified as Catholics who attended Mass regularly and so had a symbolic religious world to access, but Codd's book gave them a different way to prepare spiritually and frame their Camino memories.

The Camino Forum also had discussions regarding planning for religious and/or spiritual intent. Participants posed questions such as whether someone who does not identify as religious should walk, how to be a Christian on the Camino, and what kind of spiritual preparation one should do if you have not walked before. A question and the advice received in 2013, on the Forum regarding spiritual work captures the essence of what some families encountered through online Camino preparation and planning:

> [Question] I am building myself up to walk to the resting place of St. James in 2014. I know that for me, this is a deep calling and I wish to ensure that I do all that I can to be appropriately prepared for the pilgrimage—the walking will be arduous and I know there will be privations. They do not concern me. What concerns me is that I fully embrace my responsibility to ensure that I am prepared, so that I am "right" in my thoughts, that I can scrutinize my motives and that I can "articulate" my reasons to make this

> spiritual journey as the most natural and appropriate for me. I'd welcome advice, instruction and insights from the Camino family.

This member's question is answered through explicit religious spiritual language by a "veteran member":

> Each spiritual journey is an individual thing. . . . [F]or those on a spiritual journey (we all are, but many don't realise!: wink:) the outer difficulties of the Camino are an integral part of the inner journey. . . . [I]f you are Christian then I would suggest reading *The Imitation of Christ* by Thomas [à] Kempis. If you cannot get a copy please do pm me with your address and I will send you one.

It was also answered by another, less overtly Christian approach from a veteran walker:

> My very subjective suggestion would be to first empty your "inner backpack" ;-) I don't think there is a right or wrong way to walk the Camino, there is only our own way doing this pilgrimage. Keep your mind open, let go of your prejudices and expectations and simply accept graciously what your own pilgrimage offers you would be my advice.

The Pilgrim's Office official site has a section titled "Spiritual Preparation" that advises reflecting on "your reasons for doing The Way of St. James," and engaging other preparatory practices such as receiving an official blessing from the Pilgrim's Reception Office or your own clergy before walking.[7] There is room for individual motivations such as enjoying the "cultural side of the Way" or taking in the landscape; however, the site makes clear that these are "complementary to the spiritual and religious essence that characterizes the Way of St. James," and that "going on the Way is definitely an experience that very often brings the pilgrims closer to God."

Almost all of the pilgrims I interviewed expressed a belief that the Camino held some promise of spiritual experience, defined and envisioned in different ways, and a third of these family members told stories of preparing spiritually together, as a family. For some, like Natalie and Nell, or Brad's family, preparing involved reading texts that named and detailed the Camino as a spiritual journey. For about half of these families, such spiritual preparation together was a familiar relational strategy. Brad, who identified as a nondenominational Protestant, and Natalie, who claimed a strong Catholic identity, talked about raising children who attended religious services with them and families who spoke regularly about religious/spiritual beliefs together. Isabelle, a twenty-five-year-old woman from Sweden, and her fifty-five-year-old mom, Lisa, said they were not religious, but they spent a great deal of our interview time talking about how they had shared a "lifelong" approach to thinking about who they were "spiritually," and how they were drawn to the Camino because they saw it as a "spiritual walk." While Isabelle said that her mother was the more spiritual of the two, her interest in developing and thinking about her own spirituality, especially in doing this "spiritual walk," led her to read and discuss *The Pilgrimage* and many other personal Camino narratives with her mother. Isabella said: "Reading all those books about the Camino, once I knew I was going, I knew something was going to happen to us on the Camino." In chapter 2, I delve deeper into how families understood the spiritual as potentially active, the not yet revealed mystical elements of their Camino.

Conclusion: Possibility and Promise

> The whole Camino is a choice. You can choose to put your backpack down at any moment, you don't have to keep walking with it, and you can send it ahead. You are choosing to walk each day. No one is going to hurt you if you stop walking. It is all a choice.
>
> —Tom (twenty-two), Australia

Tom encouraged his mother to make the choice to walk the Camino after she took him to see the documentary *Six Ways to Santiago*. He made choices as well: the choice to travel on foot through Spain, to walk with his mother for two weeks instead of with the younger friends he had met while traveling, and to carry his laptop. The computer was heavy cargo, but a load he saw as essential for the writing he wanted to accomplish on his journey.

Families preparing to walk faced a Camino culture full of choices regarding routes, hospitality, method of travel, and options and advice regarding these opportunities continue to grow. As I wrote this chapter in 2019, hundreds of Camino narratives were being created and posted on blogs, and new Camino guidebooks found their way onto Amazon and phone apps. New documentaries and YouTube videos were being filmed. It is hard to imagine how the families I interviewed resemble in any way the "traditional pilgrims" that Brierley and other Camino authors speak of, those who shed all their belongings, walked out their front door, and put one foot in front of the other with no knowledge of what they would encounter during the day or where they would lay their heads at night.

Nancy Frey (2017: 11) reflects that "virtual pilgrims create memories about places and form impressions of people, places, landscapes and experiences before setting foot into them." She continues, "I am not advocating not preparing but rather encourage potential pilgrims to use common sense and reflect on the impact of being hyper-informed. Discovery, wonder and surprise are elements often traditionally sought after in such a journey into the unknown, like the Camino, and can be impacted by extensive pre-activity and engagement." The rising numbers of pilgrims each year; the pervasive and necessary presence of technology in planning, securing lodging, and communicating while walking; and the growing hospitality and tourism infrastructure on popular routes have in many ways radically changed the ability to escape the everyday, to take risks, and to find the unexpected. Still, contemporary families, like earlier pilgrims, hoped and planned together for the unknown—something life-changing—to happen to them. In this way, they were holding fast to traditional ideas of pilgrimage—traveling to a sacred place with the hope to return home transformed in some way.

While walking the Camino Francés in 2016, I passed graffiti with cartoon-like images of American pilgrims that read "Go home pilgrim tourists." The Camino is a booming cultural tourism site that benefits local businesses and the independent region of Galicia. Many smalls towns are kept viable through this contemporary revival of medieval routes and the industry that has surfaced around the Camino. The families with whom I spoke saw a piece of their walking together as such cultural tourism, learning about Spanish culture and valuing historical stories and monuments, but more in the forefront of their Camino stories was the desire to have a transformative experience. That most family members spent significant time making choices about how they wanted to engage the Camino was not surprising; such predictability in purchasing travel experiences was a taken-for-granted aspect of their lives. What made this travel experience different for most of the family members I interviewed was that their planning represented efforts to throw themselves, together, into heightened, unpredictable, and at times physically painful sacred practice. By "sacred" I mean an experience that they believed would be charged with mystical, spiritual, or (for some) explicitly Divine force that could foster individual growth and strengthen family relationships.

Families understood that to find the sacred on the Camino, their planning must leave open an element of risk. Embracing risk was at the heart of almost every book these pilgrim families read. For example, the text that almost all had in common as essential in their Camino planning, Brierley's guidebook, offers the "words of *William Ward*" as a "source of encouragement:" (37)

> To laugh is to risk appearing a fool
> To weep is to risk being called sentimental
> To reach out to another is to risk involvement
> To expose feelings is to risk exposing your true self
> To place your ideas and dreams before a crowd is to risk their loss
> To love is to risk not being loved in return
> To live is to risk dying
> To try is to risk failure
> But risks must be taken
> Because the greatest hazard in life is to risk nothing
> The people who risk nothing may avoid suffering and sorrow,
> But they cannot learn, feel, change, grow or really live.
> Chained by their servitude they are slaves who have forfeited all freedom.
> Only a person who risks is truly free.

The parents and young adult children I met told me they expected that becoming pilgrims together would be a new kind of time away together. It would not, as Maia said, be like "sitting on the porch of a rented summer vacation house." Planning and securing spiritual family time that left room for the unexpected and welcomed risk reflected their desire to partake of a larger Camino relational promise. The family members' stories I interpret throughout this book are about seizing this Camino promise, and about the social and spiritual dynamics and encounters that shaped, supported, and at times undermined their efforts.

2
Camino Promises

> I am about to share here a story about stars at dance. May I advise you to exercise a modicum of caution in attending to what follows, for the story of stars dancing over a field in a faraway land may so draw you away from the ordinary business of daily life that you find yourself, quite to your surprise, in a new world of unexpected adventures and remarkable people and some very profound mysteries.
>
> —Codd 2008, ix

Lindsey, a twenty-four-year-old college graduate from the United States who waited tables and had dreams of publishing a young-adult fiction novel, began her Camino story with her recent religious conversion and how she came to "take Christ in her life." She had heard about the Camino first from a friend, and then she watched Emilio Estevez's movie *The Way,* which made her think about walking the pilgrimage as a way to practice her new faith. She did not have the money to pay for the trip, and so she asked her mother to fund her Camino as a birthday present. Her mom agreed to pay for the trip and go with her, which Lindsey was a bit worried about given a family

Walking the Way Together. Kathleen E. Jenkins, Oxford University Press (2021). © Oxford University Press.
DOI: 10.1093/oso/9780197553046.003.0002

history of divorce conflict and ongoing arguments with her mother. She thought about asking her father to go, but he could not get the time off from work. Even though she was hesitant to walk with her mother, as she read more about the pilgrimage route she began to entertain the idea of a Camino miracle: a possible change in her mother's character that could strengthen their relationship.

> I don't have a very good relationship with my mom, but she thinks we have a good relationship and that we are close. . . . She says she loves me and all that, and I love her but . . . I thought that maybe, maybe miracles happen on the Camino—maybe if I do this thing with her, she will magically become a better person. If she just has that moment where she can feel for someone else instead of for herself, maybe something will happen.

Codd's words at the start of this chapter, taken together with Lindsey's hopes for the Camino, capture the essence of the mystical power I heard as most family members talked with me about their initial hopes for their pilgrimage. Family members spoke of a Camino promise of removal from the everyday that involved immersion in a spiritual practice with uncommon potential for individual and relational transformation. Some thought this spirituality would be found in meditative walking through nature and absorbing the mystical from Spain's landscape, people, and culture. Others talked more about spirituality born through deep connections with pilgrims they would meet while walking. Most imagined an inclusive spirituality alive in Christian rituals at churches and sacred sites they would visit together. Some saw these spiritual practices bringing them closer to God, and others as connecting them with structured Catholic prayer and rituals that might enhance their Catholic and/or Christian identity and purpose. Lindsey, like most of the family members with whom I spoke, described a number of sources contributing to her understanding of the Camino promise.

Cultivating Transformation and Connection

Lindsey, like most of the pilgrims from the United States that I interviewed, was impressed by *The Way*, a film whose message centers around family and the Camino's transformative energy. *The Way* is a narrative of redemption that captures the essence of the spiritual/therapeutic and religious worlds of the Camino.[1] The father character, Tom, is a Catholic who has lost faith; at the start of the movie he is described by his friends as not having a soul. When his local priest learns of his son's death and asks Tom if he wants to pray, he answers, "What for?" As Tom travels to France to identify Daniel's remains, his conversations with his son take place in flashback, and the audience learns that they had a strained relationship after Tom's wife, Daniel's mother, died. In one of these flashbacks, Daniel invites his father to come with him to Europe. Tom responds that he has responsibilities and cannot go. The French police officer who meets Tom at the train station and takes him to the morgue explains what his son was doing in the Pyrenees Mountains when the bad weather took his life. He tells him that Daniel was walking the Camino de Santiago, a most personal journey that draws people from all faiths. The officer shows Tom the symbol of pilgrimage, a shell on his son's backpack, and opens his Pilgrim's Passport, which had been stamped only in St. Jean, at the start of the Camino Francés. He then pulls out a passport filled with stamps and shares with Tom that he has walked the Camino three times. Tom decides to cremate his son and take his ashes on the walk, spreading them as he goes. He bonds with three pilgrims as he walks. They walk both together and alone, at times in silence and at times sharing the life issues that brought them to the Camino. At one point on the road Tom encounters a priest recovering from brain cancer surgery, and the clergymember tells him, "They say that miracles happen out here," and gives him a rosary to carry. The movie ends as Tom throws Daniel's remaining ashes onto the rocks at the sea's edge, having walked over 100 km farther west from the city of Santiago to Finisterre.

Lindsey looked forward to her Camino as she planned the trip, envisioning praying in each town, attending the pilgrims' Mass in the evenings, and making connections with others as her friend and the main characters in *The Way* had done. It is not surprising that she hoped for a "miracle" to happen, that her mother would have some change of character; she had heard this Camino potential conveyed in the movie and other texts she had read online and in hard-copy print as she prepared to walk. Lindsey, like so many others whom I interviewed, believed that the power of new friendships formed on the Camino as they listened to, shared stories with, and cared for those who walked with them might hold some transformative power for her mother, for her, and ultimately for their relationship. Anticipation that these relationships and practices could bring deep changes in one's character and social connections ran deep in Camino discourse, fueling its spiritual promise.

When I say "Camino discourse," I do not mean language alone. Rather, I refer to discourse as a more sociological concept that represents the power at work in a combination of language, relationships, texts, and rituals of the contemporary Camino inside and outside of institutions such as the Catholic Church. Discourse represents and reinforces the ideas, practices, and relationships my research participants encountered as they learned about the Camino, planned for their walk, and made their way on routes day after day for a week or over several weeks. Movies such as *The Way* and personal narratives and books about the pilgrimage to Santiago were strong producers of meaning, but routine interactions that happened as people walked Camino routes were also powerful discursive forces—*rituals* that worked to strengthen belief in pilgrim identity and transformative practice.

Pilgrims spending time together walking or as they rested at cafés or in hostels after a long day shared personal reflections of their hopes and expectations for their Camino. Some told stories they had heard about a miracle or act of kindness that had changed a pilgrim's faith in humankind. Listening and reflecting with others reinforced beliefs in the transformative power of the walk. In one lengthy conversation on the Camino Francés with a woman I had barely met, this pilgrim told me she was getting impatient waiting for her Camino lesson regarding her life's purpose—in particular, as it related to whether she should stay with or leave her life partner. She complained, "I keep thinking that moment of my Camino will come, but it hasn't." Her frustration that a lesson had not revealed itself demonstrates the power of the belief in Camino discourse that this pilgrimage was supposed to produce such mystical insight. Almost all of the pilgrims I interviewed talked about some unknown mystery of the Camino—transformative lessons, revelations, and/or miracles that would eventually come to those who walked ready to receive them.

Other regular interactions while walking reinforced the cumulative transformative potential of the Camino. The stamping of a pilgrim's passport (credentials) at establishments in towns along the way validated how far they had walked and invested in the practice. People who saw pilgrims on paths often greeted them by saying "Buen Camino"—a polite exchange, but one that served as an *interaction ritual* affirming pilgrim identity. Pilgrims' props, such as a walking stick and a backpack with a shell attached, were symbolic elements of a walker's costume that reinforced the feeling that one was a pilgrim moving forward with a purpose.[2]

Family members' understandings of what the Camino could bring reflected the relational and self-revelatory potentials that filled personal narratives they had read in published books and online pilgrim blogs or seen in popular documentaries and films about the Camino. The Camino has historically been an inspiration for works of art, music, theater, literature, poetry, and oral storytelling, with many of these creative depictions upholding the mystical, religious, or transformative nature of the practice. *The Way* promotes the Camino promise in contemporary form: at the end of the movie, Tom has clearly had some deep change in self, symbolized in the scene where he receives his Compostela. He first tells the official giving him the document his name, pauses, and then asks if the official would please change the name to his son's name, Daniel. This a poignant gesture where the audience feels some sense of completion in an ongoing process of Tom's grief work and that walking the Camino has brought him closer to his son in desire and purpose. *The Way* illustrates the Camino promise in an adventure filled with contemporary seeking, where strangers meet and come to care for each other as they search for some aspect of self-transformation or change. Through embracing and caring for others as they travel, they find the mystical in each other and themselves. The film's lesson resonates with symbolic spiritual family goals: a father whose son dies before they had a chance to know each other fully is able to connect with his memory. The father's spiritual practice brings him face-to-face with their relational history, which leads him to change how he approaches others and the world. Ultimately, Lindsey's description of what happened to her and her mother on the Camino, a story I tell later in this chapter, fulfills this therapeutic narrative of change and relational connection, even though the miracle Lindsey sought did not happen.

The heart of the family Camino promise is the soul of pilgrimage itself: the idea that traveling to a sacred place can bring transformation. This power to bring change in the form of a family "miracle" is found in one of the oldest historical legends of the Camino, that of Santo Domingo de la Calzada, a story referenced in popular contemporary Camino texts. In his book, for example, Codd tells the story soon after the point in his narrative when he sheds tears on the Camino, feelings motivated by "the most simple and fundamental postulate of my faith: God knows me" (2008: 72) and by the charity and care received from others. Codd writes that "something fundamental is happening" to him, but he does not "have words for it." The next day, as Codd walks from Nájera to Santo Domingo de la Calzada, he learns from his guidebook that the town of Santo Domingo de la Calzada is the "spiritual heart of the Camino," related to the history of Domingo, a young man who dedicated his life to serving pilgrims (82). The priest who offered the pilgrims Mass in Santo Domingo de la Calzada led Codd and others "not far from Domingo's tomb but high up on a transept wall . . . the *gallinero*, a wrought iron cage built into the wall" that held "a hen and a rooster." These, Codd writes, "commemorate a *camino* miracle that is surely more fable than history but is a great tale nevertheless" (83). He recounts the story:

> It seems that a troop of foreign pilgrims . . . spent a night in the town somewhere around or about the fourteenth century. Among them was a family with a very handsome son. A local maiden took a fancy to the lad and encouraged him in not so subtle ways to join her for a bit of a tryst. He, being virtuous, spurned her advances. . . . She hid a precious goblet in his traveling pouch and then, as he and his family left town, accused him of thievery, for which he was duly hanged. . . . [T]he boy's grieving parents chose to leave the unhappy place, but before they left town, their son miraculously spoke to them, assuring them that he was not dead but that at that moment of his perceived demise good Saint Domingo stood beneath him, holding him up by his feet so that the noose did not have its intended effect. The parents ran back to the hanging judge who was dining on, you guessed it, a rooster and a hen. They protested to the fat magistrate that their son was still very much alive, at which the judge chortled something to the effect that their son was no more alive than the two well-roasted chickens upon which he was feeding. Well, at that very moment the well-roasted fowl jumped off his plate, alive as can be, grew feathers, and began to flap about, crowing in delight at their resurrection and that of the just and chaste young man. The son was of course reunited with his parents and off they joyously continued to Compostela, and after arriving there and paying their prayerful respects to the apostle, they presumably lived happily ever after (84).

Codd identifies several morals in this miraculous story: "Stay virtuous; don't cheat and lie; the truth outs," and "don't mess around with Santo Domingo's pilgrims, for he takes care of his own" (84). I would add that there is a kinship lesson in this story as well, similar to one found in *The*

Way: family members lost through death or distance can be found again—and connections strengthened—through Camino practice.

Encounters with texts and films, social interactions while walking, and official Compostela rituals all shaped how the people I spent time with encountered, talked about, and understood relational Camino promises. For example, Peter, a sixty-five-year-old father from Australia who walked with his twenty-three-year-old son Mike, had done the Camino by himself once before and was motivated to bring Mike with him the next time because of a story that an American pilgrim told him in Santiago:

> I met a man from Seattle, Ben. His son-in-law had flown in to walk the final piece with him from Sarria. I spent a good deal of time talking with him in Santiago and he said that since the man had married his daughter they had never really gotten on. Apparently, he said, the young man had no relationship with his father. I'm not sure why that was, he had left or fallen out with him, so he didn't have a loving father in his life. Ben said that during that week of walking they learned things about each other that they didn't know before and they bonded and by the time they got to Santiago he had a relationship with his son-in-law that he never thought he would have. Before he left, he told him that he loved him! It was the best story I heard on the Camino. And so even though I didn't lack a good relationship with my son, it was a bit of a motivator for me. I thought, if we can just enrich our relationship.

Similarly, Steven, the father from South Africa who walked with his son Daniel, came to believe in a Camino promise of spiritual intimacy through his previous experience walking:

> A significant thing for me on the first Camino, I had met a lady with her young daughter . . . she was an Anglican bishop in the United States. And it just struck me as something really wonderful and she had already done the Camino and she was taking her daughter on the Camino and I just thought that gosh, it would be so wonderful to have your child with you to experience what you have experienced before. That is why I have always said to my family, "I really want to walk with you. I want to share that feeling that one gets when you are just walking, that euphoria that you get when you are just walking." . . . It is just a wonderful feeling and I wanted to share that with them so that they could love it as well.

Even those families who said they did not have a family lesson or miracle in mind when they started the Camino were aware of pilgrims' investment in the Camino's relational power. Jim (forty-seven), from the United States, who walked with his stepdaughter Anita (twenty-two) and his wife, Sheri (forty-six), said that from talking to other pilgrims, they knew families often walked "because of this reason, or that reason"; but, he said, "we actually are very happy. Our family is very fortunate. We don't really have any burdens to release, so we just did it because we wanted to do it. Because it is an amazing adventure and we wanted to do it together." In the end, Jim, Anita, and Sheri told me individual stories of their trip that included some change and strengthening of their family bond, a nod to the Camino promise. However, most family members, like Lindsey, had specific problems or concerns that they hoped the Camino would address, and talked about Camino practices and beliefs that could address them as *spiritual*.

Camino Spiritualities

> What is a pilgrim and why do people make the pilgrimage to Santiago?
>
> Pilgrimage is a time set apart from normal daily life in which people travel to a holy place. . . .
>
> Pilgrims on the way to Santiago have the opportunity for personal reflection and prayer as well as enjoying the fellowship of other pilgrims from many different countries. The pilgrimage is an opportunity for spiritual renewal and growth in personal faith.
>
> —Pilgrim's Office n.d. ("Pilgrims")

People generally started talking to me about the Camino as spiritual before I had a chance to ask them if they understood it as such. Their descriptions of spirituality included encounters with religious ritual in churches and other sacred sites along the paths, the power of meditative walking through nature, and bonding with other pilgrims. Even those who voiced confusion over what spirituality was made links between Camino practices and what they imagined the term *spiritual* to mean. For example, when I asked Jansen (sixty-one), from the Netherlands, who walked with his daughter Lina (twenty-six), if he saw the Camino as spiritual, he first noted he was not a religious or spiritual person, then said, "If walking the Camino and letting your mind wander and thinking about the universe and stuff, if that is spiritual, then maybe the answer is yes. . . . When I walked into Santiago two years ago for the first time [*he took a deep breath*] even now that is an extremely emotional experience. Um, I don't think I've ever experienced anything as powerful as that. You can tell [*his voice was broken and tearful*] it is extremely moving, so you can interpret that how you will if that is spiritual or not."

Jansen's answer speaks to the openness and fluidity regarding the way pilgrims expressed thoughts about the spiritual landscape conveyed in Camino discourse and its relational promise. Jansen was not a religious person, but he names his arrival at the end point of his journeying, Santiago de Compostela, with its massive cathedral and bustling religious tourism, as the most powerful emotional experience of his life, and welcomes me to name it spiritual. We hear acceptance of a broad understanding of spirituality as well when Brierley suggests people should do some sort of spiritual preparation for the Camino, noting that if you have "difficulty" with the term *spiritual* to "find one more meaningful to you" (8), and in Codd's discussion of how youth "are not closed to spiritual realities at all," but rather lack the "vocabulary to describe what goes on spiritually within themselves." Most of the people I interviewed went to the Pilgrim's Office in Santiago at the end of their journey to get a Compostela. They, like many pilgrims, had read the official Catholic webpage, even if briefly, to learn about what they needed to do to—how far they had to walk to receive one, where they had to walk from, the location of the office, and what they needed to say to get the document. This website's page titled "Spiritual Preparation" reinforces the belief that multiple motivations are linked to spirituality—that people walk the Camino "to find themselves, to find a meaning to life, to enjoy an atmosphere for reflection, to fulfil a promise, to meet other pilgrims, to follow in the footsteps of millions of pilgrims who have walked the same path for centuries, to learn about the culture and art along the way, to honour St. James, to deepen and enhance themselves in the Faith."[3] These reasons, the site stresses, are "complementary to the spiritual and religious essence that characterizes the Way." The characters in the movie *The Way* also represent a range of religious and spiritual positions and understandings of the journey. Taken together, Brierley, Codd, Estevez's film, the Pilgrim's Office, and other published personal Camino narratives and blogs that can be accessed online mirror the ways the people with whom I talked described spiritual experiences and, in a larger context, how people in Western cultures speak about spiritual experience.

Sociologist Nancy Ammerman's (2013) research offers a useful framework for thinking about how people draw from various understandings of spirituality, what she calls "cultural packages," to describe lived spiritual encounters and identity. One package, Extra-Theistic, includes definitions of spiritual experience that relate to feeling an awesome power of the natural world and coming to see oneself as connected to a web of being in the world, a kind of mystical spirituality that supports individual self-seeking and relational change and transformation as spiritual process. Others may pull from another cultural package, Theistic, that includes ways of understanding spiritual experience and self as located in relationship with a Divine entity. Underlying these cultural packages are expressions of spirituality as everyday acts of Golden Rule compassion, an "Ethical Spirituality."[4] These ways of talking about spiritual experience are not exclusive. People's descriptions and stories of spiritual experience often include elements from each, as was true in my respondents' stories of Camino spirituality. Lindsey, for example, wanted to walk with Christ on a journey where she hoped connections with other pilgrims might bring a change to her relationships; in particular, she thought connecting with others could provoke her mother to embrace a more Golden Rule–like spirituality. Recall her expression that "maybe miracles happen on the Camino," that her mother might "magically become a better person" if she "has that moment where she can feel for someone else instead of for herself."

Parents and young adult children talked about how Camino spiritualities related to the Camino promise that they sought. Following traditional motivations of pilgrimage to Catholic sites, Maria (fifty), a mother from Spain, went on the Camino because she promised God that she would walk the Camino if he would heal her son's knee. Her son Carlos (twenty-two), during our interview, showed me the knee brace he had worn while walking the Camino that framed the area of skin scarred from his successful knee surgery. Most of the family stories I heard were from parents and young adults who had traveled long distances to walk, and the healing they desired had not yet occurred; for them, it was still buried in a profound mystery of Camino spirituality that they hoped would be revealed. In the descriptions of investment in the Camino promise that I relate in what follows, families brought grief and loss, divorce, significant life transitions, physical injuries, and other emotional challenges to these expectations. They described anticipation of the miracles or lessons that they thought might come from spiritualities enhanced through what they described as a compressed Camino life.

Promises of a Compressed Camino Life

> The *camino* is now something much more than a physical and mental challenge, more than something to check off my life's list of "to do's," and more even than the accomplishing of my personal goal to seek the help of a grand old saint for the great cause of my life. This is now life itself. The *camino* has become my world inside and out.
>
> —Codd 2008: 79

> The Camino is like life, there are mountains to get over, challenges, smiles, crying.
>
> —Thomas (fifty), father from Germany

> Walking the Camino is like having your entire life condensed into one month and all your great experiences and all your terrible experiences happen to you in some fashion in that one month.
>
> —Barbara (fifty), mom from Canada

Camino discourse promotes the idea that walking and communing with other pilgrims resembles a compressed life: as in other kinds of liminal spaces, its structure and practice are imagined as a way of being that is different from the everyday, a life with a new set of norms, beliefs, rituals, and relationships. Each day, pilgrims generally wake up early to grab several hours of their daily kilometers in the cool morning air; they stop along the way at pilgrim cafés for facilities, coffee, snacks, and cool beverages. At the end of the day, they wash and dry their clothes, typically using clotheslines and washrooms provided at their lodging. They eat and rest, and many gather later in the evening with other pilgrims for dinner. Research participants talked of how this Camino routine, like life itself, was composed of joys, hardships, love, self-searching, and lessons learned. Many talked as well of religious or mystical Camino life practices, including stopping at symbolic points along routes to pray, attending Mass, or taking in the beauty of a piece of pilgrim art. Resonating at the center of most families' expectations of Camino life was a spirituality generated from immersion in the natural world and deep interaction with fellow pilgrims that resembled what Victor Turner (1969) called *communitas*. Such relational bonds are born in liminal ritual spaces where familiar social relationships are leveled, new connections born, and shared meanings formed.[5] Family members imagined that these bonds would bring feelings that would prompt caring for others and more deeply understanding self, intimate others, and the family issues and challenges that they hoped their Camino would address. This Camino promise of communitas was as strong in my research participants' narratives as it was in larger Camino discourse.

In *The Way*, Tom's three pilgrim friends laugh, quarrel, rescue each other, and in time reveal the reasons each is walking as they face physical and psychological challenges together—a film performance echoing family members' conviction that the pilgrimage could bring connection, intimacy, and meaning-making with strangers. In Codd's text as well, the building of the experience of communitas as the ground of the Camino life is reinforced as three pilgrim friends bond as a "band of pilgrim brothers," leaving the city of Pamplona "eminently clear" that they are "committed to be there" for each other "for the duration." Pilgrim online blogs are filled with stories about the new friendships and closeness that people have formed in bonding with what they call their *Camino families*. Even scholarship on the Camino at times reinforces the idea that a good Camino is one where a pilgrim can reduce conflict, or at least make sense of the competition for lodging or other resources on the Camino in ways that do not disturb the communitas they seek.[6] Most of the people I interviewed longed for this type of closeness with others.

I illustrate in what follows how the pilgrims I interviewed described what they thought a Camino life and its promises would bring regarding their personal growth, but even more, how they imagined their walk together affecting their family relationship. In chapter 3, I tell more of their stories, offering my interpretation of their narratives of Camino promises fulfilled and passed over.

Isabelle, a twenty-five-year-old woman from Sweden who had just graduated from a professional program and was getting ready to start a new job, walked with Lisa, her fifty-five-year-old mother. Lisa had recently had back surgery but had always wanted to walk the Camino, and she was determined to walk and bond with her daughter before Isabelle started a busy career. In their interview together fresh off the Camino, they both told me that they identified "strongly" as "spiritual people," practitioners of meditation and yoga, and that they had each read several books about the Camino before they left for Spain. They both talked about the Camino as a "compressed life," because, Lisa explained, "you experience things in a more magnified way; the stages of life and the stories that you meet from other people are heavy stories and so you get this joy of life and pain of life felt all in one trip. It was like life's ups and downs as you experience your feelings and intense life stories from others." Before they left for the Camino Lisa went to her "spiritual advisor," who suggested to her: "Don't walk as mother and daughter, walk as friends." Lisa took this advice to heart, thinking of her daughter as a pilgrim friend—even though at the same time they felt "reborn" as family, as their story of walking for a week together on the Camino will reveal.

In two of the four cases where parents were divorced, family members had experienced contentious relationships with their parent or child and hoped that their relationships might be strengthened in some way by walking the Camino together. Lindsey, the young woman from the United States introduced at the beginning of this chapter who walked with her mother, was one such case. Ariel, a young woman from the United States who walked with her father, was another. Both of these young women described conflict with their parent over the years.

Lindsey was the most vocal about how connections with others while walking might bring some sort of change to her mother's personality, and thus to their relationship. Her difficulty with her mother, Margie (early fifties), had been shaped over years of what she described as a "really complicated" family history. Her parents divorced when she was young, an event that she saw as a life disruption that "destroyed" her father "mentally and financially." Her mother received custody and her father had visitation rights; she lived with her mother and her stepfather for several years. When she was in high school, she made a choice to live with her father, a Catholic man with whom she described having a strong relationship. Even though Lindsey would have liked to have asked her dad to walk the Camino with her, she could not because he had physical issues that would keep him from being able to hike. She had "two streams of thought" in her head when she asked her mom to take her on the Camino: on the one hand, she said, she felt manipulative, in that her mother had the money and time and loved exercise and hiking, so she knew she would agree to take Lindsey on the trip; on the other hand, she saw her mother as a lonely person and did not want her to "end up that way" and thought that maybe her mother might learn to feel more for others on the Camino (the "miracle" she hoped for that I describe at the beginning of this chapter), which Lindsey thought could improve their relationship and help her mom form other meaningful friendships and intimate connections. Lindsey's belief that the Camino could bring change reflected her own spiritual expectations for an individual walk that was religious, but also a strong belief that such miracles might be found through communitas with other pilgrims—that interacting with other people might help Margie learn to bond with others in some way that would help her grow and become a better person.

Margie communicated to me that she loved hiking but that she wanted to go to spend time with her daughter and saw the Camino as a time of "self-examination" and "introspection," a time when she could "focus on life decisions without the day-to-day interruptions" of her life. She identified as "spiritual, not religious," having discovered years ago that she needed, as she put it, "connection with my higher power" but not "one church." Her descriptions of spirituality and hopes for the Camino were more about doing self-work and being with her daughter, while Lindsey's spiritual hopes were connected to her Christian beliefs and attachment to the power of pilgrimage practice to bring connection and caring for others. As I detail in chapter 3, Margie and Lindsey offered different presentations of their shared Camino, but each of their descriptions supported the belief that some kind of change took place.

Ariel and her father, Allan, who both identified as Christians, saw the Camino as a spiritual practice and held expectations that it might help them strengthen their relationship in some way. Allan talked of inviting Ariel to walk the Camino, hoping that walking with other pilgrims from across the world and facing the physical challenges would teach his daughter "valuable life lessons." Despite being warned by other family members that she was "crazy" to go on the Camino with her father given his "mood swings and controlling nature," Ariel, a twenty-three-year-old woman from California, agreed to walk for six to eight hours a day across Spain with him. As she considered going on the journey with him, she imagined that he wanted to spend the time with her to "make up for lost caretaking," explaining that when she was young he had traveled several months out of the year and that she had lived with her mother after the divorce.

Ariel began the journey with small hopes for change in their relationship, describing her father as verbally abusive and barely present during her childhood. However, she said, as she walked and came to know more pilgrims, she started to hear accounts of, and believe more deeply in, Camino promises related to transformation and the important "lessons" the Camino might bring. Eventually she embraced the idea that the Camino was "happening for a reason" and that investing in connection with other pilgrims could help her come to terms with their relationship. "I was determined to turn the weaknesses about my father into strengths," she said. "I had no illusions about fixing our relationship, but that when hard times come to us, I would be able to work in it with him in a better way." She believed that the Camino could "help you realize what it is you need to work on," and that it can bring "reflection in your soul" and help you "find God." Walking alone, she said, "you can talk to God." As someone who had been in therapy from age seven to age twenty, she described the Camino as a similar kind of "therapeutic" space where people are encouraged to reflect on their life and relationships and express their feelings to others. In chapter 3, I relate her stories of difficult encounters with her father and of the other pilgrims who helped her emotionally along the way. Ariel's story was of a difficult journey where she did a lot of "self-searching" and "cried at least once each day," but ultimately one where the Camino brought a lesson about how she should approach her future relationship with her father.

Allan did little to hide the contentious nature of his relationship with Ariel and the difficulties they encountered together and alone on the Camino. He presented himself to me as a father who was providing Ariel with a valuable therapeutic and spiritual experience. Allan envisioned that spiritual experiences on the Camino would endow Ariel with important emotional skills and help her engage in serious self-reflection regarding her life choices. He saw her as stuck in a low-wage job and controlled by negative emotions and strained intimate relationships. He likened the Camino to a "fighting ring" where Ariel could not "escape" her emotions and would have to deal with her "anger" and talk with him and other pilgrims. He wanted to build her emotional resilience: "I was trying to instill that you have to have a positive outlook. . . . Everybody's got blisters on the Camino. . . . I was trying to get her to learn to overcome pain, to work through it and listen to it, and on one hand yield to it, but to always be forward-thinking." He described investing in the Camino as an important lesson: "Even if her and I never speak again, which would grieve me, at least I would know that she is going to be okay, that she's got this [the Camino] . . . learning to use the correct tools to navigate your life and build your relationships."

In two family cases, the death of a family member was related to members' expectations of what the Camino might bring. Elise was a sixty-two-year-old Catholic mother who walked with her sixty-year-old husband, twenty-year-old-son, and twenty-five-year-old daughter. Her daughter had always wanted to do the Camino and so was a force in the family regarding learning about what the Camino was. But about halfway through our interview, Elise told me that her middle son had committed suicide just under a year and a half before. Such a tragic loss, she said, "does things to a family." Elise's attraction to the Camino came in part through her daughter's interest and her desire to get to know her two children more deeply, but she had also watched *The Way* when it came out, and then they watched it again as a family before leaving for Spain. It was a screenplay that no doubt caught her attention with its focus on the death of a son and the grieving that took place through forming close relationships with fellow pilgrims and as the character, Tom, spread his son's ashes on sacred symbols along the way. When I asked Elise whether she was drawn to the Camino as a spiritual practice, her response was about family bonds: "I wanted us to feel a connection. I wanted them to know that they are okay and that we are there for them, and that there is nobody in the world that cares more and that our family is sort of the ultimate unit." She emphasized that she did not want the family to concentrate on her son's death, that the trip was about being together and strengthening their family unit. Still, as I discuss in chapter 3, her Camino family story was full of unexpected relational intimacy regarding the son she had lost. Before they left for Spain, Elise said, they had talked with each other about why they were walking. She told them that she was "looking to fill a void." Elise used an explicitly Christian concept related to feeling God's love and compassion to express her motivations: "I said it is grace that I'm looking for. I have a void and being with all of you and being out here, doing this, is a way of seeking to fill this void." I asked to interview Elise's husband and children, but they did not respond.

Ann, a fifty-year-old mother from California, walked with her twenty-three-year-old daughter Hannah. Her husband, Hannah's father, had recently died after a long battle with cancer. Ann described an intense attachment to the movie, *The Way*, perhaps even more so than any of my other research participants. The movie had a salvific character and mystical calling for her as she was caring for her husband: "I was taking care of my husband exclusively and I ended up watching a lot of TV in my downtime, when I couldn't go anywhere, and we got Amazon and I stumbled on *The Way*, and I just wept and I could not get enough people to watch it. I had my whole family watch it with me. . . . That movie saved me . . . for the last couple of years of his illness." When Ann's husband died, she said, Hannah, knowing how much the movie resonated in her mom's life, wanted to walk the Camino with her.

Ann was a yoga instructor for years before her husband became ill, and she considered herself a "spiritual person," someone who "has to find meaning in things." She was not raised in any religious tradition and was not into "formal religion," where she felt there was too much "hypocrisy." She was surprised, given her thoughts about religion, that she was drawn to a Catholic pilgrimage and that she came to enjoy the religious symbols along the way. She reflected on her expectations: "I was really aware that journey itself is an incredibly spiritual thing and that even if you aren't a religious person, just being in that element and coming across, on a daily basis, things that have a religious, that are involved in religious rituals, crosses, arrows, shells, bridges, you know all of that, there is something about immersing yourself in that." The "whole journey," she said, "is just rich with all those symbols . . . By continuing it daily what happens is it [spirituality] is just part of you. . . . You are not sitting listening to a mass or a sermon or something that someone is saying to you. It is just you are part of it—something bigger, older, longer, bigger and stronger and more powerful than you are, and if you become open and vulnerable then it can pour into you." Hannah did not respond to my request through her mom for an interview; but I was able to access her blog. This online visual journal was a public presentation for family and friends of their family story. Hannah's blog focuses on their Peregrino friends and the cultural and natural landscape they crossed on foot. The narrative they told, related in detail in chapter 3, is a story of caring for each other and growing closer through communitas. It is a description of Ann finding confidence and purpose in life after the loss of great love, of a massive force of nature at work in their spiritual walking together, of acceptance of loss, and of the presence of angels.

A handful of families talked about motivations for walking the Camino to help a family member deal with anxiety or depression. Recall Katy's father, José, at the start of this book: a Catholic man who had received a Camino miracle of reconciliation with his older son, an experience that led him to hope that Camino practice would hold answers for his daughter's anxiety issues. While walking the Camino, I heard several parents and young adult children voice optimism that the Camino, as a space that was supposed to be removed from the everyday, would help their family members discover where their anxiety originated, and provide lessons or some guidance regarding how they might address these problems.

For example, several families talked about their family member's "addiction" to their iPhones or social media accounts. Ellen (twenty), from Australia, and her mother, Robin (fifty-four), went on the Camino with the hope that Ellen could experience healing from an upsetting experience with social media. They spoke about their hopes for a Camino where Ellen would be able to escape from her everyday digital ties, where face-to-face connections with other pilgrims would bring relief from online interactions. However, given the wired nature of the Camino, Ellen was not able to break free from the social media networks that had caused emotional trauma in her life. Even more, her mother was disgusted by the way that pilgrims took stories about them and others and put them on Facebook pages and blogs without their permission, efforts that Robin described as undercutting the more meaningful bonds that she had hoped they would form with other pilgrims. Digital habits and a wired Camino structure threatened to undermine the healing and transformative promises that families hoped a spiritual Camino experience would bring.

Jansen (sixty-one), a father from the Netherlands who identified as "not religious or spiritual," described meditating while walking as potentially spiritual: "letting the mind wander and thinking about the universe" could be considered a spiritual practice, he said. It was a practice that he experienced during a deeply powerful individual Camino, and one that he hoped would help his daughter recover from her depression associated with an eating disorder. Lina, his twenty-six-year-old daughter, had similar aspirations. In separate interviews, father and daughter talked about the Camino as a mind-clearing and spiritual practice that they thought would be good for addressing her issues. Lina, like her father, offered an open, fluid, and at times contradictory relationship with spirituality, making it clear, however, that for her the Camino was spiritual: "I wouldn't say I'm spiritual. I may be wrong. I always associate spiritual with Eastern Buddhism, yoga, and all of those traditions that are coming to Europe now, but I don't have the patience for that. I would say I'm a spiritual person. If I were to characterize why I went to Santiago, I would say it was spiritual because I really needed to clear my head, so in that sense maybe, but I'm not a particularly spiritual person." She continued: "I had to stop my studies at one point because I became seriously depressed. I had to go to a rehab, it was quite challenging. Then when I went back to school I was like, kind of lost, and I was like, okay, what now? And it was my dad who said, 'Why don't you walk to Santiago and clear your mind?'" At first, she said, she "didn't take it seriously. I was like, who walks like a thousand kilometers? I didn't take it seriously at all." But "he said it was to clear my mind because he saw that I was struggling, and I didn't know what I wanted to do." She recalled him saying to her that the Camino would get her out of her "daily surroundings and just to really take a step back and think about things." Therapy was not helping her anymore: "I was just going to therapy because I was supposed to, but I didn't feel like I was going further in therapy. So I thought maybe something like this could help me." Eventually she agreed. Lina said her father "jumped at the opportunity and said, 'Let's get this going!'" Soon they were walking across Spain together.

In many ways, all of the families described here were working through significant life transitions as parents aged and young adults made decisions about education or how they might grow in career paths. Their family relationships were shifting as young adults became independent and able to care for themselves, although most were still financially dependent in some way on their parents. A handful of families decided to walk together to celebrate graduations from high school or college. Several of the families invested in Camino promises for more specific kinds of transitioning purposes—for example, parents or young adults looking for change in educational pursuits or careers. They saw the Camino as a spiritual practice where they could experience together the lessons that the Camino might bring regarding shifts and new directions.

Barbara, a fifty-year-old mother from Canada who worked as an executive in a large corporation, walked for several weeks on Camino routes with her twenty-year-old daughter Michelle and her twenty-two-year-old-son Lance. Barbara was inspired to go on the Camino through "word of mouth" from friends who had walked and also, she said, because of "the movie [*The Way*]." Lance talked to me about watching the movie as well, although he said he had "kind of dozed off" and did not make it all the way through the showing. Still, he was intrigued by the Camino as an "adventure" and accepted his mom's invitation to walk. He was a "little worried" because he "smoked and drank" and was not as fit as his mother, who was a "marathon runner."

Barbara identified as Catholic, although not practicing at the moment, and had raised her children as Catholic, hitting, as she put it, all the "milestones" of a "Roman Catholic family": the kids were "all baptized and had their first communion and confirmation." Now, she said, "it is time for them to figure out their own faith. We don't see ourselves as responsible anymore for directing that." She saw the Camino not primarily as a Catholic practice but as a "spiritual" one where, through taking on a pilgrim identity with her children, she could let go of her mothering identity and leave behind what she named being a "type-A, alpha mom," so that her son and daughter could "become much more of leaders" and let go of their "mom dependency." With regard to her son, she thought the Camino might help him discover some meaningful direction for continuing his education and/or exploring another career path. "He works and had a year of university," she said, "but he hasn't been able to determine for himself what he really wants to do." She described Lance as "kind of at a crossroads," and then added, "We are all at a crossroads at this point in our lives." Lance told me in a separate interview that he was a "confirmed" but "lost Catholic" who did not go to Mass and did not "really agree with all these [Catholic] things," but, still, "I'm a Catholic." He had expectations that the Camino might generate some self-searching and reflection that would reveal a direction, and to that end he decided to journal during the trip. In chapter 3, I detail more of their family story as mother and son learning about themselves, connecting with other pilgrims, and the Camino bringing them closer to what they saw as their "spiritual" Catholic selves.

Rick (fifty), a father from the United States, had also watched the movie *The Way*, but he credited his motivation for walking the Camino with his younger son to a previous Camino with his older son, who at the time had been transitioning out of the military. His younger son was now leaving the military himself, and Rick thought walking for hours on Camino paths with only self-reflection and bonding with others as their task would be helpful as the son moved away from a military life that was highly planned and about preparing to be a soldier. Rick wanted to return to the Camino and experience with his younger son what he called "gold nuggets" that he remembered sharing with his older son along the route: "the feeling of peace, you are in the moment, you don't have any choice but to be in the moment. Your job is to walk west."

Rick was an experienced hiker and identified as a spiritual Christian: "I am a Christian, not a Catholic. I'm a Protestant, but the center of everything I do is my spiritual beliefs. . . . My purpose is to bring God glory no matter what I do. . . . The Camino wasn't religious per se in a Catholic sense, but very spiritual." The center of spirituality and the Camino's promise for individual change, for Rick, rested in bonding with other pilgrims. He expected that his son, like all who walk the Camino, will "take away change" that comes from the practice of walking and interacting with others:

> They [other pilgrims] may have a hard time articulating why they feel changed, but all of a sudden they are having all of these interactions with

> people from a dozen different countries and in the couple of hours that you have walked together one day you may have reached a depth of interaction that you rarely get a chance to experience. And then when you couple that with experience after experience after experience over a month's time or several weeks' time, you walk away from the Camino and you say, I'm different, my trajectory is different because I interacted in depth with all of these people.

Rick believed that the spiritual nature of the Camino in its communal manifestation would bring his son valuable knowledge and shifts in perspective regarding how to approach life after military service. As I detail in chapter 3, his son's trajectory did shift because of the Camino, but not exactly in the way his father expected it would.

One morning, after attending the English Mass in the Cathedral in Santiago, I met Ed, a sixty-year-old businessman, and his twenty-two-year-old daughter Julie, from the United States. They were both deeply tied to their identity as Catholics. Julie had just graduated from college. As I sat with them the next day over coffee at a café, a more detailed story of Camino expectations related to Ed's job came to the forefront. Julie had convinced her father to take her on the Camino as a graduation gift, but she said she had other motives. Julie was drawn to experience the Camino after spending time in the Taizé Community, an ecumenical monastic community in France that reaches out to young adults.[7] That had been her first pilgrimage experience, one in which she removed herself from everyday life, met people from around the world, and built a commitment to thinking about God, diversity and global inequalities, and social change. Julie wanted to pull her father away from his consuming, stressful job and for them to share such practice together, without interruptions. She made him promise, before they left, that he would not look at his email and that he would respect their tech-free walking time meant for discussion about life issues, interacting with other pilgrims, and prayer. She wanted, she said, a "spiritual time together when we were just quiet together, thinking about peace." Julie hoped for other types of shared spiritual experiences on their ten-day journey on the Camino Francés, including experiencing nature and the Divine in new ways together. In chapter 3 I relate their stories of spiritual intimacy born on the Camino and Ed's revelations about changing his daily life at home regarding work and family.

Conclusion: Promises Pursued

Most family members saw a compressed Camino as having the potential to bring individual and relational transformation. They hoped to explore the natural world in fresh ways with their family, to make discoveries about themselves, to form new friendships together with other pilgrims, and to grow closer to each other through sharing meditative walking and other practices they named as spiritual. Some longed to heal old wounds, others to grieve together. No matter the relational issues they brought with them as they walked, the stories most family members told me were of a Camino promise revealed. Far from the structured office of a counselor or other therapeutic, religious, or spiritual guide to whom parents and young adults might have turned for help in the past, these families were investing in personal and relational transformation through a different kind of ritual, a shared and multifaceted spiritual practice.

Anthropologist Edith Turner (2012), in her book *Communitas: The Anthropology of Collective Joy*, articulates the concept of communitas in a way that captures its essential characteristics and recognizes that such bonding can have "almost endless variations." Communitas, she writes, "has to do with the sense felt by a group of people when their life together takes on full meaning." It happens "through the readiness of the people—perhaps from necessity—to rid themselves of their concern for status and dependence on structures, and see their fellows as they are" (1–2). To understand what this concept truly means, she suggests, requires uncovering the phenomenon in social life: "Communitas can only be conveyed properly through stories" (2). In chapter 3, I offer my interpretation of the stories parents and young adults communicated to me about their experiences of spiritual intimacy. Their narratives were grounded in coming to see their family members "as just people," as many of them told me—not as mother, father, son, or daughter, but as pilgrims bonding with intimate and unfamiliar others. They are stories of finding spiritual meaning and effective practice together. While the dominant theme was building closer connections through the sharing of Camino practices and beliefs, some families also told stories of spiritual intimacy better conceived of as narratives of advantageous separation: Camino life that intensified the autonomous and healthy independent nature of individual family members.

3
Spiritual Intimacies

> It was a great thing that we shared together in life. A common experience we were both experiencing for the first time together. With fathers and sons, you tend to get this one-way traffic where the father tells the son about his experience and what he knows, but this was an experience that we both set out from the same position, you know. We were alone together, so I think it will be rewarding in the long term to reflect on it.
>
> —Peter, sixty-year-old father from Australia

Contemporary families face social and economic pressure to be dependent on one another, and at the same time autonomous. A belief in this balance and developing practices to be successful alone and together was at the heart of the aspirations and representations of experience that pilgrims shared with me.[1] Families in chapter 2 who invested in Camino promises voiced expectations of spiritual intimacy—gaining private, exclusive understandings of each other through spiritual practice, connecting as "just pilgrims" together on the road to Santiago. In this chapter, I tell their stories, organized by the

Walking the Way Together. Kathleen E. Jenkins, Oxford University Press (2021). © Oxford University Press.
DOI: 10.1093/oso/9780197553046.003.0003

types of spiritual intimacy I interpret as being central in their narratives: (1) *intimate disclosures*, fueling deeper understanding and reflexive thought about self, each other, and life's meaning and purpose; (2) *intimate encounters with nature and the material Camino*, sharing transcendence through body encounters with the world of the Camino; and (3) *intimacy through body labor*, caring for and helping each other through physically challenging encounters. These types of spiritual experience at times overlapped in their stories, and family members who identified as religious often added a layer of "vertical" or "theistic" forms of transcendence: connection to God or a supernatural power that enhanced experiences of family bonding with nature and others.[2] Listening carefully to the types of spiritual intimacy active in these stories brings to the surface how, even with contradictory remembrances or objectives, most family members came to understand their pilgrimage as impactful regarding individual and relational identity and purpose.

Intimate Disclosures

The majority of family members talked about the Camino prompting them to express feelings to their family member in new ways. For some, these were emotions and memories that had lain dormant for years. Having extended time with each other day after day, walking on paths with the space to think more deeply about their own lives, their conversation moved from benign chitchat to emotional recollections. Being "just pilgrims," two bodies in sync walking roads to Santiago together, ushered in a liminal time where everyday roles sat softly in the background and their shared pilgrim identity and practice instigated in-depth conversation. In two family cases from the United States, harsh words and arguments framed stories of intimate disclosures on the road to Santiago de Compostela.

Conflict and Discovery

> You can't change a person, people change themselves.
>
> —Lindsey (twenty-four), United States

I asked every person I interviewed if there were pictures that stood out their mind when they thought of their Camino. Lindsey said that she took tons of pictures of the road before her and the scenery, but what she remembered most about these photos was her mom, Margie (early fifties), in front of her: "My mom was way ahead. She was a fast walker and I'm a short person. . . . I felt bad about how slow I was. . . . Part of it, I like to contemplate when I walk which makes me very slow."

"So," I asked, "that's what you think of when you think of pictures?"

"Yes." She paused, and then added, "Seeing my mom in the distance."

At the beginning of our interview, Lindsey told me that she loved her mom but that they did not have a good relationship. Her parents divorced when she was ten. She lived at first with her mom and then moved to her father's home when she was a teenager because of too much turmoil in her relationship with her mom and in her mother's life. Since that time, she had had limited in-person contact with Margie. Lindsey added that she called her mom "all the time," even though she found talking with her stressful.

Lindsey asked her mother to join her on the Camino partly because Margie could make the trip financially possible, but she added, "I asked her to take me also because Mom is a lonely person." Lindsey hoped that the Camino promise of people coming together, caring for one another, and having empathy for one another could help her mother change the way she interacts with others and bring new relationships to her life. Perhaps, she thought, "even a miracle" might happen that would lead to significant change in Margie.

Lindsey said her belief in God, her connection to Christian prayer and ritual, and her membership in a community of walkers making their way to the Cathedral of St. James in Santiago de Compostela fortified her resolve to speak up and talk to her mother on the Camino in ways she had not before. Her story of expressing her feelings to her mom reflected a month-long journey filled with emotional battles and physical pain, but one that led to her discovery of how she should approach their relationship in the future.

Walking the Camino was more difficult than Lindsey expected: "My body was like, the beginning of the third day it was just like, nope, so I was limping for a week. . . . My mom had issues too, but she ended up getting better way before I did." She called the walking part a "harrowing physical experience," but one that led to her spending more time alone with her mom. One day, Lindsey said, "we had been walking long enough to where you have gotten bored about talking about breakfast and little things and you are by yourself and you are like, it's time to inevitably talk about something that will lead to something." Margie said something that prompted Lindsey to talk about her stepfather: "Something she didn't realize was that my stepdad was kind of verbally abusive." Still, Lindsey said, she was mostly cautious on the Camino about how she talked about the past with her mother: "I never really went all out and told her what it was like to be a kid with her," and "We never went all out and had that full moment of understanding each other, raw, like all broken down and this is what my childhood was, and this is what I thought about you." However, Lindsey did describe several times when she approached the past with her mom:

> I mentioned something about not being able to see friends. . . . So I just said very casually, "Remember you didn't like us going to the McNeils' house because they lived too far away?" . . . So my mom said, "You thought I was barring you from your friends!" and I said, "No, you just didn't like going driving out extra trips because you thought it was a waste of gas." . . . And she was like, "You are lying!" She freaked out and suddenly was saying that I was being overdramatic. . . . For a while we walked on in silence.
>
> I have it all in a journal. . . . I wanted to be as objective as possible because one of the things that my mom loves to do is to accuse me of lying. . . . After we walked in silence for a while, she just stopped, and I hugged her because I could tell she was upset. And she was like, "I'm sorry, I'm sorry, I wanted to give you guys everything and I guess I didn't really. I thought I was a good mother, I thought I was sacrificing all I could, and I guess I didn't." . . . I think it was genuine. . . . In that moment she was definitely sincere. But I'm not sure she learned anything. . . . That was the one time she apologized to me. Every time after that it was just one of us storming off and not talking for a while. . . .
>
> The next time we had a deep discussion about the past and I stormed off. . . . We were talking about diets and all that because she loves talking about nutrition. . . . I told her that she always used to tell me that I was overweight when I was little, and I wasn't. . . . I was kind of skinny, and she said, "No, you were always a little bit above your average percentile," and I said, "Mom, you had me counting calories since I was six." She said, "You weren't counting calories." Which was true, I was not counting calories, literally; but then she said, "You weren't counting calories, you were just counting your desserts." . . . Yeah, I was counting desserts. I was thinking, I can't have dessert this week because I will get fat. When I was six, seven, eight years old, I was already worrying about that sort of thing. And she said, "You are being overdramatic. That is a lie, I did not do that to you, I did not say you

were fat. I wanted you to be healthy." . . . I know what memories are there, and what was real, and so she was saying that a specific factual memory that I had was wrong and a lie. And I said, "No, I've worked very hard to figure out what was right and wrong."

Lindsey did not see talking about these Camino moments as making her closer to her mother or bringing a revelatory moment, but during the interview she did relate a confrontation toward the end of their journey that transformed how she understood her relationship with her mom:

There was this one specific time . . . it was very poetic. We were at the train station going out of Santiago and it was really early, ridiculously early, my mom has this thing about being early and they hadn't even opened the platform for us to go on and we didn't know what was going on, but we weren't allowed to go on the platform, and of course the poor woman who had to come down and tell us that we weren't allowed to be on the platform, my mom mouthed off to, and was kind of mean to, and I was having one of my less mature moments and was very angry at how she was being so mean to this person, and so I was stomping up to the stairs and trying to let out my anger so I wouldn't say something, and my mom's like, "Look, you don't have to be so upset about this," and I go, "No, I just wish you weren't so mean to people." And then right after that when we were coming back down onto the platform we ran into them again and my mom told her, "I just wanted to apologize for earlier if I came off as harsh, I didn't mean to do that, I'm exhausted, and I'm sorry." And I thought, wow, that doesn't happen often, ever.

Kay: What does that mean to you?

Lindsey: That she was listening. That maybe what I said struck a chord . . . I don't know if it will last in the long run, but it gave me hope. It gave me a glimmer of hope that, you know, maybe I can't change her, and the Camino can't change her, but maybe she will be inclined to change for herself.

Margie's apology brought Lindsey some hope for a Camino promise revealed:

The Camino doesn't change everybody, and the movie [*The Way*] kind of gets at that, but it really hits home when you finish the Camino and you are like, people go on it to lose weight, to maybe resolve some things, and maybe sometimes they aren't resolved, but it doesn't automatically happen, it happens in yourself. You are the one who decides that it is going to change.

Later in our interview Lindsey said: "Barring when I was baptized, the Camino was the best experience of my life." I asked her why. "I guess," she said, "because it taught me that lesson. . . . You can't change people. . . . They have to change themselves."

"My mom," Lindsey told me, "is going to tell you a story about how the Camino made us better because that's what my mom thinks it is, and that is how she is going to tell that story and that's what anyone she talks to about it is going to hear."

Margie preferred to answer my interview questions in written form, and her answers were brief. Unlike Lindsey, Margie identified as a "spiritual" person who saw the Divine as a more of an inner presence, a "higher power" that did not need affirmation by a church or faith tradition. As Lindsey predicted, her responses to my questions were about building connection and taking care of Lindsey on the Camino. Margie described Lindsey criticizing her for things from her childhood, noting that the detail with which her daughter remembered them on their walk must have been exaggerated by her exhaustion. Margie stressed their Camino as important time spent with Lindsey, and at the same time an individual opportunity for Margie to reflect about her life and career choices.

"You can do anything in this Camino Vortex."

—Ariel

I spent time with Ariel the day after she finished her month-long walk with her father, Allan, whom I interviewed a few months later by phone. Like many of the interviews with pilgrims fresh off the path, Ariel was connected in an immediate way to her Camino physical and emotional experience, recalling encounters with her father and other pilgrims in great detail. She talked with me for several hours in a café, still exhausted and in pain from a knee injury.

Ariel identified as a Christian and a spiritual person searching for God and a path to a better relationship with her father. She had a strained relationship with both of her parents, but especially with Allan. Her mother and sister told her she was "crazy" to go to Spain with him given his "great emotional ups and downs." Ariel had been in therapy from ages seven to twenty, a practice that her parents encouraged and supported to help her deal with strained family relationships. Years of working with counselors, Ariel said, made her realize that her parents' families were all in "abusive cycles." The Camino brought her extended time and opportunity to talk with Allan about his lack of involvement in her life and gave her new insight into how her father's upbringing impacted his life.

Ariel said she felt an immediate need to talk about her Camino experience; in fact, she apologized for spending so much time telling me her story. I reassured her that I was thankful she was willing to share it. Ariel emphasized that it was an "emotional Camino," where she cried "literally every day." Some of her breakdowns had to do with her father, but issues with other family members and her current job provoked tears as well. Ariel called the Camino a "cleansing and renewal" and a "time for serious reflection." But, she stressed, it was also about learning to love other people: "When you look back on life, all you really want to do is give love. Nothing is guaranteed in life." Most important, she said, is "reflection in your soul."

The Camino was a deeply reflexive and laborious practice for Ariel: "There were so many f— yous and emotional lows and stress. The Camino isn't a good thing unless you are ready to do the work." My dad has kind of a "mad-scientist personality in that he likes to be in control." They walked together sometimes, and separately at other times because of blisters or other injuries and illness, or because she chose to walk with another pilgrim. She recalled arguments, their origins, and accompanying emotions in great detail. One fight stemmed from her father's interactions with two young Korean women talking on their phones in an albergue:

> He [Allan] said out loud, "Oh great, we'll be up all night." And I was embarrassed, and I thought it was selfish. I called him out later, I said, "You shouldn't say anything until something happens." I found out later they spoke English, so it was really embarrassing. . . . I told him, "Honestly, you need to change your attitude." And he said the trip was a "favor to save my soul." I stood up and he grabbed my arm and I said, "I'm twenty-three years old, don't touch me like that. I'm not doing this." I was in tears and exhausted after that and thought I might quit right then. It was embarrassing because it was in an albergue and everybody else was around. I texted with my mom and my sister and they said I was tough and would "figure it out."

Ariel said she "realized . . . after that first fight . . . that everyone has their handicaps, and just because they are your parents it doesn't mean they don't. I told my dad that morning that we are all on the Camino to make our lives work somehow, and that the most important things in life are understanding, kindness, and giving love." She described several times when Allan would "start out happy in the beginning of the day," walk ahead to find a place for them to stay, and then at the end of the day, he was often unhappy and moody. I became caught up in the intensity with which she told her stories; at times, sitting in the café, we were both tearful.

Ariel emphasized that despite the arguments she "had several moments of new understanding" with her father, and realized that he was "trying to work through many issues from his childhood:"

> He made a point of telling me one time that the reason he acts mean or uncaring sometimes is that he is "working through his childhood." He said, "It has nothing to do with you." I had told him that I wanted to quit, and he said, "I don't want you to go." He cried. He burst into tears. That was the first time in my life that I saw my father cry. He said, "Please don't go. I want to do this with you. Take some days by yourself and then let's finish together." That showed me a lot. Parents are supposed to be the stronger one, and for him to let himself let go of that emotion in front of me. It was the first time in my life really that he took me completely out of the equation. After that moment on the Camino he did not walk ahead so quickly, for him to say he was sorry—it was not him, it was like a breaking point for him.

"The Camino doesn't fix anything," Ariel qualified, but it "teaches you how to love each other."

Challenging his behavior and coming to see her father's emotions in light of his childhood brought new relational understanding that, in her words, was "finding God." She said she still had "huge issues" with Allan. She was relieved to have left his constant presence and was not sure when she wanted to see him again, but she "walked away knowing how to love him."

When I spoke with Allan a few months after their Camino, I asked him if there were pictures that stood out in his memory of their trip. He said: "I look at the pictures and they are so endearing. I've got so many pictures of her and everything else." He added that while there were a lot of "good things about the trip," "honestly, the real warm and fuzzies were few and far between. There really was just a chasm between us." Later he described an enduring image: "On the last day I took a video of her walking away and it's just the greatest thing in the world; it's her flipping me off. It's such a great, how do you want to say, encapsulation of the moment. She is smiling but flipping me off."

Allan identified as a "believer," a "spiritual person" who was raised in a Jewish household and converted to Christianity. Because he told me his story a few months after their Camino, he was able to reflect on how their journey might have brought change to his daughter and their relationship. Allan decided to take Ariel on the Camino because he believed in its transformative power. He thought she might become a stronger person through its physical and emotional challenges and by forming close relationships with pilgrims: "I wanted her to experience the Camino and come back with something that she could say was truly hers, something that was real and tangible, and also meet some people that see things differently, and for Ariel to be able to see the bigger picture." He reflected on his life lessons as he defended his hopes for Ariel:

> I was on my own at an early age and I learned that you could basically do whatever you wanted to, you just had to put the work into it, and with Ariel I was trying to instill this with her on the Camino. That you can start your day out with things in your head that are going to derail you . . . You have to have a positive outlook. . . . And when she had blisters and everything else, I realize that I could have been more empathetic, but I was like, everybody's got blisters around here. It was one of those things. I had an MRI before the trip and my back is messed up and I was like, nothing is going to stop me on this, I'm not going to let it. I'll do it. I know I will because I want to do it, and she was in better shape than I am.

Allan described routine defiance: "It was a fight during the whole trip, I mean she was in such resistance, the better part of it, and if there was anything I said or did, it was wrong. It was tough. It was very difficult."

He also told a story of having spiritual alone time on the Camino when he could remember and reflect. This reflection, he thought, had brought him to a place where he was able to express his feelings in new ways to Ariel. Ariel was injured and sick at one point and so spent about a week a pension healing and later bused ahead. During that time walking alone Allan had a lot of time to think about his early relationships: "I basically had a couple of parents who had things to do other than be a parent. So, for me to try to be the best parent,

I'm not perfect, but for me it's important because I did not have good role models."

"Everyone has a little spiritual moment on the Camino," Allan said, and "some are greater than others." He found spirituality and Divine energy through walking: "I think you realize that if you keep your cadence through the trip, whatever that might be, and you just push yourself down the road, I think you will have that little walk with God." Walking alone is "spiritual in itself. It kind of frees you up and allows you to think. You don't have any distractions." His reflexive spiritual work culminated in his crying in front of Ariel. He said Ariel "was ready to quit," but he "wasn't going to make it easy." He told her: "You know, if you want to go, you are welcome to go. If you stay with me, I'll support you all the way through." She looked up at him and said, "What's the difference?" He told her that there was a big difference. He emphasized to me that "the whole thing, honestly, the whole thing was to do this, it wasn't really about me. It was about me and her . . . it was about her and getting her out, spending some time with her and learning about her and you know, building a relationship and just getting in the ring with her in an area where she had no escapes."

Allan and Ariel did not see each other for months after their Camino. Allan offered some assessment of what he saw as the long-term effects of their Camino discoveries and the growth of intimacy in their relationship:

> She's got some stuff to work out between me and her, but at this point, I have to think we built a trust, and I think that is the most important thing any two individuals can have, emotional trust. . . . She is coming over this afternoon and we are going to do something together. We are going to work on a project she is working on. . . . I don't know that she is a different person, but her outlook has changed. . . . Everything I wanted to happen has happened, except it took coming back home as a benchmark to see her own growth and to understand the Camino—she has it under her belt, nobody can take it away from her.

I asked pilgrims what the most challenging part of their Camino was, and the most rewarding; but I also made sure to ask, about midway through interviews: "Does anything stand out in your mind that you learned about your mom [dad, son, daughter] from your Camino?" Lindsey and Ariel's stories represent how disclosure of feelings long left unspoken led to Camino lessons about relational ethics. Ariel learned how to love through frustration and disappointment. Lindsey came to understand that she could let go of feeling the responsibility to change the people she loved. As pilgrims together, family members had access to a new kind of space and time for listening.

Leveling and Spiritual Connection

At the beginning of conversations I asked what family members thought was most important about their Camino, and at the end if there was anything about the experience of walking that they wanted to share. These broad questions often lead to descriptions of familiar family roles and responsibilities fading into the background and becoming "friends" or "just pilgrims." Shedding familiar social roles is common in experiences of pilgrimage, and in the case of these families, new relational equality was central to the intimacy they described in searching for meaning together.

> As a mother who is used to taking the front seat . . . I had to let things go and if everybody wasn't in bed at night, forget about it . . . distancing my maternal instinct . . . I had to remind myself on several occasions. I still wonder a little bit if I achieved this—walking the Camino for myself and they are walking the Camino for themselves. I would start to worry about my son learning from this. . . . Your mind can get into the nuts and bolts of who they are and what you are together because you are managing—your instinct has been for so many years to be the mother. On the Camino you can be a bit more distant and a little bit less in charge and less responsible, but it is hard work, and I had to put effort into doing that.
>
> —Barbara, mother from Canada

Barbara was a fifty-year-old executive in a large corporation who had spent much time meeting her children's educational and emotional needs. On the Camino, she wanted to let go of being a "type-A, alpha mom" so that her children could "become much more of leaders" and let go of their "mom dependency." She pushed aside her family role: "The whole experience was very much an equal playing field. When we met people, they would know I was the mom, but we met them as equals. . . . They were people in their own right that we were meeting, no history or context, no definition around us." Being with children on equal ground allowed her children to challenge her in ways they had not in everyday life. For example, at the end of one painful day of walking her daughter told her: "Why are you looking miserable all the time if this was your idea?" Barbara explained: "I didn't understand the way my inner conflict was translating itself across other people. She [daughter] called me out and it was painful, and we had some conflict around that. I pushed back, and we had a long, difficult discussion, but it was a good one for us, a very healthy one. So I gained insight into how my behavior affects others."

Ann, the fifty-year-old mother from the United States who walked with her twenty-three-year-old daughter Hannah, said that she was a "protective mother," but that she also let her children "make their own choices about what they do." On the Camino, she said, "it was a mutual looking out for each other. Watching out for each other, but we both felt very free and individual." The Camino was a space where they could be together as mother and daughter, but where leveling through pilgrim identity brought some sense of freedom to abandon social norms of mothers as family caretakers. For example, Ann noted that in the past, she had basically always "done what was right for the girls" and put herself "second." So when Ann wanted to stay in hotels or a pension rather than an albergue, even though she realized that it was something her daughter "didn't want to do," Hannah had to "step up and do it" for her: "I think that she just thought differently on the Camino. Our roles were reversed in some ways that were really nice for us. . . . I don't think we could have done that at home in regular life. . . . Just being in a situation [on the Camino] where so much is leveled."

Jansen, the sixty-one-year-old father from the Netherlands, walked with his twenty-six-year-old daughter Lina on two occasions. His son, twenty-two-year-old Jacobus, joined his father and sister on their second Camino. Jansen described the leveling and disruptions of routine family roles as they walked. The first time he walked with Lina he saw them as being "on a one-on-one equal basis," where Lina made reservations and he planned routes. The second time, he said, "I had much more sense that they were beginning to look after me."

In the previous chapter, I noted Jansen's investment in the Camino promise. Having walked alone several years before, he found the Camino had helped "clear his mind," and he thought it might help Lina with her depression and related psychological issues. Lina did describe feeling less anxiety and more able to handle life on her return home, but the spiritual intimacy born between them on the Camino was more directly related to how Camino space brought them together as equals, pilgrims on the road to Santiago who were present to listen to each other's self-discoveries. I was not able to speak with Jacobus, but both Lina and her father put great emphasis on how, as pilgrims, they shared a new depth of conversation, and at the same time became comfortable with silence born through extended walking practice. Lina described a conversation sitting together resting at a café after a long quiet morning's walk:

> "I've decided I'm going to retire. I haven't actually talked to your mother about this, but I've decided that I'm going to retire." . . . I knew that was something he was thinking because he started working for this company when he was twenty-four and I knew that it was going on in his mind, but he just placed it on the table like, "That's it. I've made my decision." So that was the most memorable moment and we talked about why, what he was fed up with, and what he wanted to do with his life that made him think, "Oh, I want to retire now." . . . I learned that one of the main reasons is not that he is fed up with the company, it is really that there was so much more he wanted to do in life, and he needed time to do it.

Jansen described a similar connection with Jacobus when the three of them walked together: "I've always been close with my daughter, but with my son it was a little bit different. But it is very clear that since the walking we understand each other, I've seen things in him that I didn't know were there."

> Kay: What sorts of things?
>
> Jansen: Before, I tended to see him a bit as somebody who needed to push himself a bit more and get more out of his education and life. . . . I had a bit of an impression that he—not just him, but a big part of his generation in the Netherlands. We older people look at this generation and say, God, they are a bunch of softies and maybe we raised you in too much comfort and too protective an environment. . . . But then I saw him sort of toughing it out thirty kilometers a day and, you know, becoming more and more determined to finish and get there and actually enjoying achieving that. He said, "I just need to challenge myself a bit," and I actually saw that happening in front of my eyes. In general we live in very different worlds, but on the Camino, what the trip has done for me is a huge reconnect with him because we were so close for six weeks and we learned to appreciate each other so much more.

John, a sixty-year-old father from Canada who walked with his twenty-eight-year-old son Richard, said that he had "always wanted to be friends with" his children. But now that his son and daughter were adults, he wanted to foster even more of "a mutual respect," and to make sure he and Richard are "not just father and son" but that they "enjoy certain things together and get on as people." He saw the Camino as bringing a space to do so, a practice where he and Richard could build their friendship and listen to each other in a different way: "When you spend two weeks together, twenty-four/seven, he listened to me talk about myself and my history and my childhood." Richard also, he said, "opened up to me on the Camino more than he ever did before . . . Richard is a bit of an introvert, so he is reticent, not forthcoming with things, but he was more forthcoming on the Camino about his feelings and wants for marriage, children. These are things I would have liked to have known before, but never got that deep with him until we were together and it came out naturally." One time when they were walking, John said, they talked about how you can "use moments of massive challenge in your life as a springboard to become better." He saw walking together on the path as bringing this self-work: "We're walking and we're talking about this, about how you can come to a better place in your life and use challenges. So what do we, how do we each, you know, as equals here, I'm still your dad and I'm still paying your tuition and you still depend on me a little bit for now, but that's gonna end quick. But here on the Camino I said, 'You don't depend on me, you know. That said, here we are. We're just a couple guys, walking.' " Their reflexive work together brought what John described as a "bond."

Robert, a father from Madrid in his mid-sixties who had recently retired and just completed his second week-long Camino with his twenty-eight-year-old son Martin, said that the Camino brought "rare time to think together" and to "breathe peace, while talking about every type of topic, from the trivial to the most deep ones like love or faith—something that you aren't able to do in your everyday life." Robert noted a tradition in Spain for fathers and sons to walk the Camino together and felt "very lucky," given "that all dads" in Spain "want to do this with their sons, but not all can do it." In walking, Robert said, Martin "became not only my son, but my friend."

Bart was a father from the United States in his mid-fifties who walked for two weeks with his son Charlie, a college student in his early twenties. Bart attended a "spiritualist church" back home, which he described as a community that was "just people getting along and just having a social conscience, allowing your personal spirituality to manifest the way you feel it should manifest." Bart had gone on hiking trips before with his son, but he saw the Camino as different because it was a spiritual space full of energy that brought them together in conversation and knowledge of each other:

> Charlie and I would talk about this, we would say, we are walking right now where you know millions upon millions of pilgrims went. . . . These were people that had a purpose, that energy still—it's flowing, it's bouncing off of you. The stories, the old stones, and we talked about what's that mean to you? So we had some real depth of conversation. And every day, walking side by side, you just, there's moments of that comfortable silence, then there's moments of this great conversation, and then on the third or fourth day you're like, geez, that's my son, you know, that's my son. That's the one I haven't really talked to in four years since he's been in college. You know what I'm saying? Comes home for Christmas and it's "Cat's in the Cradle": "Hey, Dad! Christmastime, wooo! I wanna see the guys—can I borrow the car keys? See ya later, can I have them please?" You know, maybe I wasn't around that much when he went away to college. So I want to do another trip with him like this, maybe the Appalachian Trail.

Charlie said he believed in a "higher power" but that his "philosophy is a similar philosophy to what my dad has regarding spirituality and peace. It is just kind of there, it's around us, mostly in nature is the best way to get connected to it." The Camino, he said, "since you're surrounded by nature and by other people, this community of walkers . . . it definitely had a spiritual peace." Charlie remembered, in particular, "having a lot of self-reflection time where you're walking, you're moving, sort of a moving meditation sort of situation where you really get connected to yourself and you're talking to all of these people and it's sort of an open-boundary sort of relationship with people." For many, spiritual intimacy between parents and young adult children was strengthened through conversations and other kinds of meaningful encounters with pilgrims.

Connection Through Pilgrims

At times, shared relationships with other pilgrims brought a unique window into family members' emotions, character, and life issues. Other times, pilgrims served as important therapeutic advisors who helped make sense of their family relationships. Pilgrims also played a role in naming parents and adult children walking together as exceptional, an acknowledgment of family togetherness and connection.

During Ariel's Camino arguments with Allan, she at times used her technology to contact her sister and boyfriend back home, who gave her counsel and encouraged her to continue walking with her father. These distant intimate others encouraged her by saying that "God" was with her and that she was on the Camino "for a reason and may never get this chance again." But Ariel was also deeply influenced by close relationships with other pilgrims to stay with her father and finish the Camino with him. These pilgrims, she said, would "fill me up with love and kindness each time I got emptied out," so she could work on loving her father again. For example, she described Allan becoming "impatient" with her injuries: "He would point out other people around me with pains and aches that you could tell, and he would say, 'See, they are not complaining!' " On another occasion, she recalled, she had had her headphones on and her father yelled something. "I didn't hear him so I took off my headphones and told him he should have more support for me and he yelled, 'I'm not showing support for you because you have your head so far up your ass.' I yelled at him in the street, 'F—— you!' " After such intense confrontations, Ariel at times found guidance and emotional support from an Irish woman who she said cared for her like a "mom." After one father-daughter argument, this woman gave Ariel a purple crystal, a "reflection stone," and told her, "Now you have to finish the Camino." Ariel said other pilgrims would approach her and say they had heard that she was upset with her father, and they would talk with her about the importance of "loving through your Camino weakness." The Camino, Ariel stressed, became a practice to learn "love and patience." The whole trip, she said, she was "praying to God" that she and Allan would be able to "work on communication." The Camino responded with a lesson: "The most important thing is to develop patience, love, and most of all happiness with oneself." Ariel became "determined," she said, "to turn the weaknesses" she had with her father into "strengths:"

> I had no illusions that I would be able to fix our relationship . . . only that when hardships come, that I would be better able to work on it with him and with myself. The Camino helps you realize what it is you need to work on.

> Through it all, I was able to try and give love to my father. . . . Each time I got emptied out by a fight or big blow-up, someone else's love and kindness filled me up, so I could work on loving my father again.

Lina and her father, Jansen, told stories of making friends together on their first Camino. There was one Frenchman in particular "whose English was also very good," and so they were able to talk with him in some depth. "He had just retired and had such a wonderful dry sense of humor. If he was sitting at your table that evening, the whole table would be laughing." Lina and Jansen stayed in touch with him and visited him when they were in France again on their Camino with Jacobus. "He was an important person that definitely shaped the Camino for me," she said. This French pilgrim in many ways affirmed the intimacy and specialness of their time together: "I think he really liked the fact that Dad and I were walking together, he really thought that was a beautiful thing." Lina remembers him saying to her dad at one point, "I like seeing you walk together, you have a kind of fusion together. It is really beautiful to see father and daughter walking together like that. Yeah, he enjoyed the fact that we were walking together." Other pilgrims affirmed the exceptional nature of their walking as a family:

> There was this other guy the second time we walked as well, this Canadian guy. I wrote it in my journal because I said I have to remember this, because he said: "The three of you are walking together. Wow, I can't imagine doing anything like that with my family. You guys must be close. You are lucky." That is literally what he said. When I started out I didn't feel like it was special or magnificent at all, but I'm coming to realize that maybe it is. Maybe I'm luckier than I thought that I have a dad that I can do that with and a mom that I can call every day. It made me realize that maybe it is magnificent and that I'm definitely lucky.

In parents' stories, being together with other pilgrims at times offered a captivating window into the emotional world of their children. Barbara, for example, talked of observing her son's decision-making processes and interactions: "We would be sitting at dinner and other pilgrims would explore with my son: 'Do you want to stay in that industry, and have you thought of changing?' They would be genuinely interested, asking really open questions that he would answer and *I would be present for* [emphasis added]." She marveled, "I would not have that opportunity at home. . . . It would be like you would be witness to things in your kids' life that you are not always witness to. Sometimes I felt like I was sitting in the counselor's office next to my kid."

Danielle, a fifty-year-old mom from the Netherlands who walked a week with her twenty-two-year-old daughter Sophie, saw the Camino as a "calming life" where pilgrims shared caretaking and where she could "step back from mothering." She hoped that Sophie could be introduced to the meditative power of the Camino and bond with pilgrims. Indeed, Sophie stressed that "we were friends on the Camino, not mother and daughter." As I talked with them together early one morning in Santiago over coffee, they shared a photo that stood out in their minds: at one albergue their "Camino family" put chairs in a row and formed a "massage chain," where they worked to heal shoulders aching from carrying heavy backpacks.

Several young adults also noted seeing their parents differently as they interacted with other pilgrims—such as recognizing they had a sense of humor or other character qualities they had not seen before. Danielle, for example, had walked the Camino several times by herself before inviting her daughter. Sophie was brought deeper into her mother's spiritual life by watching her live out a seasoned pilgrim practice with others.

Ann, the mother from the United States who walked with her twenty-three-year-old daughter Hannah, made it clear that they had individual, separate time on the Camino: I was "very comfortable with the couple of times that I walked alone, and I was very comfortable letting Hannah walk by herself." But Ann also described feeling social distinctions between parent and child disappearing as they formed connections with other pilgrims: "It was a monumental thing to do. The few people we bonded with we both bonded with. It was obvious—the people that we communicated with it was really some strong communication, and over the six weeks it was mutual, we both had the same exact feelings about those people."

As I noted at the start of this chapter, the types of spiritual intimacy I have outlined are not exclusive. Bart and his father, Charlie, offer an example of how a pilgrim community and experiencing transcendence in nature come together to shape this intimacy. I note earlier how Charlie and Bart found connection with each other through walking and extended conversations with each other. Bart also talked about how the conversations he had with other pilgrims brought him closer to understanding his life goals and how they related to his father. Dialoguing with other pilgrims was different from routine greetings and surface-level exchanges:

> You skip the "How's the weather today, what'd you have for lunch?" and you go straight to the "What do you really care about in your life? What are you working towards?" You kind of really get deep into people's personas and where their goals are, and I felt open and easy to communicate my personal beliefs and goals, etc., to other people who were walking the Camino with me. It was definitely a spiritual experience. I remember having a conversation with this German guy. My dad and I spent maybe three, four, or five days of the trip walking with him and so we all got pretty close. I remember his just asking me, because I had shared with him that I was studying international business and management, and he asked me why I wanted to be in business. Why was I studying that exactly? I felt like no one had ever really asked me that question. There are a lot of negative and positive connotations with being a businessperson, so I had to try and think about it and give him a genuine answer. It really kind of made me reflect on, why do I care about this so much? So I thought about my dad in business and how I grew up around his businesses and his success and how it inspired me. I gave him examples of stories of working with my dad, and so I came to the realization that, yeah, I really do want to go into business because my dad's in business. So it was one of those kinds of moments where I was like, wow, this is why I'm doing this.

Having such depth of conversation while walking through nature on a physically challenging path with others was at the center of why Charlie named the Camino a spiritual experience. He spoke too of how barriers were broken as people's physical bodies were strained:

> Everyone's tired, everyone's got this backpack full of junk, everyone, so, the physical kind of barriers, you're kind of broken down a bit. Everyone's tired, and you kind of, once you break past that physical, you get more in the spiritual and the mental/emotional areas. I felt like that definitely happened with me. I didn't feel like putting up a front with anybody. I was tired, and all these things were happening around me and all these connections and all of these—the nature, the natural beauty of the walk itself. It kind of put me in a *real* mindset. You know, if I was crabby, I was crabby. If I was in a good mood, I was happy in a good mood. I didn't have to pretend. You know what I mean?

It was this openness and what he saw as a more genuine state of mind that brought him closer to other pilgrims, and thus to his father.

Intimate Encounters with Nature and the Material Camino

Many pilgrims on the road to Santiago described communing with nature and the "natural beauty of the walk" as prompting spiritual intimacy. Jim, a forty-seven-year-old stepfather from the United States who walked with his forty-six-year-old wife, Sheri, and his twenty-two-year-old stepdaughter Anita, told me during our phone interview: "The twenty-one days together I will remember as peace of mind walking as a family because you are either by yourself, or with your family and you are just walking and certain parts of the Camino, it is just beautiful and it is so peaceful." Almost all family members at some point during their interview described a spirituality induced by feeling connected to their parent or adult child as they experienced, together, a sense of awe from nature and the material landscape of the Camino. These were largely stories that featured shared bodily experiences of the natural world that provoked emotions, or feelings of physical presence in spiritual transcendence together.

Cocoons, Thunder, and Angels

> We have always been very connected. She is strong and thoughtful, but careful. I'm a person who shares things and she is a person who is not willing to share intimate details. Being with her and walking with her, you know she called our beds the "little cocoons," you know, the sleep sacks, little side-by-side cocoons, and . . . I don't know, it just, I think she saw me in a different light. Always as her mother, but as someone more independent than I think she had seen me before, and I saw her as someone more independent and less someone who needed me.
>
> —Ann, mother from California

Ann told me that her daughter was a private and extremely busy person, which might keep her from talking with me. She was right. Hannah did not answer my request to be interviewed, but I did have access to her Camino blog and film. On her blog, like her mother, she noted being tucked away close together in their beds at night. She also shared images and video that focused on important structures and symbols along the way and the landscapes and life they passed through. In her interview, Ann described this natural world and the structures and symbols as a shared spiritual experience with Hannah:

> I was really aware of the fact that the journey itself is an incredibly spiritual thing. And that even if you are not a religious person, just being in that element and coming across, on a daily basis, things that involve religious rituals and symbols—crosses, arrows, shells, bridges—there is something about immersing yourself in that, in nature. One day we had decided to go a more difficult route and then, the biggest thing, a storm happened. The thunder—the way it thundered and the way it hailed! At first, we were feeling almost like a victim, realizing that it was nature pouring itself into us. It was that power and strength and energy was just being pounded into us in a way that I really feel was real. It was very powerful, and it was almost as if that force of energy that came from nature, from God if you will, was given to us to continue and keep walking the difficult route. I know that may sound a little far-fetched, but I don't know.
>
> Kay: That makes perfect sense.
>
> Ann: The whole journey is just rich with all those symbols. From the paths to the crosses to bridges—there are so many bridges. . . . I think what happens is that by continuing the walk daily, what happens is it is just a part of you. You are not sitting listening to a Mass or a sermon or something that someone is saying to you; you are just a part of it. Part of something bigger, older, longer, bigger and stronger and more powerful than you are, and if you become open and vulnerable then it can pour into you. And so I was really glad in the end that it happened that way for us that day because we were really just at the point of exhaustion.
>
> Kay: Did you talk about these things with Hannah?
>
> Ann: Yes. Yes.
>
> Kay: And she felt the same way?
>
> Ann: I think she did. We felt it was no mistake that the weather happened like that that day. No mistake at all.

These types of mystical, transcendent experiences are represented in vivid form through the photographs and videos in Hannah's blog—a heavy dark sky enveloping them as they walked together through the rain with ponchos over their backpacks. Hannah also describes hail hitting them in their faces, covering the road in front of them, threatening thunder and lightning flashes, and pouring rain in high elevations. She wrote about walking after the rain in wet ponchos and shoes, and how the sudden intense rainfall made their path risky. She described watching her mother's body show a new kind of strength, different from her role as family caretaker.

Like many contemporary individuals, Ann distanced herself from organized religion: "I would consider myself a spiritual person. I have to find meaning in things. . . . I'm not into formal religion, there is too much hypocrisy for me in formal religion." In an effort to underscore the magnitude of the transcendent nature of their shared experience of connection with the natural world, she leaves open the idea that others might define the kind of power they felt as "God."

Families spoke of the intimacy that came from shared emotions related to walking. For example, Steven, a sixty-year-old father from South Africa, had walked the Camino before by himself and wanted his twenty-two-year-old son Daniel to have the experience. "I wanted to share that feeling that one gets when you are just walking, that euphoria that you get . . . you've done it yourself . . . having walked." He said, "It is just a wonderful feeling and I wanted to share that with them [his children] so that they could love it as well." Steven had taken his son hiking before and understood walking the Camino as a chance to reexperience that closeness born in traveling together:

> He and I had done a lot together in past. I had taken him to India and hiking in the lake district of England, in the highlands of Scotland, I'd taken him to Spain before, but not on the Camino. And so it was really nice to be with him once again, just the two of us. It was really wonderful to relive that, just having him to myself. We share a lot of interests together. We have a common sense of humor, and we just get on so well together, it was wonderful to spend that time with him again.

Steven identified as a spiritual Buddhist: "My son and I, we have taken Buddhist vows." Meditation was a daily practice shared with his son when they were together. Since Daniel had gone away to college, he had missed walking and "talking nonstop" with his son in nature. The Camino brought them together again spiritually in this way.

Only We Will Understand

While I was talking with Ed and his daughter, from the United States, in a coffee shop in Santiago, Julie used the word "transcendent" at least three times to describe the ten-day pilgrimage they had completed two days before. As I noted in chapter 2, Julie wanted to spend concentrated "spiritual time" with her father to pull him away from his work environment. They were practicing Catholics, and their descriptions of spiritual experience drew from theistic language; for example, they talked of "praying each day" and holding a "small cross they brought with them." However, they also pulled from understandings of spirituality that involved expression of feelings and self-searching. Julie spoke of having time to talk with her father more about his family history, capturing "family stories that might have otherwise been lost." In the evenings they read and discussed a book about spiritual connection together. They expressed a fresh understanding of each other born through immersion together in the natural world where they could walk and be "quiet together, thinking about peace." All of those Camino practices, they said, "rejuvenated" them in "spirituality" and "relationship."

Their story was also filled with descriptions of mystical moments where, like Ann and Hannah, Ed and Julie felt the presence of the natural world overwhelm them. They talked about feeling challenged yet refreshed by walking hours in the rain. "There was so much rain," Ed said, "when our boots filled up with water, we just kept going because, what were we going to do? They can't get any wetter. You just keep going." They told a story of soaking their swollen feet at the end of a long day in a hot spring while a woman doing laundry made the water soapy around them—a moment, Julie said, they named out loud the "transcendent." Such shared corporeal encounters provoked spiritual intimacy. As Julie articulated, this was "an experience that only two people can share."

Ed and Julie shared a physical and a spiritual connection in the material structure of the Camino as well. Like many of the Catholics I talked to, the Cathedral in Santiago de Compostela was a space that magnified their sense of family connection. Julie said that being there, where "so many diverse people for so many years" had come together, made their experience "deeper." The physical experience of sitting in the wooden pews and feeling the stone walls surround them made Julie feel as if they became, together, a part of the pilgrim flow across time. Her connection to her father in this historical space resembled Bart's description of growing closer to Charlie as they felt energy flowing from the paths where millions of pilgrims had walked with purpose. When Julie and Ed went to the Pilgrims' Mass in Santiago, Ed was struck by how much they knew was going on in the service, even though he didn't know the language. He was taken aback by how Catholics around the world were reading the same scripture that day, and he felt "this [Catholic people] is a family after all," something he had been told in his home parish but had never really felt in this deep a way. Julie added that the moment was particularly powerful for her because the spiritual book she and Ed read together on the Camino was about different types of people coming together to worship, and there they were "sitting in this beautiful space with all different kinds of people; it made our experience of the Camino deeper." At one point during our interview Julie turned to me to try to explain the depth of experience of their shared Camino: "In a word, transcendent." She added, "We may show our photographs to others and tell stories, but only *we* really can feel what happened and experience it in this way."

Experiencing the natural and material world of the Camino together felt like a "rejuvenating" of "spirituality and relationship" for a father and daughter who were already close. Ed was able to tell a story of fulfilling the Camino promise through a "rebirth" and what he named several times as a "cleansing." Ed had high hopes of how the experience would impact family relationships and day-to-day life. He anticipated weekly walks with other family members and starting a family book group. He wanted to play the guitar again. He loved animals, so "maybe," he said, "I will volunteer in an animal shelter." The Camino was a "restart," a "reboot," a "jumping-off point" for him after decades of parenting and caring for aging parents. Ed and Julie smiled at each other as they told their story. Only one moment of tension surfaced as he frowned and looked surprised when Julie recalled her friend's words: "You will have a cool story to tell at his funeral." She quickly added, "Maybe she should have said wedding, but the point was, she said that it was going to be a 'story forever' that we would have." They laughed. The Camino, she stressed later, "is something that nobody can take away from us. We walked it, together."

Silent Presence

In some stories, walking through the natural landscape of the Camino brought an intimacy with loved ones who had passed away. Pilgrims described figures in clouds that indicated mystical presence and expansive landscapes that summoned memories of those lost. I talked with one father who carried the ashes of his aunt on his family pilgrimage, leaving them along the Camino as he had watched Martin Sheen do in the movie *The Way*. I walked for several days with a woman who carried the walking poles her late husband had planned to use for his Camino; walking and remembering over 800 kilometers brought his spirit to her side. Walking on the Camino for several hours one day with a young woman, I witnessed her tears as the smell of fresh-cut grass reminded her of childhood summer play with her deceased brother.

Feeling the presence of a child or parent who had died affirmed deep loss and shared grieving for some families. Ann and Hannah, having recently lost Ann's husband, Hannah's father, to cancer, experienced moments where they felt the essence of his life fill their immersion in nature. Hannah writes in her blog that about halfway through their trip she felt an intensity of physical pain and fatigue. As she faced these physical challenges of the Camino, she could not help but see her father and feel his struggle. She became intensely aware of the grueling nature of his disease, how he had fought it for years, and how her mother had cared for him. Ann's Camino journey was, in many ways, about connecting with Hannah, but also about "reclaiming" her life after so many years of taking care of her husband. She and her husband had wanted to walk the Camino together. Like the woman I met who carried her late husband's walking poles, Ann carried the spirit of her husband with her. Ann was working to "let go" and affirm her power to live a full life alone: "I had cared for him for so long that I had to give up the sense that I was responsible for him somehow. . . . I could give him over to God in whatever way I was hanging on to him." Ann and Hannah attended the Pilgrims' Mass together in the Cathedral, where they saw the Botafumeiro (a famous large censer) swing. Feeling the blessings of the pilgrims at the Mass brought release: "You could hardly hear what they were saying, but we had this incredible view, and when the Botafumeiro swings, we were both just unbelievably moved. I can't tell you the sense of gratitude and peace I felt from what we felt in our hearts at that moment. It was amazing."

Elise, the sixty-two-year-old Catholic mother who walked with her sixty-year-old husband, twenty-year-old-son, and twenty-five-year-old daughter, described one time on the Camino when she felt like the son that she had lost to suicide was walking with her: "He was there with us. He was very much there with me." However, Elise was determined that their family Camino should not focus on his death, and so they spent time together talking about the spiritual excerpts from Brierley's book and worked to relate his message to their own life experiences. "I wanted us to feel a connection," she said. "I wanted them to know that they are okay and that we are there for them, and that there is nobody in the world that cares more and that our family is sort of the ultimate unit." She explained how silence in Camino practice shaped this intimacy:

> We were amazed at the beauty of the walk, walking through vineyards and the beauty of the towns and the eucalyptus forest, and we had perfect weather, absolutely perfect. . . . One of the things that happen when you are walking day after day, you are not looking each other in the eye at the dinner table, you are walking side by side, and when you are not looking people in the eye all the time and you have lengths of time the talking is different, you know, it is just kind of pours out. Or the silence, silence is—it's good to be silent with one another, to be able to walk. . . . It feels very comfortable . . . you are not trying to press conversation.

Elise recalled the spiritual power of the Camino to affirm her family's deep connection with each other:

> The Camino was spiritual in our own way. We laughed a lot. We sang. I cried at one point. [*She hesitates and starts to cry.*] . . . Ummm . . . we did cute little things, like we'd say, okay, first time you see a cross say a prayer . . . and there was . . . um, just a minute . . . let me compose [myself].
>
> Kay: Sure, sure, take your time. . . .
>
> Elise: There was a Canadian woman that we met who didn't speak much English, only French, and we had seen her along the way. She was with other people, but she was also walking alone, and one day we had taken our wine and chorizo and cheese and bread and carried it, and we stopped and we were having our little picnic and along she came and she stopped and she said, "I just want to tell you [*she starts crying*] . . . you are the most beautiful family."

Sitting outside sharing a familiar ritual midday Camino meal, this fellow pilgrim reminded Elise of the intimacy she shared with her children who were present, and with the one who walked with them in spirit.

Intimacy Through Body Labor

In some cases, spirituality was about support and care related to the physically challenging nature of the Camino. A body may be able to walk for one, two, or three days six to eight hours carrying over ten pounds on the back, but when you add another day, and another, and then move into weeks, the stress felt from strained muscles and blistered skin can be quite painful, and for some debilitating. The first time I walked on a Camino path in 2012, I met a man at a bus stop who was heading home only one week away from his Santiago destination. His knees had given out. He called his wife, sobbing, and told her that he had to stop.

Several families told stories of moments where the younger family member became a physical force that helped push older bodies to continue walking. For some this was literal, as young adults put their bodies next to their parents' bodies in ways that helped propel them forward. Others described holding and nursing each other as they healed from exhaustion or other body ailments and illnesses.

In the case of Isabelle, a twenty-year-old woman from Stockholm, and her mother, Lisa, fifty-six, the Camino represented an enormous challenge from the start. Lisa had wanted to walk the Camino for eight years and had even purchased boots a while back with the hope of walking. She read Paulo Coelho's book *The Pilgrimage* (1987) and talked with others about the power of the walk as a spiritual practice. Unfortunately, serious back issues made walking the Camino and carrying her pack out of the question. As companies started to pop up everywhere on the Camino that provided services for sending luggage ahead, she decided to try the approximately 115-kilometer walk from Sarria to Santiago with her daughter's help. Isabelle had a little over a week between ending her graduate studies and starting her new job and had hopes of using that time to walk a "spiritual Camino" with her mom. She too had read books about the power of meditative walking and finding spirituality in nature. In large part, though, her Camino was about being there for her mom. Isabelle carried their daypack with all the water, food, and other items they needed, and when they got to a steep hill, she would literally push her mother from behind, offering support so that Lisa could make it up the hill.

As I noted in chapter 2, Lisa's spiritual advisor had told her, "Don't walk as mother and daughter, walk as friends." In my interview with Lisa and Isabelle over breakfast two days after they had walked into Santiago, I asked them if they had been able to do that. Isabelle quickly replied, "No." To which Lisa added, "Well, you were sometimes my mother." Isabelle said, "Yes, because I took care of you." Her mother turned to me and said: "We gave birth again to each other."

Kathleen was a sixty-two-year-old mother from Ireland who had had hip replacement surgery. She walked the Camino from Sarria to Santiago, about 115 kilometers, with her two daughters, Lauren, age twenty-five, and Emily, age twenty-two. I sat with the three of them one morning over breakfast in Santiago the day after they finished their Camino. Her daughters had made the arrangements for them to travel with an online booking company that would send their bags ahead each day. Lauren and Emily helped Kathleen continue when her hip and legs hurt. When she would see a big hill up ahead, they would talk about "strategies" for conquering the incline. "My daughters told me to do it in four steps—just four-step increments," Lauren said. "It was just like in the army, how they count 'one two, one two, one two.'" Lauren and Emily stayed by her side, their bodies in sync, counting, making their way up the hill.

Young adults received physical assistance from their parents as well. Lindsey's mom, Margie, described caring physically and safeguarding the physical well-being of her daughter as they walked:

> My daughter and I had one particularly hard day when traveling between distant stops because several public water areas were marked as contaminated. Lindsey and I nearly ran completely out of water in 100-degree heat with no shade. It actually turned out that her Camelbak hose was twisted and therefore it was not empty. However, not knowing that, I dispensed my water to Lindsey a mouthful at a time every hundred feet or so. . . . She was somewhat weak, and she actually struggled more than I for most of the Camino. . . . I became concerned because I started having a bit of chest pain—likely due to dehydration and being overheated.

Such a presentation of feeding Lindsey in light of her own struggles was in line with Camino norms of ethical spirituality, but it was also about caretaking, a performance of good mothering woven into her Camino story.

Allan talked about caring for Ariel when she was ill or injured, of making sure she was getting sufficient food and drink along the way even as he too was feeling worn down:

> One time I walked back on this trail and she wasn't there. I walked back into town and I, this is, it's getting on late in the day. . . . I end up walking

back more on the trail and . . . I was livid. I hadn't eaten, I was worried, and she said, "I just got here," and, um, you know, it was like blazing hot, and I asked, "Have you eaten" and she was like, "No," and I had left her money, every day I'd give her money and said get something to eat—instead of using your food in your pack, buy food if you can because you will save your food when you can't get food. I gave her, I was always making sure she had 25 or 30 euros with her every day. . . . So I said go get something to eat and drink, we have to get going. . . . She goes in and I'm waiting, and she comes walking out with a beer! And I look at her and she said, "Well, I'm having a beer, I deserve a beer." I said you haven't eaten all day. I was irked at that point, I really was. . . . I may have made an idiot of myself, but it was just one of those . . . she doesn't get it.

Ariel spoke of this encounter as well, naming it as an example of how the Camino "was precious time together, where my dad got to play the caretaker he never was." She added that during the final week, after her father had told her how much he wanted her to finish with him, he was "caretaking" all the time, buying her tea and making sure she was okay. "He was so excited," she said, "because he was not there for me caretaking when I was growing up. To have that much time together, to spend that much time, he had time to figure out how to do it."

In several family cases, parents told stories of their son or daughter caring for them unexpectedly in ways that instigated new forms of intimacy. Caroline, a mother in her mid-fifties from the United Kingdom, walked for a week with her twenty-five-year-old daughter Leisa. I spoke with Caroline two months after her return home. She was impressed by the leveling dynamic of walking as pilgrims together. On the Camino, she said, they laughed, joked, and were even relaxed about sleeping in the same bed. They met the same people and walked the same number of kilometers with equal weight on their backs. "It doesn't really happen in any other aspect of your life," Caroline said, "that you have this completely shared immersive experience." It was a journey she saw as making them "companions, sharing on equal ground." She recalled a story about body caretaking that had great emotional weight:

Some of the Camino is really difficult, the last day we did well over forty-two kilometers, we must have done about forty-five kilometers and I was absolutely exhausted. I had already done a very demanding walk that I finished about ten days before we started on the Camino. I did the GR 20, which is a high mountain route in Corsica. It is meant to be the most demanding route in Europe, and it is really demanding, and I kind of probably hadn't recovered from doing that. So when we did this last day going into Santiago, I was exhausted, and I pretty much collapsed in the Pilgrim's Office. I couldn't stand at the desk. I was just exhausted, they quickly gave me lots of sugar, and we experienced something in terms of our relationship that had not happened before. She became, she looked after me, completely, and, um [*pause*] . . . That felt quite important. It also felt slightly scary because I do a lot of looking after for my mother and I kind of thought, oh no, this is far too early for her to have to be looking after me and this is crazy. Even for her, I felt uncomfortable about reversing that parent-child, which kind of taught me a lot really; I find it very difficult to let go of wanting to care for my children, and to reverse it and having her need to care for me was kind of odd. Um [*pause*] . . . yeah, that felt a big thing to have happened. . . . Who knows what might happen in the future. We never know how much time we have.

Mary Ann, a Catholic from the United States in her early sixties, told a story of her eighteen-year-old son George carrying her backpack and keeping her warm when she had a severe case of hypothermia:

The second day I got hypothermia and he carried my backpack. . . . At the albergue, he piled sleeping bags on me. It was kind of a scary thing because there was no hot shower at the end and the next day, and the days after that, people would come up and say, "Is that your son that took care of you?" We would run into them on the Camino and they would say, "Well, you know, you are a legend on the Camino! We heard what your son did." And they would look at me and say, "You are looking a little better, looking a little better, you looked awful."

Hundreds of significant others back home, both from their parish and from their family, became emotionally invested in their physical struggles and George's caretaking through Mary Ann and George's co-authored blog. During her interview, Mary Ann spoke of him as her "savior" on the Camino. Mary Ann also took care of George when he came down with an illness during their trip.

The Camino promise of ethical spiritual practice that family members imagined as they planned their Camino journeys, of being simultaneously alone and together as just pilgrims caring for each other, manifested in their stories of transcendence through physically sharing body burdens and needs. For example, one mother from Australia who walked with her son noted that they would help each other along, that they were "each other's motivation," especially when they were feeling sick. Other family stories were of doctoring blisters, relieving the rashes from bedbug bites, locating and applying medication, and—as in several of the stories mentioned here—making sure family members had adequate food, drink, and a warm bed to sleep in.

Some narratives included instances of carrying a family member's backpack when exhaustion or injury took over, and parents and adult children caring for each other through illness or injury. Peter, the father from Australia quoted at the start of this section, was a repeat pilgrim who took his twenty-three-year-old son Mike on the Camino. Mike walked part of the way with friends he had met on the Camino, but Peter asked him to spend the last week walking just with him: " 'Look, I really wanted to do this Camino with you, and while it was great to have your mates join us, remember that that is what we wanted to do originally, and I would really like to spend some time walking with you.' So he stayed with me for the last week, which was a very bonding experience." Peter's description was of being "connected" during that week together.

He recalled that week together as a unique "bonding experience" where Mike was able to tune in to "my needs and my mentality and we connected." He told a story of illness, sacrifice, and caretaking:

> I became ill one day and had a bad case of vertigo and my son woke up with a terrible itchy rash that we learned was bedbugs. We were turned out of the albergue at eight a.m. and were sitting in a cafe having breakfast when I had another attack of dizziness. I asked a man in Spanish if he could get me a doctor. Ten minutes later an ambulance arrived and two paramedics rushed in and began attending to me. They walked me out to the ambulance while my son gathered up our bags. We were taken to an emergency medical center. I was able to produce my travel insurance documents and got full treatment including an EKG and an injection. My son was not able to get treatment for his rash until two days later, where we found another emergency medical center. Nobody spoke English, but he got an injection and some medication which cleared up the rash. I guess this illustrates how we had to look after each other when a crisis hit unexpectedly. The story will be retold many times in the coming years, I expect.

Peter continued, "Another time I was struggling on the road and he had to take my load off me and look after me. I think we saw each other at our most vulnerable. A boy grows up seeing his father as a sort of very strong and sort of strong type of person, but I'm sure it was educational for him to see me in a more vulnerable position, you know." He added, "Mike had his own pack and mine on his front and would share his water with me when I ran out. He was my savior. . . . He would chastise me for not drinking water. . . . It was like 'the child can be father to the man,' that saying like, when your folks get old and you have to be like a parent to them." Young adult children taking on the burden of their parents' load had numerous levels of significance for their relationship. As Peter described, it was a moment of family role reversal, but it was also an affirmation of their shared pilgrim identity, where they were alone on their journey but at times extraordinarily together, in this case physically through carrying another's backpack, a practical yet sacred pilgrim object.

It is hard to communicate the body intimacy that happens when one carries another pilgrim's backpack. Once when two members of a group I was walking with insisted on taking my pack because I was feeling faint, I felt like I was incomplete. They had taken the pack that carried all of my Camino belongings, that symbolized my physical ability, and that held my identity on the road as a pilgrim. When it was gone, it felt like they had taken on a body appendage. I asked them to give it back. They did not, observing better than I my uneven gait and washed-out skin tone. I was thankful and angry. On another occasion, I carried a pack for an elderly German man I met in the Pilgrim's Office. He was too weak to walk to his hotel. The large backpack was covered in his sweat, which bled through my T-shirt and onto my skin. As Mike, George, and others may have felt when carrying their family member's backpack, I was touching and incorporating the physical body of another in ways previously unknown.

Intimacy Through Separation

The choreography of the Camino, walking together with the family members you came with or with new "Camino family" members you met while walking, was a natural part of Camino culture. Young adult children often found people their own age whom they wanted to walk with, socialize, and build separate "Camino family" groups. A few parents whom I encountered while walking told stories about their sons or daughters leaving them for a while to walk with friends. Like Peter, they thought it was "natural," the way it should be. One man, whose son was already several towns ahead, heard from him only through digital messaging and Facebook. He told me this was fine, expected, and that "children are supposed to have their own lives." The Camino experience, he added, was about meeting people from across the world, just as he was doing as he walked with other older pilgrims. As father and son, they were sharing a Camino practice, marking their independence through engagement in communitas with other pilgrims. It is not surprising that most of these descriptions came from field observations and informal interviews. My official interview call asked for parents and young adult children who walked together. Individuals who traveled to Spain with the intent of walking with their family member and then separated may have assumed that I did not want to hear their story. However, this theme of separation and independence as shared Camino experience did arise in formal interviews. They were narratives that affirmed the autonomous, healthy, and independent nature of their family relationships.

Rick, the fifty-year-old father from the United States who walked with his twenty-three-year-old son David in an effort to help his son transition from the military, told a story of Camino family separation with connective purpose. Rick had been diagnosed with Parkinson's disease in his mid-thirties and spent a good part of our phone interview detailing his journey of learning how to manage his condition with exercise and nutrition. In fact, he had been able to climb and hike several challenging trails in recent years. The Camino gave Rick a chance to prove to himself, and to his son, that he was capable of taking care of himself. Rick said that when David was growing up,

> I was not in a good time with the Parkinson's and he was my helper. I reached a point where I couldn't drive by myself, he had to go with me. It was a different life than what I lead now. For me to be able to show him [through the Camino], I'm capable, I'm capable, I'm slower than you but I can bear it until the end of the day. And we reached a point where he was . . . like, "Okay, Dad, I can't walk this slow as you, so I am going to take off." So we would walk together for thirty minutes and then he would take off, and we would pick a point where we were going to meet for lunch. So we'd meet there and share that time together and walk together a little bit more.

Rick said that David was "more wanting to get away from me than me wanting to get away from him." David also met a woman he became interested in. Rick said, "Between Roncesvalles and Santiago you couldn't separate them at all. . . . They are the same age, she is from the States, so basically they were together the whole time and they have been talking nonstop since we got back. She is coming to visit us next week. . . . Who knows, the whole reason he may have walked the Camino with me was to meet his future wife." Much of Rick's story was about demonstrating his independence and David forming an intimate bond with a young woman. Still, Rick described their experience as creating a long-lasting connection. David might not realize it now, Rick said, but "I helped give him a gift that as he gets older, will settle in. He might be in a stressful point in his life and he might say, 'I'll take a walk.' . . . Maybe that is something that carries on, that when he has children he feels that, 'My dad did this with me, I want to do that with you.' A legacy, something nobody can ever take away from us."

In many cases, parents whose adult children walked ahead on the Camino described keeping an eye on what their children were up to and sharing their Camino practice through digital technology. Facebook posts of their family member ahead a town or two hanging out with their new friends brought comfort that their son or daughter was enjoying the Camino and bonding with other people. The pervasive presence of digital technology on the Camino, which I address in chapter 4, in many ways enabled this kind of spiritual intimacy through separating. They were watching and traveling in mediated space with their family member. It was a filtered, somewhat distant experience of their child's Camino, but a practice that, at the same time, they understood as accomplishing together.

Conclusion: Spiritual Intimacies as Moral Performances of Family

The stories in this chapter of building spiritual intimacy reflect wider social expectations associated with parenting and young adulthood. Narratives of emotional disclosure, shared intimate encounters with nature, connecting as friends, and doing intimate body work were ultimately performances of engaged mothering and fathering, of being there in intense ways.[3] They were stories of a radical presence with adult children accomplished through spiritual practice that also fulfilled gendered expectations in contemporary parenting. Fathers who stressed becoming friends with children, growing close to them emotionally, taking care of them, and endowing them with important emotional strength and self-knowledge were living up to tenets of contemporary fatherhood.[4] Gender was salient as well in how mothers talked of "letting go of mothering," becoming friends on equal ground with their children, and at the same time being exceptionally present in their children's lives and caring for them emotionally and physically.[5] Ultimately, the alone-yet-together discourse of the Camino provided an effective backdrop for parents' performances of helping daughters and sons become independent adults while distancing themselves from negative stereotypes of overinvolved parents. Young adults also affirmed their position as healthy individuals as they talked about learning more about themselves through Camino practice and by talking with their parents about their emotions and concerns.

Scholars have shown that emerging adulthood represents a time in life when many young adults move away from parents' religious traditions, identity, and practices, but this is not true for all.[6] The stories of families I relate here who shared spiritual intimacy through Camino practice offer examples of young adults engaging in and affirming spiritual beliefs and practices with their parents. In several cases—for example, those of Ed and Julie, Steven and Daniel, and Mary Ann and George—stories were of claiming an explicit religious identity (Catholic) alongside their parents.

Most of the pilgrims I interviewed understood a moral family as one that cultivated emotional connection and learned how to communicate well, listen, and open themselves to express and embrace others' feelings. They saw the spiritual practices of the Camino, in all their various forms, as vehicles for attaining these relational ideals. Digital habits and the pervasiveness of Wi-Fi in Camino structure came up often in family members' stories of seeking shared spiritual practice. Like Katy's story of the Hospital of the Soul that I told at the beginning of this book, family members often acknowledged digital devices as a threat to both individual and shared spiritual practice. In fourteen family cases in my formal interviews, families told stories of planning and controlling how they would use technology on the Camino. In chapter 4, "Intimacy and Discipling Technology," I explore the strategies families adopted to discipline technology in ways they hoped would enhance spiritual connections.

4
Intimacy and Disciplining Technology

> Instead of a global, bracketed time away mentally and physically in a unique place and space, Internet Age pilgrims progressively tend to have a fragmented experience. . . . Rather than being in the Camino people seem to want to constantly get out of it. It's harder and harder for people to simply be content and be where they are.
>
> —Frey 2017: 15

A week and a half after departing on foot from Saint-Jean-Pied-de-Port, at the end of a twenty-kilometer day and after enjoying a shower and change of clothes, I strolled through a small town whose streets were home to cafés, private pensions, and a couple of upscale restaurants. I was content, proud of the kilometers I had accomplished, and ready to enjoy a cold beer and plate of something fried and salty. As I walked from my hotel to the café, the sun was still bearing down, so I stopped under an awning in the center of town and leaned against the stone wall to rest. Across the street was a twenty-year-old woman who I knew had been walking for a couple of weeks with her mother and father. She sat on a bench a block from a pension where I saw

Walking the Way Together. Kathleen E. Jenkins, Oxford University Press (2021). © Oxford University Press.
DOI: 10.1093/oso/9780197553046.003.0004

her mom talking with the owners, checking the family in for the night. The young woman was slumped over, staring at her phone and holding it with a frustrated grip. She seemed to have been crying. She looked up from her mobile device to take a sip from her water bottle and saw her dad walking toward her. He sat beside her and appeared to lovingly touch her shoulder.

I could not hear his words, but the intensity of his concern and love seemed unmistakable. She looked up at him, smiled, and then focused on her screen. She turned to him and then back to her phone again; with each glance in his direction she fought a stream of tears. After a few rounds of struggling to pull herself from the device and listen to him, he appeared to convince her, with whatever words he found in his exhausted state, to pull her tired body up and walk toward the pension. I was overwhelmed in that moment by the father's gentle love and care, and the daughter's tears and frustration born from what I imagine was physical pain, exhaustion, and her relationship to the device she held in her hand.

The contentment I had felt from a long day's walk and hot shower sharply faded. I had spoken with the father several days earlier while walking and knew from other pilgrims that he and his wife were hoping the Camino would help their daughter disengage from her online world and become more physically active. Screen time, they thought, had made her antisocial. Tears flooded my eyes as I watched this young woman on the bench. My feelings came in part from my status as a fellow pilgrim, albeit not fully, as I routinely reminded those with whom I walked of my research question and intent. But more than that, I was overwhelmed by a sociological imagination fearful of the weight and cultural power of digital technologies in contemporary lives. In just four years I had seen a change in this pilgrimage into wired space for a generation of families for whom phones, tablets, and social media connections had grown even stronger on and off the Camino. When I first spent time with pilgrims in Santiago in 2012, people carried cellphones, but the presence of these devices and use was not so all-encompassing. Encountering this family several years later pushed me to think more deeply about how technological forces might hinder or facilitate families sharing spiritual beliefs and practices.

The first time I had seen this father and daughter was after an exhausting mountain climb. I'd passed a picnic spot at the top for pilgrims with tables and a covered shelter. Most of the pilgrims, including her parents, were at the tables with others talking and eating snacks. The daughter was sitting about thirty feet away on a rock, staring intently at her phone; because of the others who were using their technology at this spot, it was obvious that the phone signal was strongest there. Her engagement with the phone was somewhat different from the relationship most others had with their devices. They would look up occasionally, stretch a bit, and turn their head to acknowledge another pilgrim. She created a private space when she stopped to rest, sitting farther away from the others, her shoulders pulling down and forward as she read and typed. This posture, and her relationship with the phone, happened each time I saw her at a café or rest stop. At one rest stop when I was talking with her father she looked up from the phone to say one sentence about her food order, then quickly went back to the phone. This young woman was not alone in her digital focus at café stops. Many of the pilgrims sitting around her were occupied with texting, social media, and securing reservations.

A number of the parents I formally interviewed spoke about how the Camino could help both parents and their young adult children address digital habits and the impact of devices on relationships. Charlie's father, Bart, said the Camino was an "opportunity for people who are in a struggling relationship to know their kids because cellphones and texting are distancing us."

BART: People blame the kids, but when I go to work at my restaurant each day, I can see the dads on the cell all the time; and by the way, I'm not pointing any fingers, I'm just as guilty. You know, put it away when you are with your kid, but we need to stay connected, and things like the Camino, these old traditions, can be used as a process for bringing people together in ways that nothing else could.

KAY: Did you feel that people were using technology on the Camino that pulled them away from each other?

BART: The sad thing is that's the hypocritical thing. Even when I'm talking I feel hypocritical in that I am just as guilty.

KAY: We are all guilty.

BART: Exactly, so I'm one of those, "Yeah, you guys shouldn't," but there I was doing it. It's just like texting when you drive—you are like, was that dumb! Almost like alcoholism—boy, was that dumb to get drunk again. Well what the hell are you doing it for? There is an interesting thing. What the heck are you doing it for? Because at the moment, this present moment awareness, you are not aware, you are doing it because something beeps and there is something important there . . . but it is a sad addiction and I hope, I don't know if . . . I think it's going to get worse.

The physical act of walking each day on the Camino, Bart suggested, offered structure to push digital devices to the background for several hours at a time. He admitted that he was on his phone each day on the Camino, but qualified that it was primarily during the evening hours. He called this his set-aside "tech time," when he managed his employees and did course work online for his doctoral program. He found this necessary engagement with digital devices frustrating but knew that his ability to work online also made it able for him to continue working and pursuing his graduate degree while traveling for several weeks with Charlie. His story was of being able to build intimacy with his son and absorb the spiritual material and relational world of the Camino through controlling how and when they used their technology. Bart became a *digital controller* of sorts, sending messages back home to Charlie's mom so that his son could enjoy the Camino free from the tethers of a wired world.[1]

Family members spoke of the benefits of technology in their everyday lives and how it allowed them to stay in touch with each other, especially as young adults attended college or took jobs far from home. But they also recognized how their habitual use of digital devices and social media platforms in daily life, Facebook "friends," and a world of online work tasks threatened to muddy the waters of their desired Camino practice. In fourteen of the forty-one family cases where I conducted formal interviews, parents and adult children told stories of deliberately working together to discipline technology for the purpose of creating pockets of tech-free time. A Camino structure saturated with Wi-Fi made such navigating and controlling of digital devices an important practice for the creation of liminal time and shared spiritual connection. As Nancy Frey implies on her website, Walking to Presence, thinking about one's relationship with technology is an essential part of processes of reflection and meaning-making on the contemporary Camino.[2]

In chapter 1 of this book, I highlighted the growing influence of an online world in choosing and securing a family Camino journey. In this chapter, I illustrate families' stories of digital technology on the Camino, how these experiences related to their expectations of individual and relational transformation, and the multiple ways they used and disciplined information and communication technologies (ICTs) during their pilgrimage. While members of these fourteen families named the increasingly digital nature of the Camino as a severe threat to relational connection, several of them also used social media platforms to engage in online visual journaling that brought them closer to each other in the retelling of their shared spiritual journeys. Securing tech time for this shared practice was another force driving their disciplining of digital devices. The contemporary Camino reflects a broader cultural phenomenon of ICTs infiltrating basic modes of communication, social processes, our most intimate relationships, and, inevitably, spiritual and religious space and practice.[3]

The Digital Camino

Walking the Camino has been profoundly shaped, especially in the last twenty years, by ICTs.[4] As I addressed in chapter 1, there are changes in the ways pilgrims plan for and navigate Camino space and hospitality, but also, as Nancy Frey (2018) has suggested, in the mental aspects of the journey.[5] Frey (1998) notes in her ethnographic study of the Camino in the 1990s that the liminality—feeling "out of time and out of place" through walking and the bending of time—enables pilgrims to have unique insights on and assign new meanings to intimate connections. Her more recent observations on Camino routes lead her to argue that wireless internet has brought a more "fragmented" experience of pilgrimage. While Wi-Fi signals can at times be weak, for the most part pilgrims on popular routes are able to use their electronic devices to secure reservations for lodging as they walk, contact friends and family, stay in touch with work colleagues at home, and maintain interactions with the people they meet on Camino routes. Contemporary pilgrims' continual virtual connections then, as Frey suggests, put them firmly "in" rather than "out" of time, which hinders their ability to move into a space that is liminal, a time different from the everyday where social norms and concerns seem distant. Remaining in everyday time impacts the opportunities they have for making new connections with nature, others, and oneself.

My observations on Camino paths and interviews with these fourteen families who talked explicitly about controlling and managing their use of digital devices reflect the desire of many pilgrims to limit the intrusion of technology into their spiritual pursuits and fall "out" of time. Recall Maia from chapter 1 who walked with her mother, father, and brother in 2013. Maia had memories of walking the Camino with a professor and other students as an undergraduate. The Camino, to her, was a place where she had enjoyed being away from phones and computers. When she walked with her father, mother, and brother several years later, she was just finishing graduate school and in between education and full-time employment, relatively free from workplace or academic online obligations. She had a phone, but turned it off and rarely used it, "pretending" with friends back home that she was "unreachable." Maia told me she longed for that loss of awareness of time that she had felt walking with her college group years earlier. However, on this trip in 2013 she knew she had to keep track of time, especially traveling with her family, who, despite their detailed Camino "battle plan," were somewhat dependent on making online reservations and Maia's knowledge of the Camino and Spanish skills. "I don't wear a watch in everyday life," she said, "but on the Camino I had to wear a watch because I lose track of time. It is the only way I can keep track of time. When I am on the Camino, I forget sometimes the day and the time." Maia's father, Kyle, noted that even though they had phones, they "rarely used them," and that at night, rather than being separately engaged in individual social media platforms, they "took turns contributing to a family blog for relatives and friends."

The way that Maia and her family talked about and approached digital devices on the Camino seemed different from how Katy and many others I encountered in 2016 and 2017 did so; the later participants seemed more attached to their Instagram feeds and/or Facebook Camino performances. While I am sure that there were pilgrims in 2013 who felt bound to their digital devices, in my observations three years made a significant difference in degree and habit regarding smartphones and tablets. This is not a surprise in our increasingly mediatized world, where—whether by choice or because mandated by work or education pursuits—people are more and more tied to their digital devices.

In my interviews with the other two-thirds of the forty-one family cases, parents and their adult children did not seem overly concerned that digital devices would undermine their experiences. Whatever their individual or family digital habits were, they did not see them as a threat to spiritual intimacy, and they valued the information and communication that online access brought. Jim, for example, a man from the United States who walked with his stepdaughter and his wife and booked their trip with an online Camino company that secured lodging for them on a planned route, commented:

> You know, one of our bigger topics of conversation was "Imagine what this was like before the internet," because I was so surprised by how much information was available so that you almost overprepare, in a sense. You are like, okay, this town is going to have this, and this town is going to have that,

> before you even get there. You can also do a google map and you can literally see a street view of a very large portion of the Camino itself.

Jim did not see this overplanning or having constant access to the internet through his phone as risking the relational and spiritual rewards of the Camino. In fact, he talked about growing closer to his stepdaughter as they captured their trip on social media and gathered hundreds of photographs of each other on paths and with newfound Camino friends. Most families I interviewed, and those I encountered while walking, generally carried one or two pieces of technology. Even families who worked together to control and limit their technology assumed that at least one family member should carry a small computer device for practical reasons. Most had a smartphone or purchased basic phones in Spain that would allow them to make calls and text with other pilgrims. Some, despite the extra weight, brought tablets, and a couple of young adults and one father carried laptops in their backpacks.

Being able to find reliable Wi-Fi on the digital Camino was a common perceived burden, especially for those attempting to maintain blogs. At the end of the day, as pilgrims were checking into albergues and hostels, demand for online access at times weakened signals, and I observed people grow frustrated as they tried to update Facebook blogs. This concern surfaced in interviews as well; for example, when I asked Mary Ann, whose Facebook Camino journey was followed by other pilgrims, her family, and members of her Catholic parish at home, if the albergues she stayed in had Wi-Fi, she said:

> I wouldn't say most, I would say some, but then it was frustrating because it would say outside of a restaurant "Wi-Fi available," but it wasn't really. Sometimes when we went into a shop we'd have to "Oh, look it's here," and "No, oh, right here, here it is connecting." See, I didn't find any compelling reason to connect. I would be like, I know we have to connect, otherwise it will be hard because I just knew that they back home would be worried. I think my son felt the same. It wasn't that we wanted to connect. . . . And so it was kind of a burden to have to connect.

In eighteen of the forty-one family cases, members created digital journals together, a type of shared creative engagement with technology that necessitated managing tech time in the evenings or at café stops to post, read comments, and/or create visual narratives.[6] For example, Allie, the mother from the United States who walked with her daughters Melissa and Jessica, had readers who validated the spiritual nature of their time together as they walked: one follower commented, "What a wonderful spiritual enlightenment for you all!" Reading these affirmations together and alone became a ritual during their journeys that strengthened their close knowledge of, and participation in, each other's spiritual experience, and this ritual necessitated securing tech time. Ann, the mother from the United States in chapter 3 who walked with her daughter Hannah after Ann's husband passed away, talked about their combined efforts to digitize their Camino experience. Hannah was diligent, Ann said, in curating their Camino trip through her public blog. She described her daughter writing stories to accompany the photographs and videos they took together. They captured images of windy landscapes, farm life, streams, staged photos of enjoying a beer or glass of wine together, and selfies of the two of them that reflected the closeness they were experiencing. McKenzie and her sister Victoria from Canada, who walked with their mother, Lauren, described a practice of working together to compose captions for their Facebook blog. Most nights, Lauren said, they would sit together and "yack about the day and go 'Okay, what's the theme, how are we going to string our blog together for today?' " Lauren emphasized that theirs was a collaborative effort: "It was really cool because we were all trying to be respectful of each other's unique creative ideas and make sure that we were trying to incorporate each into the blog." These were collaborative journal entries of shared mystical transcendence, and the journaling was made possible through securing tech time. For example, one post read: "As we passed through the groves, we were focused on yet another exhausting climb when a ghost-like woman on a white mare with foal at her side accompanied by three dogs galloped by. It was such a strange unexpected sight that we wondered if it had happened at all."

Creative engagement, while strengthening spiritual intimacy in families, also imposed a burden of frequent online connection. Stories like Mary Ann's and others led me to attempt to send back photos and descriptions of my Camino experience when walking in 2016 on the Camino Francés with my husband, Mark. When we stopped at the end of the day we would write about our encounters and decide which pictures we would send back for our children and my mother to see. While it was a rewarding shared creative project that the family back home looked forward to each day, it was also burdensome and required discipline in locating a strong Wi-Fi signal and setting aside time to be online. It was a task that at times took me away from meeting and talking with other pilgrims. In addition, being online instantly brought relationships and issues at home into the forefront of my Camino experience.

Pulled Back

> Digital age pilgrims typically embark on the Camino *physically* but do not make a clear *mental* break with home. It is more common now to have *collaborative* pilgrimages in which friends, family, unknown followers and even the boss come along *virtually* on the Camino. The pilgrim may maintain a significant mental back and forth via the cloud with this audience.
>
> —Frey 2018: 153

Family members were drawn to life off the Camino through various kinds of digital relationships. Some, like Mary Ann, carried the emotional weight of responsibility to online followers with whom they were sharing their journey. When Lindsey's phone broke and she was not able to make her regular Facebook updates, she borrowed another pilgrim's device to update her Facebook page so that people back home would not worry: "My phone is broken," she wrote on her blog, "so you won't see me anymore. Don't worry. I'm not dead." The expectation that pilgrims needed to check in with friends and family to assure them that they were safe and to read the comments they posted was a common sentiment on the part of almost all of the pilgrims I met, and a task that routinely pulled them back to everyday life.

Several parents, like Charlie's father, Bart, were drawn back into their everyday lives digitally through work responsibilities. Bart had to spend a couple of hours each day online completing his coursework and managing 400 employees at his restaurant. While their situations were not as extreme, several other parents were pulled back into their everyday lives when they took time to check in at work. For example, Ed, Julia's father, said he only looked at his email once during their week-long journey, and then sighed with frustration as he described the number of work problems that had invaded his Camino space in that one session. One mother who worked in real estate checked in with her office every few days. Her daughter complained that at times she would "disappear for hours" to work. I met and walked for a couple of hours with a father from Mexico City who was with his two sons; one had just finished his senior year of college, and the other had just begun. He had his laptop in his backpack and what he called a "satellite locator" so that he could, he said, "pretty much have Wi-Fi anywhere." He said he had to check in online each day with his company, given the nature of his business. Brianna, a twenty-one-year-old college student from the United States who walked for a week with her father, talked about how she and her father hiked on weekends and during vacations at home. While she felt like the Camino gave them valuable time together after her being away at college for several years, she was disappointed because there was Wi-Fi in so many places: "We already knew how to be together and be introspective hiking together, but I like hiking in the mountains in California better; actually, there we could walk for a couple of days with no Wi-Fi." Even though they would have preferred not to use the phone or check email, because they had Wi-Fi every night her mom expected them to check in and her father felt compelled to check his email. One day, she said, "he had 107 messages from work that he had to take!"

Some family members were pulled to people back home through therapeutic dependency, a need to obtain frequent advice and assurance from loved ones. Ariel, for example, often in tears and exhausted, sent her mother, sister, and boyfriend many texts, called, and even FaceTimed to find guidance in how to deal with her father, Allan, as they argued and struggled to stay together on the Camino. She said that after his first big "outburst with the young women talking on the cellphone," she sat in a café and emailed her mom and sister and told them it was really time for her to come home, that her father could not be happy, and that "this wasn't what I signed up for!" They convinced her that she was a "tough girl" and had the strength to stay and "walk it through." Ariel also emailed her boyfriend every day, and when she was held up in a pension for several days with an injury and illness while Allan walked alone, she spent a good portion of the time FaceTiming with her boyfriend, who encouraged her to keep walking and told her that the Camino was what God wanted her to do. God was with her, he said, and assured her that she was "there for a reason" and that she "may never get this chance again." He encouraged her to "reflect and spend time with God" as she was healing and preparing to return to her father on the path. Ariel believed this contact with her boyfriend gave her the strength to continue her spiritual journey and continue working on her relationship with Allan.

Lina from the Netherlands, who walked with her father, Jansen, also stayed in almost daily contact with her mother and her boyfriend via email and FaceTime. Jansen told me that Lina was "very close" to her mother and that they talked daily: "Lina's anxieties and worries and difficult moments are shared intimately with my wife, so she is very involved with trying to help her." On the Camino, Jansen said, they thought it would be good because "my wife could have a break, and we had decided to call her only every other day," but, Jansen said, "my wife started fairly quickly calling us each day less than a week into our six-week trip, and so we ended up having daily check-ins."

In family cases like Ariel and Lina's, intimacy with others was strengthened via technology, but it was not always with a family member or intimate other who was physically with them on the Camino. For example, Ariel described her sister growing in compassion and experiencing something new between them: "It was the kindest my sister had ever been to me." Ariel stressed in her interview how important it was for people who are doing the Camino to "have people back home, or someone at least, who can help you through this." Such relational work with significant others back home mediated by technology had the potential to weaken intimacy with the family member they were walking with. Emotional digital outreach was also, as Ariel firmly believed, understood by some as essential to building connection through a demanding physical and emotional practice: "While you are on the Camino, you need someone back home to talk or email because you become delusional . . . everything starts to seem like a wash on the Camino."

Others were in touch daily with close family members back home for whom they were emotionally responsible. Several parents were also caretakers for younger children or their aging parents and so contacted them frequently while on the Camino. Caroline, for example, the mother from the United Kingdom who walked for a week with her daughter Leisa, used WhatsApp to be in touch with her mom: "She is eighty-seven and she needs to be in contact with me, so I called her probably almost every day." For Caroline and several other parents with whom I spoke, their willingness to take such a long time away from home was contingent on being in daily contact with dependents. Many of them, like Caroline, posted pictures on WhatsApp, Instagram, or Facebook for these family members to follow their journey. Once family members made the decision to post on a social media platform and send frequent photos and postings to family and friends, those back home became invested, offering encouraging posts and following their family member's Camino journey each day. One woman in her forties whom I walked with for several days one summer wondered out loud what her aging father's daily life would be like without what had become his morning ritual: finding her location on the large map posted on his kitchen wall that he used to follow her progress and reading online about the towns she passed through each day.

Many of the pilgrims I interviewed voiced irritation and concern regarding the family member they were walking with being pulled back home emotionally. For example, Allan said, "I was hoping that she [Ariel] could disconnect from her friends, but she couldn't." Lindsey said her mom, Margie, "used her iPod" to "connect to Wi-Fi and was constantly sending email to boyfriends, various guys she was dating on the internet." Lindsey saw this as a problem because she felt it led to her mother not absorbing what the Camino had to offer and also because Margie complained about not being able to get online at times.

Most family members talked about digital devices connecting them with newfound pilgrim friends as they walked. Texting and Facebook helped them locate people they had walked with for a day or two on the path, or share digital journals when they became separated from other pilgrims. Pilgrims of the digital age also carry information about global politics and tragedies at their fingertips, which provoked parents and adult children at times to feel a sense of communitas with pilgrims as global citizens. In June 2016, as the Brexit vote came in, pilgrims were immediately aware through digital news. Family members I spoke with talked about sharing conversations and tears with each other and pilgrims they met while walking who were concerned about the implications for Europe and beyond. Several family members from North America talked to me about the sympathy pilgrims from Europe offered as photographs of mass shootings in the United States appeared on phones and tablets. This immediate appearance of current events on a wired Camino prompted families to build connection together with pilgrims from across the world.

For some pilgrims, the wired nature of the Camino brought them to an abrupt sense of disconnection at some point during their journey. Katy, for example, whose story I told at the start of this book, found an unfamiliar and startling peace at the Hospital of the Soul. Separated from her cellphone and directed by the structure of the space to spend time reflecting, she felt alone for the first time with a sense of Divine presence. She and her father, José, recognized the weight of her revelation. As Katy explained to me sitting at the café with her father, she had tried to replicate that feeling when she saw other opportunities on the Camino, but she was always pulled back to her technology—communication with other pilgrims, documenting her journey visually, and posting photos on her Instagram. José and Katy, concerned about anxiety that bothered Katy in her daily life, recognized the power of this digital pull away from the calm and peace that Camino spiritual practices could bring. While they wanted to combat this force, neither of them talked about devising concrete strategies for limiting their use of technology on the Camino.

Several family members also talked with me about individual pledges to discipline their use of digital devices. Lina, for example, made a choice not to be active on social media while on the Camino with her father:

> I really felt like I was going there to have time to myself and to get things straight and work things out, and a phone is intrusive. It goes off every two seconds, your Facebook goes off every two seconds, and you know if you don't respond people automatically assume something, so I thought it would actually be better just to not have it with me. I did take an iPad, but just to stay in contact with my mom and boyfriend, so I FaceTimed and emailed with them. They were the only two people I reached out to while I was gone.

Pilgrims also made pledges to stay away from various types of social media. For example, Anita, a twenty-two-year-old from the United States who traveled with her mom, Sheri, age forty-six, and her stepfather, Jim, age forty-seven, made a pledge to stay off Twitter: "I didn't use my Twitter for the entire month I was there. . . . It was good, kind of refreshing, like not worrying about what was going on, so that was a nice way to kind of break it. But I would still upload pictures to Instagram, just to keep people up to date." Melissa, a twenty-three-year-old woman from the United States who walked with her mother, Allie, age forty-nine, and her sister Jessica, age twenty-five, made an individual decision to leave all of her devices at home to enhance the spiritual aspects of her Camino:

> It was more of a spiritual thing for me to just go and see what I could accomplish. . . . You become in tune with your strengths and weaknesses and things like that . . . getting away from all the technology. You have anywhere from really eight to twelve hours, however long you decide you want to walk, and all you can do is think. You think about your life a little more because, like I said before, we are so in tune to technology and we don't,

> no one ever really stops with the technology, so it was nice to put that aside and actually think about things like, what am I doing with my life and, um . . . where am I going. So that's really how I explain the Camino, is that it was very mind . . . mind . . . mind over more than body.

Allan also talked about keeping his email at a distance and not engaging with family or friends at home so that he could connect with Ariel and "not contaminate it [Camino] with anything from the outside."

Family Digital Designs

The preceding are examples of individual family members telling stories of purposively controlling technology use. In a third of the family cases, parents and young adults talked about collaborative negotiation in planning how to approach technology. They wanted to discipline their use of digital devices in ways that would strengthen shared experiences of spirituality on the Camino. These strategies of reducing, containing, and controlling digital engagement constituted their Camino digital designs.

I did not ask family members directly if they had approaches to limiting technology use; their illustrations of disciplining technology were born from in-depth responses to my open-ended questions about the kind of technology that they brought with them. Digital designs, for the most part, revolved around how the families constructed "tech-free time" and "tech time." Tech-free space was uninterrupted time where they could self-reflect, connect with each other, contemplate nature, and engage in walking meditation or prayer together and alone. For the most part, these families designated their walking hours during the day as tech-free, with short café stops as space and time where brief digital check-ins were allowed. Sacralizing—making sacred pockets of liminal time while walking—felt liberating, and the space they created was described by many family members as spiritually filled. Pilgrims who identified as Christian also elaborated on how disciplining technology supported sacred time for contemplation of religious texts, prayers, and meditative walking that would bring them closer to God. Controlling technology enhanced the various types of relational spirituality that I outlined in chapter 3, in particular intimate disclosures and intimate encounters with nature and the material Camino. Family strategies for disciplining technology and creating sacred pockets of time took two basic forms: (1) designating a family member as manager of digital devices, and (2) coming to a consensus regarding how and when family members would use technology.

In four of these fourteen family cases, I heard consensus-building in their descriptions that involved designating a family member as the manager of digital devices. This digital manager was the person who carried, and was in charge of, a phone, iPad, or laptop for the family. In some cases, this person was the family member who posted to blogs or other social media that kept extended kin back home apprised of their Camino progress and experiences. In other cases, the designated controller simply carried the device(s) and they all used the device(s) for communication back home and to reserve lodging and/or navigate Camino routes. These family members suggested that coming to a designated-controller agreement before starting their trip, or in some cases as they walked, allowed other family member(s) to disconnect and enter into more spiritual, meditative periods of time.

For example, Victoria let her mother, Lauren, carry and control their digital device, which the family used together to create their blog entries. Victoria said this made it easier for her to disconnect from social media. In fact, she said, "neither my sister nor I brought any type of technology." Victoria talked about spending hours talking and connecting with her sister, McKenzie, and their mother, and also walking with them in "silence" without the temptation of occupying her mind with social media or music. Bart, Charlie's father, is another example of adoption of a designated-controller digital design and also of family members coming to a consensus regarding how and when family members would use technology.

As I noted earlier, Bart had to spend time each day online completing course work for an advanced degree program and managing 400 employees, and so he carried their technology. Bart and Charlie decided that Bart would carry his phone and laptop, but that when they were walking, they would not use technology. Bart noted: "We saw a lot of people with their iPhones and their iPads and we made a decision . . . not to do the music, iPhones and ear buds and listening to music. So, we made that decision so that we were walking together, we weren't texting. When we stopped, I would send a message back to the business or I would make a quick call." While Bart knew that he would be pulled back into his everyday educational and work tasks at designated times, Charlie was able to remove himself from any online activity, an absence that he talked about as enhancing the spiritual connectedness and reflection they experienced together while walking. Charlie spent more concentrated time with his father and was able to bond with other pilgrims with whom he felt a sense of community. Charlie said he walked for weeks and did not even pick up a phone: "Instead of worrying about taking a picture, I'd just enjoy it [nature and people encountered] and kind of engrain it in my memory." He characterized this set-apart, unmediated space his father helped provide as spiritual: "You're surrounded by nature and by other people, this community of walkers—definitely had a spiritual peace. . . . It's sort of a moving-meditation sort of situation where you really get connected to yourself and you're talking . . . an open-boundary sort of relationship with people."

Barbara, the mother from Canada who walked with her son and daughter, made the decision with her children that their goal was to do without technology altogether. "We did have our camera," she said, "but that was it." She continued:

> I guess I had the impression that you are encouraged to let go and not encumber yourself with technology, and we had debated one phone, but we decided against it. And we decided about perhaps purchasing, you know, a cheap throwaway phone once we arrived, but we were astounded that old and young, almost even with the older generation, they were very attached to the technology and we were without it, so . . . My kids certainly did not say, "Why were we so stupid?" and they didn't resent the fact that we had landed with that decision about the phone. There were times that it made it more complicated, for sure. But being without it didn't rob of us any of the experience, and probably would have cut into our experience.

Danielle, the fifty-year-old mom from the Netherlands who walked for a week with her twenty-two-year-old daughter Sophie, talked about working to maintain the Camino as a "calming life" and introducing Sophie to the meditative power of the Camino. To bond with each other and new pilgrim friends, mother and daughter worked together to limit their use of technology and social media, as Danielle had done in her previous Caminos alone. They agreed to try to use their phones only for "practical reasons, to arrange things, and for safety." They did this because they wanted to be "free from obligations and not available" to family and friends by phone.

John, the sixty-year-old father from Canada who walked with his twenty-eight-year-old son Richard, said that they decided to bring only "one cellphone to share." Similar to Danielle and Sophie, they understood this phone was "just to find places to stay," and as an emergency contact point for his daughter back home. "The only person who could get a hold of us was my daughter." John also used the phone to take hundreds of photos, which he later uploaded on Flickr. "I really wanted to be incommunicado; I tend to check my work emails when I'm on vacation and I was adamant, adamant, that it was not going to be that kind of vacation, so I shut myself off, after twenty-eight years in the same job. I was shut out and it was wonderful!" John said that his son brought a hard-copy journal and took notes each day.

Danielle and John introduced a digital plan to Sophie and Richard, but in some family cases it was the young adult who took the lead in suggesting how and when family members should abstain from or set aside digital devices. For example, Julie and Ed, the father and daughter from the United States who described their shared spiritual experience in chapter 3 as "transcendent," agreed together that they would limit their use of technology. In fact, putting technology to the side was one of the behaviors that Julie set as a rule and expectation for her father, who she thought was too tied to his stress inducing workplace. In their interview together, Ed described his job as "like a razor," and proudly repeated the promise he had made to Julie before they left that he would not look at his email. Ed said that she was clear he needed to turn off the email, that she did not want his office to be with them on the Camino: "Julie told me I couldn't check my email, I couldn't contact work, and so I didn't. Everyday emails are drudgery. . . . The Camino gave me an escape. It was so freeing. It was, and all the problems, all of it will be there when I get back. I did it because I knew it would make her happy." Limiting their use of phones and computer devices throughout their trip produced uninterrupted time for shared religious practice: "We prayed together each day the St. James novena," Ed said, "with the cross that my older daughter gave us before we left." Julie credited their limited use of digital devices with producing time where they could be "quiet together, thinking about peace." It was during their tech-free walking on Camino paths and extended time in the evening at cafés that Julie said she had time to ask Ed more about his family history and to capture those "stories" she said might have otherwise been "lost."

Ed and Julie also pledged not to use technology for entertainment; rather, they wanted the evening hours to be more meaningful. Ed talked about how this was different from the way it was at home, where they watched a show, news, or a movie at night. Instead, on the Camino tech-free evening hours were saved especially for the discussion of a spiritual text that Julie had picked out for them, a book whose plot centered around people who came from radically different backgrounds and shared a spiritual connection. They read this book with each other in the evenings and talked together before going to sleep about how the many pilgrims they had met while walking reflected themes in the book. Experiences like these were, in Julie's words, "transcendent," heightening shared practices during a ten-day journey where Ed checked his email "only once."

I interviewed an evangelical Christian family of five from the United States in Santiago early one morning at a coffee shop. The parents were in their late forties, their son was in high school, and their daughters were in college. They spoke of agreeing together to each bring "one piece of technology," but, as with Sophie and John, family members made clear that their aim was to use digital devices only for "practical reasons." The parents and adult children each named a purpose for the phone or tablet they carried: journaling, using maps the family had downloaded, and referencing the family calendar that had details about what person back home they were saying prayers for and walking for on a particular day. The father, Brad, talked about his device as being a way to "check in at work"—not too much, though, just enough to make sure that the employees at his business were doing okay. Ellie, his wife, stressed that having books on her Kindle was important to her practice of reading something meaningful at night. She was a women's ministry leader in her home church, and many of these texts were books she might use to offer spiritual and religious guidance. While it was, of course, highly possible that some family members used their technology for something other than these "practical" tasks and did not tell me, the story the family told together was one of efforts they made to not engage media forms that would take them away from their Camino experience. Interestingly, they described their tech-free walking time using media concepts to underscore how they had replaced digital entertainment with creative relational interactions. Ellie explained, "We had what we all called our 'personal podcasts.' One family member would introduce a topic and then we would talk about it, for a long time, for hours while we walked." Brad gave an example: "My podcast was about the Spanish government and the difference between socialism and capitalism and high rates of unemployment in Spain." Ellie said her "personal podcast" was about "marriage and family and feminism and the breakdown of the family." The two daughters chose less politically infused topics, such as "What is the cutest animal?" The story they told was a performance of making decisions together about controlling technology on their Camino and connecting, as a family, during tech-free time.

Isabelle, the young woman from Sweden who helped push her mother, Lisa, up steep inclines, decided with her mother before they left home that they would only use their phones for taking photos while walking. Their deep desire to have the "spiritual Camino" they had read about in so many Camino blogs and published narratives shaped their pledge to not access social media while walking on Camino paths. Isabelle reflected that this agreement of setting aside tech-free time gave her permission and time to "slow down," to truly leave everyday relationships behind without the constant temptation to check in with friends and other family members. Their pledge made her able to be with her mother in nature, which to Isabelle represented the "spiritual part" of their relationship. Her mother, Lisa, said that disengaging from all social media while they were walking on paths helped them "experience all things in a magnified way." How often, she asked me, "do you have time to talk so much about things without something else getting in the way?" Lisa named these tech-free moments in total as giving "birth again to each other on the Camino," noting that they "laughed and cried together and sang songs together and remembered stories from Isabelle's childhood," things that they had not talked about in a long time. In their co-authored account of tech-free Camino time, they had a rare kind of time and space where they could listen carefully to each other.

Natalie, the mother I introduced in chapter 1 who had a neck injury and was able to walk for a week because they used a service that carried their luggage, told a story that illustrated how tech-free walking and limiting technology use allowed her to embrace a different quality of being with her daughter, Nell. Both Nell, age twenty-one, and Natalie, age fifty-five, decided that they would try to use technology only during designated times for checking in with their booking agency regarding travel plans and communicating briefly with family and friends back home. Natalie emphasized the practicality of having Wi-Fi and her phone and iPad and, for her, their absolute necessity given that the luggage service, Camino Ways, was what gave her the strength to walk: "Technology allowed me to be brave. I am not a risk-taker. Technology allowed me to be a risk-taker." But, she said, "I wanted to have time to sit with my thoughts that I don't have at home," and so she used her iPad "once a day," for the "least technology possible," in order to send photographs and texts to friends and family. Nell had her own impressions that shaped her desire to work together with her mother to discipline use while walking and in the evenings: "I did not want to be as connected as I am usually. I think in my generation there is a rejection of the constant online presence. I think, actually, that we push tech away because we are so used to it."

Natalie and Nell said that even though their journey was not as physically demanding as that of "the pilgrims who carry everything," carrying lighter backpacks during the day and not having to worry as much about checking in online to secure lodging allowed them to walk on less crowded paths, as they were not trying to rush to get rooms on the last 100 kilometers into Santiago on the French route. They were able to, they said, take their time and "smell the roses." Like Ed and Julie, Natalie and Nell brought a text to read to fill evening hours, a "small spiritual book" that a priest back home had recommended to them: *A Field of Stars*, by pilgrim Father Kevin Codd. They read Codd's text aloud to each other at night. They both used Codd's language in talking about staying "humble in the walk" so that that the walk would "humble them." They spoke of developing an "intimate bond together in walking," due in part to their pledge to disconnect, which opened space for deeper discussion and reflection on their individual concerns and mother-daughter relationship. For example, Nell talked about having the time to finally talk with her mother about the pressure she felt to pursue a career that her mom and dad approved of. Natalie said that she was able to make her daughter understand that she and her husband were fine with whatever career Nell wanted to pursue. Natalie also talked about how they learned to "listen" to each other "more deeply," identifying different species of trees as they walked and relating them to experiences from Nell's childhood. Even though Nell considered herself a Catholic, she was able to talk with her mother about how she was at a point in her life where she wanted to "explore" and "listen" to different religions. By designating tech time, mother and daughter ensured a wealth of tech-free time for spiritual reflection removed from everyday relationships and concerns.

How family members measured the success of their efforts to work together to adhere to their family digital designs varied. For example, the family of the young woman at the start of this chapter felt that their efforts had paid off. I had a conversation with all three family members at the end of their Camino in the Pilgrim's Office as they arrived in Santiago. I was meeting someone at the office, and the family recognized me as they stood in line. They called me into conversation, and we talked for a bit about the other pilgrims we knew. The daughter lifted her head from her phone and talked with me for the first time, asking my opinion about colleges she might want to attend. Soon after they received their documents of completion, she returned to her digital cocoon and sat under a tree in the garden away from other pilgrims celebrating this ritual moment. Yet even though she was still attached to her phone, she had made it to the end of the Camino and had been out of her room and away from her digital world for an extended period of time every day for more than four weeks. Another pilgrim who knew the family well told me that the mother was pleased her daughter had begun talking and interacting with other pilgrims, even if only briefly, as she did with me in the Pilgrim's Office that day.

Several families told stories about having a day or two where they broke their family digital plans, and one family talked about failing miserably throughout the entire trip. Ellen, age twenty, from Australia, and her fifty-four-year-old mother, Robin, went on the Camino with the hope that Ellen could experience healing from a social media trauma. Through consensus-building, they agreed together to search for ways to limit use of their digital devices. For example, they turned off their Facebook apps on their phones, and Robin shut off her email settings. They had decided to use their phones only to book lodging, check news, and send photos back home. Unfortunately, because "Wi-Fi was everywhere," Ellen was able to connect to Facebook and was pulled back to a social media world that had caused her much anxiety. Both mother and daughter expressed disappointment that Ellen became engrossed again in Facebook dramas that took much emotional energy that might otherwise have been used to connect with each other, bond with other pilgrims, and experience the natural world of the Camino. Despite the pair working together on a family digital plan for tech-free time, Ellen's social media habits and the wired nature of the Camino weakened their pursuit of spiritual intimacy.

Conclusion: Lasting Digital Practices

It is striking that a third of the families in this ethnographic sample told me stories of disciplining technology. Their concern reflects a larger cultural discourse about the intrusion of online obligations and relationships into everyday life and the need for people to develop new digital habits regarding ICTs.[7] Brierley's text, online Camino forums and blogs, and published personal narratives of this extended walking pilgrimage shaped family members' stories of controlling technology for sacred purpose. However, in an increasingly mediatized world where human relationships and social ties are so deeply shaped by ICTs, the stories they told me were also larger cultural performances of moral family digital discipline and togetherness.[8]

Their stories suggest as well that disciplining practices can be extended upon return home to foster spiritual intimacy. In five of the fourteen family cases where I found the disciplining of technology, family members were interviewed in Santiago soon after finishing their Camino. These family members talked about hoping to find similar spiritual practices in their everyday lives where they could be away from digital worlds and connect with their family members. Three of the fourteen families had even walked the Camino before and told me about establishing family practices in the pursuit of spiritual intimacy at home using strategies similar to those they practiced on the Camino. In one family case, Kirsten, a forty-nine-year-old woman from the Netherlands, served as the designated controller so that her daughters, Maud, age twenty-three, and Sarah, age nineteen, would not be tempted to text or use Facebook. She talked about their Camino experiences as a "detox from life," a relief from school and friendship groups. After returning home, Maud and Kirsten made a point of going on long walks together and leaving their tablets and cellphones at home. Kirsten said: they wanted to replicate elements of their Camino escape from work, school, and social media through walking in and appreciating the "beauty of nature" together. When I interviewed Kirsten, she had returned to Santiago with Maud and her parents to walk for two weeks.

Thomas, age fifty, and his daughter Marie, age twenty, from Germany, had walked the Camino three times since she was fourteen. They decided together to limit ICT use while walking on the Camino, a practice that they replicated at home where they would take long day hikes without phones. Thomas called this creation of time at home to walk in nature a meditation practice. Marie noted that over time, experiencing this "meditation in nature" with her father made her feel comfortable expressing her feelings to him: "I'm not someone who tells what I'm thinking. . . . Walking—on the Camino and at home too—I can tell him things." Their story of tech-free walking time together over six years was of fostering a strong emotional energy connected to the practice of being together in nature; it was a ritual energy that became a familiar and desired way to be together.

Spiritual intimacy, as noted in previous chapters, involves individuals sharing private experiences and feelings related to practices and beliefs. As

I have shown in this chapter, engagement with social media platforms could challenge the exclusive nature of this intimacy for family members, but it also had the potential to enhance experiences through parents and young adults writing and composing visual journals to share with online followers who then validated the exceptional nature of their spiritual practice.[9] In chapter 5, I argue that the creation of such digital memories opened up new possibilities for experiencing spiritual connections as pilgrims returned home. I illustrate as well in chapter 5 how other material and non-material memory forms, as constructed recollections of intimacy through practice, surfaced in family members' stories and held ritual energy. Family members' boots, poles, printed photos, jewelry, tattoos, and other objects and images rich with exclusive relational meaning had the power to build connection and spiritual intimacy in their everyday lives, as did quiet memories, those experiences that were generally more private.

5
Connective Memories

We walked for a while with a Frenchman whose English was very good. He really liked the fact that Dad and I were walking together. He really thought that was a beautiful thing. I remember he said to my dad at one point: "Yeah, I like seeing you walk together. You have a kind of fusion together. It is really beautiful to see father and daughter walking together like that." . . .

And there was another guy the second time we walked . . . he said: "The three of you are walking together. Wow, I can't imagine doing anything like that with my family. You guys must be close. You are lucky." . . .

When I started out, I didn't feel like it was special or magnificent at all, but I'm coming to realize that maybe it is. Maybe I'm luckier than I thought that I have a dad that I can do that with and a mom I can call every day. It made me realize that maybe it is magnificent and I'm definitely lucky.

—Lina, the Netherlands

Walking the Way Together. Kathleen E. Jenkins, Oxford University Press (2021). © Oxford University Press.
DOI: 10.1093/oso/9780197553046.003.0005

I spoke with Lina (twenty-six), and later with her father, Jansen (sixty-one), after they had returned home from their last Camino. Their experience of walking with Lina's brother, Jacobus, was still fresh in their minds, as was their first Camino practice together, which they remembered as making a difference in their daily individual and relational lives. The "most rewarding part," Lina said, was after they returned home:

> When I came back, I genuinely realized that I had found somewhat of a peace of mind. I was a lot calmer. I was a lot better able to handle daily stress. You know, things that usually broke me up before, I went, I realized, oh, I can actually handle this a lot better. So it has actually done something for me.
>
> Kay: Can you think of an example?
>
> Lina: I think whereas before little things could really get to me. I think before, a stupid thing like somebody driving in front of me who is not going as fast as they could be, I'm impatient, that would really irritate me. And now I'm really more relaxed about things. Like I can say, okay, so it's going to be a bit longer. So things like that. I still have a lot of the, you know, the mental problems that come with anorexia—I'm still always scared to gain weight, scared to eat too much. But I can put it more in perspective, I can feel like, okay, I feel like crap today, but I know that it is in my mind and I can put it to rest more and get on with daily life. Whereas before that, would just completely overrule everything—days were spent just thinking about that. And now I'm better at that. . . .
>
> Kay: So you think the Camino offered something?
>
> Lina: Yeah, I'm still not sure what it was. It has made me calmer, and the funny thing is that I think it's true with my dad as well. My dad used to get extremely worked up about work and things like that, and you can really see—yeah, he still gets worked up and still gets irritated when things don't go the way he wants them to go at work, but at the same time . . . now he is far better at saying, okay, whatever, we'll see what happens, or not. And so I think we both actually have that, but I can't actually explain where that comes from, I think it is because you are out of it for six weeks and you come back and you realize, well, the world moves on, everything is fine, even though I didn't do all of those control things that I usually have done. So I think that has something to do with it.

Lina and Jansen's memories of their Caminos together took several forms. Her perception of the effects of the Camino in their daily lives was a quiet memory of shared encounters and emotions, an exclusive experience with her father that summoned feelings of their calming, compressed Camino life together. When Lina told me the story of the Frenchman's comment, she was offering a private recollection that in the telling validated her family's special bond. Her story also reflected exclusive body/emotion memories of physical and mental challenges accumulated through walking more than 800 kilometers together, memories that shaped a shared approach to life. Jansen's quiet memories of his family Camino affirmed a new relational quality and connectedness with his children as well. Jansen remembered being terribly homesick during his second Camino, and missing his wife to such a degree that he wanted to go home. Jacobus and Lina, he said, "talked me through those moments." Through these and other encounters, he came to see his son as stronger physically and emotionally. Jansen spoke as well of the "2,000 photographs" that followed them home on his son's camera and phone as digital memories. Lina told me about a handwritten journal from her first Camino with her father that she read at home to remind her of what they had accomplished together and their new approach to chaos and conflict in everyday life. When she walked the second time with her brother and father, she built on this collection of shared Camino lessons, this time using her iPad to construct a digital journal. In my formal interviews with seventy-eight family members, thirty-three after their return home, pilgrims imagined and experienced ritual memories as long-lasting and carrying emotional weight, symbolic recollections of intimacy that would bring, or had brought, new understandings and shared family identity.

Randall Collins (2004), building on sociologist Emile Durkheim's (1912) ideas about how collective emotional energies can produce group membership and Erving Goffman's (1967) research on collective social sentiments at work in everyday interaction rituals, offers a helpful way to think about rituals, connectivity, and memory. Interaction rituals, whether a simple daily greeting or a more extensive practice of walking together for weeks to a sacred site, can bring a range of feelings and emotions connected to how people think about what is moral or right regarding interactions with individuals, groups, or larger social relationships. For example, Lina and Jansen talked about Camino ritual teaching them to take in the world as it comes and letting go of the need to "control things"; this shared approach to daily life, born through repeated practice, reinforced their identity as family members who held similar life values. Their journey also affirmed their individual commitment to self-work; for example, Jansen worked to let go of tension and anger, and Lina faced her control issues related to food. These ritual memories reflected larger cultural expectations that families should be both alone and together. They are remembrances of becoming strong individuals who are both supportive of and dependent on kin.[1]

Rituals have the potential to produce a high level of "emotional energy" that can promote solidarity and affirmation of ideal family relationships and their imagined long-term consequences (Collins 2004: 48, 108). Emotional energy at work in ritual life can shape how people feel about what is good in the world and about how we interact with each other, nature, mystical forces, and/or Divine beings. To touch the soft wood of the pew where one's grandmother sat each Sunday and sing the hymns she knew by heart, to bake challah as one's mother did and smell the sweetness of the bread in the air, to speak a relative's oft-repeated adages—these are all practices where the weight of connective ritual memory may carry forward into the participant's life, where ritual objects, language, and other sensory elements can define and shape individual ethics. Such ritual memories can reinforce family intimacy and identity by tying individuals to a particular symbolic worldview regarding what is meaningful in life and by propelling repetition of rituals that solidify group meaning and worldview.[2] They are connective memories that echo some of the broad ritual effects of communitas, feelings of shared life that become meaningful in the embracing of similar beliefs and practices.

Almost all of the pilgrims I encountered walking Camino routes and in the city of Santiago, whether they were walking with family of origin, alone, or with their newly constructed "Camino family," expressed concern about wanting to bring Camino revelations about time and relationship with the natural world and others back home. They thought about how they might replicate distance from technology, care more deeply for others, and push aside anxiety in their fast-paced daily lives. Some were concerned about taking physical Camino practices back: how they might move in a purposeful way for hours at a time, challenging their bodies with a daily routine that made the experience of eating a simple meal exceedingly satisfying. Many of the families with whom I spoke contemplated how they could continue to experience the pleasure of sitting at a table drinking a coffee or sharing a glass of wine or fresh-squeezed orange juice with family members without the interruption of digital screens. They wondered if they could replicate the sense of connectedness and meaning in sitting in silence together and with other pilgrims.

When Collins (2004) speaks about the emotional energy that rituals can carry, he is talking about a continuum: practices can also sustain moderate emotional energy that does little to bind people together in common purpose or identity, or low emotional energy that could distance people from common ideals or goals. In Ariel's and Lindsey's cases, the emotional energy carried in their walking practice regarding family intimacy was connective, but in a more moderate sense. At the end of their Caminos, they were not ready to identify with their parents' worldview, but they did feel closer to them and a sense of ritual success in revelations regarding how to continue forward in their relationships. Ariel, seeing her father cry for the first time when she threatened to leave the Camino, had "new moments of understanding" of his life experiences. The Camino, for Ariel, did not "fix anything," but, she said, "it teaches you how to love each other." The miracle Lindsey had hoped for through communitas and the religious/spiritual energies of the Camino did not change her mother, but her storied memory was of ritual progress, an encounter that brought the revelation that she could not change her mother. Lindsey believed that this new understanding would help her to be a daughter in a more positive, supportive role. In my research I also heard some evidence of what I call *distancing memories,* reflections of ritual practice with low emotional energy. These were memories that reinforced differences in worldview and spiritual practice among family members, or memories of the Camino as a failed spiritual endeavor.[3] I heard a few distancing memories in interviews, but these were generally not the stories people wanted to tell. Most descriptions of distancing memories came to me during field work through informal interviews and observations. For example, a young man at a café described his father spending most of his Camino time socializing in bars, and a mother and daughter felt the Camino was too crowded and full of people more interested in their phones than in engaging with them.

In this chapter, I illustrate three types of connective memories born of shared Camino ritual that surfaced in family members' stories.[4] The first is *quiet memory*: storied and sensory memories that are generally more private and shared with intimate others. Quiet memories are quiet because they sit more in the backstage of relational social performances. Their largely private, exclusive nature reflects the potential for heightened emotional energy to build spiritual intimacy, as such memories represent family members' exclusive knowledge of each other's spiritual beliefs and practices.

The second type of connective memory I illustrate here is *digital memory*. Digital memories can be quiet—for example, digital images shared only with intimate others, such as the video Allan fondly recalled taking of Ariel walking away and "flipping me off" and which he described as an "encapsulation of the moment" because she was "smiling" at the same time. But digital memories today are also likely to be frontstage performances of spiritual intimacy shared with wide networks of extended family, friends, and, in the case of public blogs and social media platforms, an endless well of possible audience members. Digital memories have strong potential to carry emotional energy and reinforce spiritual intimacy both in their creation and through their immediate accessibility in daily life.[5] Family members' descriptions of digital memories capturing shared transcendent experience suggested high emotional energy through the generation of new memories of ritual connection.

The third type of connective memory, *material memory*, can be private or more frontstage performances of family ritual experience: printed photographs, symbolic objects like jewelry, a pilgrims' stamped credentials, and even tattoos. Material memories appear in various forms and represent and remind family members of mutual ritual experience and family identity. They may be displayed permanently in homes and offices, like printed and framed photographs on living room coffee tables and on refrigerators. Others can be more present in everyday life, especially tattoos or jewelry that adorn and travel with bodies throughout the day.

Quiet, digital, and material memories are not exclusive and frequently overlap; however, they do have distinct characteristics. They are distinguishable in how individuals experience their creation and how they are recorded, remembered, and made accessible as connective memories.

Quiet Memories

It was probably the third or fourth day, and so we were about halfway done with our walk. I remember this moment really clearly because we had a really great conversation. We were sitting in this really cool café that was like elevated, looking over a river, and it was early in the morning, it was like six in the morning, and prior to the Camino, I never wake up that early.

> Waking up that early and being functional doesn't happen, so it's this kind of this mystical weird thing that the Camino does. Everyone wakes up at four in the morning and starts walking—it's just kind of wild. . . . So we were sitting at this café just sipping on a nice cup of coffee just overlooking this river and we were just talking about the day and . . . where are we going today or, you know, where are we stopping, and then we just kind of like stopped talking and had this little moment of just looking around and we were both silent for about five minutes straight. And the reason why that sticks out to me is because both my dad and I are very talkative people. You know, we feel like we need to continue the conversation and say something. And we were both silent and looking around and kind of absorbing the moment and it was just, um, we had a really good connection there.
>
> —Charlie, son from the United States

The preceding quote is a quiet memory from Charlie about embracing quietude with his father. Quiet memories—those stories, encounters, and emotions that come alive in telling them to intimate others—were often about what pilgrims imagined as the special nature of shared family Camino experiences. They were generally reflective of private emotions and experiences. At times such memories contained details of other pilgrims' lives that they knew would not have been appropriate for sharing on blogs or in other public venues. Quiet memories often magnified ritual emotional energy, feelings of being connected in a special way to their parent or child, as they saw themselves as the only ones who knew what those memories felt like. I imagine this type of memory was triggered by the private nature of the interview process, ushering a sense of intimacy into our conversations, which at times brought me to share my own private feelings regarding my Camino experience.

Sophie, the young woman from Amsterdam who walked with her mother, Danielle, was struck by how other pilgrims saw their walking together as mother and daughter as something special: "People liked to take pictures of us because we were a mother and daughter walking together. They liked to see us together." Danielle responded to Sophie's comment with a story of a member of their "pilgrim family" who was drawn to them in an intense way. This woman was from Germany and had a bad relationship with her son. They walked with her, prayed with her, and spent time talking with her about her son and how she might reach out to him. Danielle suggested that perhaps, together, they had helped this woman believe that reconciliation with her son was possible. Danielle and Sophie shared this memory of caring together for another person, an exclusive understanding of being a point of inspiration and hope for another pilgrim by demonstrating a strong parent-child bond.

Memories of others naming the beauty of their family connection were dominant in family members' stories. They were points of interactions with other pilgrims that lived quietly in their memories, recollections of others affirming their family as a model, an ideal representation of what family was supposed to be. Elise, the mother from the United States whose middle son committed suicide, shared quiet Camino memories that resembled this affirmation of her family as connected. Recall from chapter 3 Elise's memory of the Canadian woman who, on seeing the family together sharing a picnic of cheese, bread, and chorizo, stopped to say, "I just want to tell you . . . you are the most beautiful family." Remembering this woman's statement summoned a ritual memory that brought tears to Elise's eyes, a testimony to the unity and connection of her family in the face of devastating grief and the social shame of suicide. Lance, the twenty-two-year-old from Canada who walked with his mom, Barbara, and his younger sister Michelle, also remembered the attention they were given by other pilgrims because they were a family: "The amount of people we met was amazing. It was one of the highlights of the trip, the amount of people we met. And I think that was because we were walking as a family. People kind of stopped and noticed us. They introduced themselves and got to like us because we were walking as a family." His mother, Barbara, carried this memory as well: "So many times people would say along the route, 'Who are you? Who are you with? Oh, you are a mother and two kids—ah, really!' They always seemed to be taken aback by that. In a kind way, in a generous way, but they would always remark on it."

Mary Ann, the Catholic from the United States in her early sixties who walked with her eighteen-year-old son George, shared quiet memories that she saw as having lifelong implications. She described attending prayer meetings with her son where the intense suffering and hardship of fellow pilgrims from across the globe were spoken of. She mentioned the people they met along the way who commented on the special nature of how George cared for his mother during her hypothermia. Mary Ann saw these quiet memories as being of consequence: "I pictured myself before we left that I would be eighty something . . . and in my mind there would still be those memories because we remember these, without saying anything." Upon return from the Camino, she continued to see these as enduring recollections that would bring mother and son an exclusive point of spiritual memory and communication:

> I know for the rest of my life and his life, it is just a connection, and that we can say things, or I can. For example, when he went off to college, he was there for about a month and he was saying, "Wow, this is really difficult." . . . And I wrote him a note that I could never write to someone who had not done that [Camino] with me. I just said, "You know, remember to stay hydrated, keep up your energy, watch out for the Gypsies, and you will get there one step at a time. It may not be Santiago, but it will be graduation."

Several parents and their young adult children, like Mary Ann, projected the impact of such shared quiet memories into the future. Julie said she had time to ask her father more about his family history and "captured family stories that might have otherwise been lost." Julie also talked about the memory impacting end-of-life ritual; as I interviewed both daughter and father in a café, Julie said that when she had told her friend back home that she wanted to walk the Camino with her father, the friend told her that she would "have a cool story to tell" at her dad's funeral. Julie quickly corrected, "Well, maybe she should have said wedding, but the point was, she said that it was going to be a 'story forever' that we would have." The implications of Camino memories at the end of their parents' life came up in a handful of conversations. I interviewed Mitch, a fifty-one-year-old father from the United States, and his son William, who was twenty, over dinner and a walk through the streets of Santiago one evening. When William and I were walking alone, I asked him if he would do the Camino again if he had the chance. He said yes, and that he had had a conversation with his father during their Camino about whether or not his dad wanted him to take his ashes on the Camino when he died. His father told him that he would but that "I hope that won't be for a long time!"

Ed and Julie also spoke about how the memories they accumulated on the walk were exclusive—experiences that only they would understand. Julie, as I noted in chapter three, used the word "transcendent" to describe their journey several times during our interview. Recall too that they told a story about sharing an extraordinary experience of soaking their tired feet together in soapy water at the end of a long day, an experience Julie gave as an example of the exclusive understanding each of them had of spiritual practice together: "We may show our photographs to others and tell stories, but only we really can feel what happened and experience it in this way. . . . Only we will fully understand the moment." As we were leaving the café, Julie pulled me aside and motioned for her father to wait outside for us. "I have something to say privately to Kay," she told him. He obeyed, and I indicated to Ed that he could talk with me privately too if he liked, although he did not take me up on it. When Ed was outside, Julie held my arm and told me a story about something she had learned about her father on the Camino that she greatly admired. This quiet memory was born through spiritual intimacy with her father and told to me as intimate other.

Toward the end of our interview, before Julie gestured for her father to leave us alone, they asked me if we could have a photo together. Julie recruited the Spanish couple at the table next to us to take our photograph, and we stood with our arms around each other as the patron captured our encounter. I became, as I did with others I interviewed in Santiago, a part of their family story, a relationship that somewhat resembled the sharing of feelings and personal stories that exists as an ethic on the Camino. Ed then asked me, "What about your family? Have you walked with your family?" I became vividly aware, in the shadow of their story of transcendent experience together, of my relationship with my father. I had just spent time visiting and taking care of him before he died and had my own quiet memories of being close with him as his cancer spread. For some reason, Ed and Julie's relationship became, in a moment, a symbol of what I had hoped I could have with my father when he was alive. I was overwhelmed with emotion, captivated by the beauty of the story they told, perhaps as was the Canadian woman who latched onto Danielle and Sophie as they were walking. "I would have liked to walk with my father," I said to Ed and Julie. "He died in January." "I'm so sorry," they both said. I thanked them and then quickly shifted the conversation to how busy my children were with school and how I did hope that one day one of them would walk with me.

Pilgrims often talked about these exclusive experiences of Camino spirituality as making a difference in their relationship as they aged. While I cannot say if the intensity of these connective memories would last over the years, the confident manner in which they communicated this expectation was dominant in the majority of family stories. Those who had been home for several months, like Mary Ann and her son George, offered examples of effective remembering, quiet memories of shared laughter, caring for each other, and giving to others, moments they said only they would completely understand. Sheri, a forty-six-year-old mom from California who walked with her twenty-two-year-old daughter Anita and her husband and Anita's stepfather, Jim, age forty-seven, talked about how Jim, the "storyteller" in the family, made them laugh in recalling even their most painful Camino days where a stolen camera or painful blisters slowed their journey. Sheri recalled the most important part of the trip was the "bond" that it created with her daughter: "We share that experience together . . . we will always have that trip together . . . a bond, a common . . . I mean, we can talk about it together and it is just between her and I . . . it's very close to us."

Some families who had been back home for several months talked about quiet memories that focused on physical, mind/body shared experience. Mary Ann said, "If you both, in reality, walk exactly the same million steps as the other one, in exactly the same type of weather and you went through the same, it just can't help but bind you in a way." Recall Bart as well, who spoke about his Camino with Charlie, remembering how they were walking together "where millions upon millions of pilgrims went," and of the "energy" that was still there "flowing" and "bouncing off" of them. It was an energy that he described as bringing them closer together in conversation, a ritual he wants to repeat: "So I want to do another trip with him like this, maybe the Appalachian Trail." Caroline from the United Kingdom, who walked with her daughter Leisa and who in chapter 3 described collapsing in the Pilgrim's Office, spoke to me about how, in hiking the Camino with Leisa, she was sharing with her something that was "an incredibly important thing" and part of her "sense of identity." When she was young, hiking was a "big family activity." "I was kind of brought up in a wilderness area in the United Kingdom," she said, and "so as a child I spent a lot of time walking." Being by herself, she said, "was not an odd thing to do." Caroline likened this memory of families walking together to a basic human drive: "I guess some of us, long, long way back, were nomadic, so maybe just the physical presence of walking with our loved ones was a central part of what we did, day to day, and I think that must be something to do with why it feels so right." Leisa was, she said, "already at work planning to walk the Pacific Crest Trail in the United States." And, she said, "as a result of this Camino walk," we are "going to do more." Families in Europe were closer to the Camino and could walk week-long sessions over time with more ease and less cost. Caroline talked of continuing this family practice in part because of her early family memories and those she shared with Leisa. They had plans to walk a new Camino route together, "in pieces," and start with the first distance the following year.

I talked to Thomas, the fifty-year-old divorced father from Germany, and his twenty-year-old daughter, Marie, whom I spoke of in chapter 4 regarding their disciplining of technology. Walking over several years together on the Camino and on trails at home had become a repeated ritual, a fundamental part of their relationship. These were quiet memories; in fact, Thomas said he had a hard time articulating how their meditation walking together was "spiritual." Largely, he noted, its spirituality was tied up in how the Camino "mirrored life," with challenges and joys. Marie shared this understanding of walking and elaborated that its spiritual nature came from meditative walking through nature. She said walking brought them closer because "I have had to show another side to my father," and "that makes it easier to show him that side at home." Thomas and Marie had quiet memories of walking in meditation together, something they shared exclusively. He did not have the same level of intimacy with his son, whom he described as more "laid back" and not as physical, and Marie did not have a similar shared practice with her mother. She nodded in affirmation of the special connection she and her father had through their memories and desire to return to walking paths in their everyday lives together. In addition to these quiet memories of spiritual intimacy, like almost all pilgrim families, Marie and Thomas had hundreds of digital memories on their smartphones and tablets that carried emotional energy.

Digital Memories

Digital memories are distinct in how they reinforce spiritual intimacy through instant accessibility and digital presence in daily lives.[6] The families that I spent time with all had smartphones and/or personal computers that they carried with them routinely, and so they could revisit visual memories almost without limit. These devices brought digital photo albums, social media pages, and blogs into offices, classrooms, cars, coffee shops, living rooms, and kitchens—accessible via Wi-Fi in most of the spaces they occupied. Digital memories also had the potential to generate new memories of ritual connection.

Pilgrims told stories of how they invited family or even the public to performances of photographs and videos put to music or told with scripts to accompany the images. Families' digital albums and videos resembled travel slideshows of old, but in addition to being accessible with contemporary speed, they took vivid form in our visual culture, where words are second to images that capture our attention and render realities. Digital photo enhancement, video manipulation, musical soundtracks, and other editing tools that were previously unavailable to amateurs made family members' creative assembling of digital memories effective. George took photos as they walked and his mother posted them on her Facebook page, but he also assembled them in a slideshow for family members, friends, George's Scout troop, and their local parish. These frontstage digital memories of shared spiritual experience had a life on social media and were shared with others in person on a large screen when they returned home.. One photo was of Mary Ann kneeling and praying in a chapel—a moment that she did not know George had captured. George's creative slideshow for public presentation, as ritual, also brought a new level of connection, a discovery of spiritual intimacy for Mary Ann.

About a month after returning home from the Camino, Mary Ann was talking with a good friend about how she wished she had had more in-depth conversations with George. George, she said, had a discerning nature that led him to speak only when he had something "important" to say, a quality that she said made her tendency to offer a verbal comment about everything seem excessive. On the Camino, she came to appreciate his approach and began to think about things before she spoke. Still, she told her friend, she was slightly frustrated that she had not been able to talk with George about what the Camino meant to him. Mary said that her friend, who was among the "500 people" who had seen George's slideshow in their hometown, answered her complaint with: "Are you dumb or stupid?" Mary Ann qualified:

> Well, not really, but it was pretty clear. She asked me: "Did he ask for your input on which pictures he chose?" And I said, "No." And then she said: "Did he ask what music?" I said, "No." Then she said, "You need to understand that . . . the art of him putting this together, this is his view of what was most important, and he is telling his story." And I finally put it together and I said, "You are absolutely right. He is showing me, not telling me."

The digital memory came to have this new form of connection for Mary Ann in public and private viewings, and it had a long life for George as well. When I interviewed him close to a year after their Camino, he was still at work on their slideshow, making it "way better, a lot better," he said, with a new photo editing software package that his cousin had just given him. "I took over 3,000 photographs in thirty-eight days," so, he said, "the first slideshow was long," and he was working to make a "shorter and better-looking" version that would be more appealing to show to his friends when they said they wanted to hear about his Camino trip. The slideshow, for George, was a representation of this spiritual trip with his mother, a trip that he described as a "rite of passage," a marking of their connection before he went into the world: "You know, you spend eighteen years with your mother, she raises you and all that, and then you go and do this together. It's hard to describe. I don't know, it's the last big thing that you do together." His ongoing perfection of this digital memory, returning to these images to mark this "rite of passage," brought him to repeatedly reflect on his quiet memories as well.

Melissa, the daughter from the United States who walked for four weeks with her mother, Allie, and her sister Jessica, spoke of the enduring meanings at work in digital memory. "We made a slideshow," she said, "a beginning-to-end type thing." Jessica put together all of the selfies that they took together with other photos: "One thing we did that was really fun for us, every day we would take a selfie with the three of us." Their selfies appeared often in their blog, where, as I noted in chapter 4, friends and family cheered them on, affirming the spiritual nature of their journey. "They were true-to-life selfies," Melissa said, "so if we were feeling like crap, it would have whatever face was on our face at that time. So in one of ours there is one person really upset and the other two are having a great time, and there is another time where all three of us just look like we are flying high." The selfies provided, she added, a "chronological order of where we were on this day and this is how it felt." Melissa's family faced a number of injuries and physical challenges as they walked the Camino, including bedbug bites and falls into thorny shrubs, and many of their photos captured these injuries in the form of swollen arms and cuts on knees and thighs—harsh reminders of how they cared for each other through painful experiences. Their morning selfies lived on in the blog as memory of what they had overcome together. Jessica used them, along with other photographs that captured the natural landscape and pilgrims they met along the way, in her digital slideshow.

Several months after they returned home, Jessica, Melissa, and their mother watched Jessica's slideshow together for the first time with friends and family. Allie described the setting:

> We were at a barbeque and she put it up on the TV and it was the first time we had seen the entire slideshow. So that was pretty cool and emotional. We had to stop it all the time and tell people the story behind the picture, or the story behind the person in the picture. . . . Then we just kind of cried at the end because it was just kind of this almost reliving it thing and it was nice to go back and kind of relive it and share it with all of our friends and family.

The digital memory shared with others pushed them to tell quiet behind-the-scene stories about their family photos and the daily selfies. Like slideshows presented from projectors in years past, their digital show on the television screen was an opportunity to remember together again and recall humorous stories and experiences. Like their blog, it gave audiences the opportunity to affirm their journey together as exceptional and transcendent. Allie talked about how the images helped her to recall forgotten memories: "Memories that come back and you are like, I remember that, and you are like, oh, I had totally forgotten that." Allie noted that on each revisiting of the assembled photographs, "different pieces come back to each of us at a different time."

Blogs served as electronic journals that family members could return to and use to recover feelings and memories of their shared experience. I spent significant time reading through and analyzing the blogs of the people I interviewed, but I also found numerous other public Camino blogs from families from across the globe as well as from other types of groups who walked the Camino together. These digital memories of family Caminos all had similar shots of well-known ritual stops such as the Cruz de Ferro, a stop along the way where many pilgrims bring their prayers and purpose in walking and a stone to symbolize their intentions, which they leave along with thousands of other stones in a large mound at the foot of the cross. Almost all had photos of family members beside shell markers on paths as well. Mary Ann and others marveled at how large their digital audiences were and how others seemed to find such meaning in their posted writings and photographs. Jan, for example, the mom from the Philippines, used her phone "to post pictures and updates on Facebook" each day: "I wanted Facebook friends to know about the Camino and hoped that some would be encouraged to make their own Camino. To my surprise, my posts were followed by 60 to 120 persons every day, and I have friends who tell me that the first thing they did when they woke up each morning was to see if I had posted from the Camino." Blogs had the force of spiritual intimacy in their creation together as family, in audience affirmation of their spiritual journey, and in their constant accessibility in their daily lives.

For Ann, the mother from the United States who walked after her husband died, digital memories of her time on the Camino with their daughter allowed Ann to continue what she described as a process of reclaiming her life, gaining strength in a world without the man she had deeply loved. Recall from chapter 4 that Hannah kept a detailed blog with stories and personal reflections to accompany the photographs and videos that Ann and Hannah took together. Hannah, like other family members, created a digital memory for her parent. She used footage that they had taken together and set it to music, offering it to Ann on Christmas as a holiday present the year they returned and then posting it on her blog. This video, for Ann, summoned a transcendent Camino—a mystical, divine connection that came to her only after seeing her daughter's visual composition that captured their shared experience. Ann said that she was not a religious person, but that her experience of the Camino had been palpably spiritual at specific points. As described in chapter 3, they felt together the power of a storm, the thunder and hail, "nature pouring itself into us," and that it was "almost as if that force of energy . . . came from nature, from God if you will." Those transcendent spiritual moments they shared in nature were captured and lifted up with song in Hannah's video. Ann described one particular shared moment captured in video that had long-lasting impact:

> I felt that I had cared for my husband for so long that I had to give up that sense that I was responsible for him somehow, that I could give him over to God in whatever way I was hanging on to him. . . .
>
> We went out to Finisterre, the coast, and I was the one videoing those scenes of the sunset when we were there, and what I was videoing was the two birds that were flying. I didn't even see that the sunset that evening looked like a big angel and there is a shaft of light coming down from the angel toward the rocks, and I didn't see it until she made the video and I was just like dumbstruck . . .
>
> During the first year I would watch the video a lot and it reminded me every single time that I can do anything. I am strong. I am getting older, but shoot, I'm still here and have a lot left that I want to do, and I can do a lot, so

> it's not over. It's not. And that's what made me—it was the video that, seeing the video and just remember[ing] each time the emotions and the feelings and, you know, watching Hannah walk . . . seeing all that and remembering that. Especially when I first came back and when I felt like I needed a boost of strength and to remember those emotions and feelings, that feeling that yes, I did that, I walked one hundred miles.

Hannah's creative assembling had lasting ritual value for her mother. Ann was reminded each time she watched it of what she had accomplished individually and how Hannah had been a part of this healing and grief work through Camino spiritual practice. They felt overcome by the beauty and force of nature together on the Camino in so many different ways. Hannah's video captured each of those moments, the thunderous sky and hail, their sitting together and bonding with newfound friends from across the world over wine and a meal. Ann was able to use the viewing of this digital memory that captured so much of the spiritual energies of their practice as therapeutic ritual of power and claiming new life.

The process of creating and sharing digital memories of spiritual experience appeared as ongoing spiritual practice in Kirsten's family as well. I met Kirsten, from the Netherlands, one morning in Santiago. She was with her older daughter, Maud, and her mom and dad. The family group was getting ready to bus together to a starting point two weeks out on the Camino. I introduced Kirsten in chapter 4 as an example of a family member who had served as the designated controller of digital technology for her daughters, Maud and Sarah, and noted that Kirsten and Maud had also adopted a walking practice back home. As we drank coffee at a café together that morning, Kirsten shared that she was introducing the Camino to her parents this time and was also excited about walking again with Maud. Their first Camino walk had given birth to a "hobby" for Maud that Kirsten talked about as helping them communicate and understand each other in a deeper spiritual way.

Kirsten could take this extended time to walk with Maud on the Camino because she was not employed outside of her home and received funds from the government to stay home and care for Maud, who she said had "brain issues" that affected her communication and speaking. Maud was "better on the Camino," Kirsten said, and walking helped with her condition. That first Camino experience, Kirsten explained, helped them escape from daily work and social media and allowed the "spiritual" experience of taking in the "beauty of nature" together. Maud and her younger daughter Sarah became more "independent" and "responsible," more "positive," in their daily lives at home. Maud, in particular, found pleasure in taking videos of flowers, mountains, and other points of natural beauty as they walked. The family watched her Camino videos when they returned home, and Kirsten felt her daughter's impressions of the natural world in ways she never had before. At home in their daily life they began to take long walks as well, and Maud carried her camera. Watching these videos together became a routine family practice that, Kirsten said, brought deeper connection, appreciation, and understanding.

Families also brought home other forms of digital memories that followed them in their daily lives. Jim, the stepfather who walked with his wife, Sheri, and his stepdaughter Anita, told me that the hundreds of photos he took now have a "virtual life." He described a humorous photo as his "screensaver" that he looks at throughout the day: "My wife and I were taking a selfie, and in the background Anita is a little ways back behind us, maybe twenty or thirty yards, making a goofy face and dancing around behind us. It was a really cute picture." When I spoke with Jim, Anita had just walked the Camino again. Jim and Sheri followed her through a Camino app that allowed them to track her walking. As she stopped in each town, on mountaintops, and at symbolic Camino religious markers along the way, Anita and Jim would return to their photos, remembering when they had walked together in the same places. These memories and the digital app brought them closer to their daughter, who was in Europe on her own.

Like shared quiet memories, family members talked about how they imagined their digital photographs and enhanced slideshows as being effective throughout their lives. The Camino, Caroline said, was unique in being a weighted experience of role reversal with her daughter Leisa and in their "sharing on equal ground" as "companions." She told me, "I think, having done this, it's something that we will always have. I think when I look back, when I'm old and I can't walk anymore, when I'm like my mother is, I'm really glad I will have this to look back on, and I think it is one of the reasons I took the photos." Caroline said her diligence in taking photos of their trip was "to have that connection." She paused, and there was silence for a few seconds on the phone line. When she spoke, it sounded as if she was about to cry: "You know, maybe when she goes to my funeral she will sit and think, 'Well, I had that time with my mom.' "

Material Memories

Digital and quiet memories can take material form through symbolic objects that are displayed or worn as reminders of spiritual connection and shared experience with family members. Family material memories have long been essential forms of transmission of family identity. Material memories that involve religious or spiritual ritual gatherings are particularly salient, such as printed and framed photographs of christenings, weddings, and bar mitzvahs on fireplace mantels and on refrigerators. Photographs and family videos come to shape how we remember our families, how they are connected to our lives, our identities, and what we find most important in life. I have a faded 1964 photograph of two-year-old me on top of my father's shoulders, and framed beside it is another at the same age with my mother holding on to me at a community pool; these images, in their simplicity, remind me of the protection and comfort I felt as a child, and the values my parents shared with me that have become a part of who I am. In our daily lives, we see glimpses of what others have decided to remember about family in photographs on office desks, refrigerators, and walls, but we know little of the quiet memories these images might hold or their connective memory potential.

Computers and phones are material objects that can give digital memories life, and for most of the pilgrims I interviewed and spent time with, these devices followed them throughout the day as a prop, part of their costume, just the way things are. But digital photographs also took printed material form, as they did in the stories of several mothers who spoke of making or wanting to make hard-copy photo albums or scrapbooks with travel souvenirs pasted beside photographs (train ticket stubs, restaurant receipts, brochures from museums and other cultural tourism sites). Caroline, for example, shared her online slideshow with her daughter Leisa, but she was also planning to assemble the images in hard-copy album form to give her for Christmas. Sheri talked about future plans to assemble the photos together with Anita, a creative revisiting of memories: "The photos are all in a box now [*laughs*]. It's a process. I want to make a scrapbook and do it with my daughter's journal because she kept a good account of where we went and remembers better than me. . . . I have everything together but, you know, whenever we can get together to do it. We might have to go somewhere and get it done! [*Laughs*]." Natalie, the Catholic woman from the United States who had a neck injury and was able to walk with her daughter Nell by booking their trip with Camino Ways, talked of making a "shell collage" together with the photographs of yellow arrows that they had taken. During our interview in Santiago, Natalie talked about using a photo of their boots hanging together on an albergue wall that they had staged together. She imagined the image at the center of a collage with shells and arrows surrounding it. It would represent the "intimate bond" they said they had developed through shared Camino practices: reading Codd's book *A Field of Stars*, praying, "listening" to each other "more deeply," and absorbing nature in a slow and purposeful way.

Natalie and Nell, like several other pilgrims, also talked to me about their desire to mark their Camino on their skin, material memories on bodies. Tattoos have become more acceptable over the last twenty years across class and especially in the United States, and a number of tattoo shops have opened in Santiago. As Annie Hesp (2018) has suggested, these designs drawn with indelible ink under the skin serve as permanent *sellos*, stamps, on the body.[7] One can easily access images of various tattoos of shells, crosses, and other Camino symbols on the public Facebook Camino tattoo page. This desire to make permanent markings is driven by the popularity and accessibility of tattoos in populations that in the past would have been taboo. In the case of the Camino, and in particular Camino journeys shared by families and other small groups, the permanent sello (stamp) can be a particularly potent symbol of group membership and identity, a totem that cannot be washed away or hidden in a desk drawer. In many cases, the tattoo was placed in a body area that was visible to others, such as forearm or calf.

Toward the end of our lunch, Natalie and Nell talked to me about their tattoo deliberations. Nell said she had "convinced Mom" to get matching small shell images. I understood from Natalie's tone that she was trying to embrace the new turn in their relationship of being on more equal ground, of sharing as companions the world and experience of the Camino. Natalie liked the idea of having matching symbols permanently etched on their skin in the exact same spot. This was surprising, Nell noted, given that her parents had been "anti-tattoo" for years. In fact, one of the conditions of paying for four years of college for their kids was that they would wait until graduation to get any "tattoos or piercings." As they talked about the process of getting a tattoo and how it would be a reminder for their entire lives of this spiritual journey together, I could hear the thrill and hesitance in Natalie's voice of doing together with her daughter something she had previously considered so radical. "What do you think?" Natalie asked me after they talked about a local shop they had seen while walking earlier in the day. "Well," I said, "I don't know a lot about tattoos, but I do know they have to heal in a certain way." They quickly agreed that because they were going to do a bit more traveling together, it would be better to wait to get the tattoo until they were back home. Besides, Natalie said, they had a cousin who was a tattoo artist, and so it would be special if he designed and did them. I was trying to be impartial, but as I write, I wonder if my response influenced their decision; was I a voice of caution that gave them an excuse to wait?

There are likely many individuals and family groups who consider getting a Camino tattoo and do not follow through, but many do. While in Santiago one spring I spent several hours watching individuals, couples, and some groups who looked like families walking in and out of a popular tattoo shop on a busy street in the city.

As noted in chapter 2, Maria, a mother from Spain in her fifties, had walked the final week of the Camino into Santiago with her son Carlos as fulfillment of a promise to God for healing Carlos's knee. He still lived with his parents and was at a point in his life where he was thinking about what kind of career to pursue, given his limited options and the country's high unemployment rates. He decided to walk the entire French route and Maria joined him in Sarria. Carlos was surprised when she agreed to get matching tattoos in Santiago. "She is not a tattoo person!" he told me during our formal interview. The Camino, Maria said, was where she had gotten to know her "son as a man," and she wanted to mark this knowledge of equal adult status. The next day, I ran into Maria and Carlos walking out of a tattoo parlor. Both had gotten tattoos, though not matching ones. His was on his left thigh: a yellow arrow with a cross at the end. Maria smiled and showed me a small shell on her wrist, a discreet sello marking her care work of prayer and the spiritual walking practice that had brought her to see her son as an adult.

Handwritten individual journals were another form of connective memories in pilgrims' stories. Lina, for example, understood journaling as therapeutic in the moment and in reflection on her return home:

> On the first trip I had a little notebook with me that I wrote in every day. I wrote every day for a couple of reasons: I wrote every day because my therapist had told me to because he said you really need to figure things out, and because it was good for me, it was a good reflection. I have the feeling that writing helps me, but I never do it in everyday life because I feel like I don't have the time. Well, that is obviously not the case going on the Camino, so

I wrote every day and eventually I really enjoyed it because, you know, you move from place to place every day and there is no way you are going to remember all of the places you visited. So, I actually enjoyed the writing and I still have them and I look at them from time to time just to see, oh yeah, we did this and this. So, it was a way to clear my mind and a way to remember the things you did. I did that the second time as well, only then I didn't have a notebook, I wrote on my iPad, basically because I feel that typing is faster than writing, so I can get more of my thoughts down than on paper. It was a practical reason.

The pilgrims' passport itself and the Compostela are material memories of walking with family. More recently, pilgrims can also get a certificate of distance that documents the number the kilometers walked. In the city of Santiago there are numerous tourist shops and items for sale: T-shirts, jewelry, crosses, shells in hundreds of different forms, pottery, and other physical representations of Galician lore. There are also a number of street vendors and artists selling hand-crafted items. When I asked Thomas, the father from Germany, if he had any photographs that stood out to him, he got excited. "I have a photo of—wait, oh, I love this one. I have to find it for you." As he searched through his phone he asked, "Have you seen that guy, the one on the corner near"—and he named a shop on a street. "No, I haven't seen that artist," I said. He smiled and showed me the photograph of a man selling small figures made of thin wire. "Look at this. Wait." He started looking through his backpack and eventually pulled out two figures, both with pilgrim staffs; one had a heart formed at the top of the walking stick. The wires had gotten tangled together in his backpack; he separated them carefully and set them on the table in front of us.

In the café, the three of us—Thomas, his daughter Marie, and I—looked at the figures on the table for a few minutes, admiring them and studying their form.

I asked him, "What are you going to do with them, do you think?"

"I don't know," Thomas said with a shrug. "They will be a nice memory."

"Did the artist make the figures like that for some reason for you?" I asked.

He said, "I don't know. Maybe the heart on one because he thinks my daughter loves me to walk with her."

The wire figures on the table in front of us were reminders of his daughter's love for him and their shared development of an appreciation of spiritual walking practice.

Thomas had told me earlier in our interview that a mystical force had brought him to the Camino when he walked it the first time by himself. It was the memory of that first walk that had led him to introduce Marie to this walking practice, a "gift" he offered with the hope that she would make walking a part of her individual daily practice. Marie spoke of adopting her father's beliefs about finding spirituality in walking through nature and of having to come to love hiking by herself and with him. Through their Caminos and other walking trips together, she said, she learned that "the walk is meditation in nature," a repeat ritual reminder of what she and Thomas understood as valuable spiritual practice that reinforced their love for each other and the natural world.

Distancing Memories

As I noted at the beginning of this chapter, not all family Camino memories were connective. I heard quiet whispers of memories that fed distancing, a lack of shared understandings of worldview and purpose between parents and their adult children. A few pilgrims, when they learned of my research topic, told me about young adults they had met who traveled to Spain with their parents to walk, but who instead fought and ended up traveling with new pilgrim friends. While walking I encountered pilgrim rumors of families quarreling and abandoning each other to walk alone. I observed a young woman as I was walking on the French Way who talked of wanting to stop walking with her mother because they kept getting into arguments and because her parents were more into the Camino as a ritual. She spoke of how nice it would be to stop walking on painful blisters and to enjoy instead the culture of Madrid while her parents finished the Camino. My field notes contain several brief and informal conversations with pilgrims that suggest additional forces at work in distancing memories; for example, for the young man I mentioned at the start of this chapter whose father spent too much time "drinking and socializing," their trip was an affirmation of disconnection. His memory of these frustrations underscored the lack of a shared family understanding of what was right and moral regarding relationships with others.

Another kind of distancing memory surfaced as well in observations and interviews: ritual memories of people alienated from others by technology or the commercialized nature of their Camino experience. Such recollections of Camino ritual had the potential to reinforce a lack of shared values, interests, or belief in the Camino as a transformative/spiritual practice. Recall Ellen and her mother, Robin, from Australia, from chapter 4. They hoped to leave their digital connection behind, especially a painful social media trauma that Ellen had experienced at home, but the presence of Wi-Fi everywhere and other pilgrims' sharing private information on Facebook pages inhibited the creation of a memory of Camino experience as spiritual. A mother, father, and their three young adult children who walked from St. Jean to Burgos and then took a train to Sarria to walk the final 100 kilometers into Santiago described crowded summer paths, and they remembered the Pilgrims' Mass in Santiago most clearly as tourists taking photos. Ultimately, they found their trip, which they expected to be spiritual, more of a family vacation with affordable lodging and great food and wine, and where they interacted mostly with each other. A ritual memory of intimacy and connection through consumption, perhaps, but not through the spiritual discourse of the Camino.

These memories of distancing through Camino encounters are faint voices in my research, and they are not in the form of rich narrative descriptions like detailed connective memories, but they are nevertheless equally important to consider, as they suggest how ritual memory with low emotional energy can impact relational connection.

Conclusion: Connective Memories in the Crucible of Pilgrimage

> When you are doing something like walking, and everything you see is new and every town you walk into is different and you are experiencing this together, it is like buddies at war, which is that type of experience, common experience, in a crucible-type situation. It's a situation that changes your relationship and makes it stronger, and just by doing this with my son, this is something that we will always have.
>
> He doesn't realize it right now, but I helped give him a gift that as he gets older, will settle in. He might be in a stressful point in his life and he might say, "I'll take a walk. . . . Maybe that is something that carries on, that when he has children he feels that, "My dad did this with me, I want to do that with you." A legacy, something nobody can ever take away from us.
>
> —Rick, fifty-year-old father, United States

Rick, who walked with his twenty-three-year-old son David, describes their Camino as creating new relational connection and building long-lasting life habits. He imagines their memory of the Camino having relational force, creating a family "legacy." His use of the term "crucible" is apt given the new individual and relational connections and abilities he sees as born of shared Camino ritual. His story and those of the other family members I have relayed in this chapter suggest important outcomes of shared spiritual experience, memory, and family connection.

The forms that ritual memories take and how they are constructed and communicated can play a role in how family members understand who they are, how they should be in the world with others, and what is most important in life. Oral and written narratives of pilgrimage and travel for transformation have, throughout history, been charged with social meaning when shared with others. Maria's wrist, while she goes about daily chores, now carries a sello, a permanent symbol of intimacy and caretaking with Carlos. Today, digital memories in our mediatized world have new potential to continually refashion and affirm high emotional energy from ritual memory. Ann's digital video memory became a therapeutic tool for individual growth and grief work. Maud's hobby of capturing nature on video became a valuable mechanism for communicating her appreciation of nature to family members. George crafted a digital memory presentation for family, friends, and community groups that brought him together again with his mother in new ritual space and form.

Most of the people who agreed to talk with me at length for a formal interview related memories of a successful Camino that involved building some level of trust and/or understanding of each other. Lina, like Elise and other family members, carried quiet memories of others naming their relationship in walking "special." They understood the value of this social performance of being a family who could commit to walking together and who respected the spiritual and therapeutic value in the practice. Sam, a twenty-one-year-old woman from the United States who traveled to Spain with her mother, Bess, age fifty-one, told me that their relationship grew stronger because of "all the different shared [Camino] experiences we have now that are completely different than really what almost anybody else in the world has." Ann spoke of how she and Hannah developed close relationships on the Camino; she described Hannah as more open and accepting of all people, and she stressed that they bonded with and helped people together: "We both did. It wasn't a question . . . we both offered something to them that they must have needed at that moment." The lasting memory of their shared emotional ties to these pilgrims was significant: "I don't know how to explain it . . . we both have the same exact feelings about these people. I don't know if that makes sense." Even those who shared memories of constant arguing with their family member eventually gave the experience and ritual memories connective weight. The Camino promise, as reflected in popular books and films, was not one of always smelling roses and moving over mountains and through towns without conflict. Like the characters in *The Way*, the movie that so many of my respondents had seen and that had pulled them to the Camino, fighting, drinking, and misunderstandings were integral scenes in a larger Camino script of building connection, feeling the presence of loved ones departed, absorbing nature, and touching Divine energy together.

Family members wanted their connective memories of Camino practices to have a continued impact on family relationships and individual spiritual endeavors. At the beginning of this book I told Katy's story of her experience at the Hospital of the Soul. Recall that José, her father, in response to Katy's shock at the realization that she had never been truly alone in the presence of God, said that the Camino was "worth every penny." He saw her ritual memory as effective, an encounter that might help lessen her anxiety and bring her closer to God. Katy was not so sure: "I wish I could feel that again. I don't know how. I don't know how to stay away from it [social media] and worrying about what people say." The encounter already seemed a potentially haunting memory, of peace embraced and then taken away. It was a memory only two weeks old, but one she was struggling to understand and make effective in her daily life. Her father, José, saw the experience and its resonating memory as the "miracle" for which he had prayed.

In the concluding chapter, "Engaged Spiritual Sensibilities," I consider the relationship between families' memories and the development of a more engaged kind of ethical spirituality, a recognition of their privilege, and a commitment to caring for others and the natural world. I reflect on how their stories push contemplation of the social forces that stand in the way of practices like the Camino and highlight differences in access to spiritual practices that may foster relational intimacy and the building of a social consciousness.

Conclusion

Engaged Spiritual Sensibilities

Professional sociology and the sense-making world of the pilgrims I encountered share some purpose. Sociologists conduct research based on impressions born from other scholars' work, personal experience, and a desire to produce knowledge about the social world. For many of us, our inquiries are grounded in a concern with how we might better our local communities and build a global society that is more caring and just. Most of the family members I met invested in the allure of the Camino promise to build close relationships with each other and unknown others, telling stories about the Camino as representing and teaching a larger kind of peace, direction, and fellowship that should be present in daily lives. Their experiences speak to contemporary social, economic, and technological forces that both help and hold back the creation of such connective relational energy through spiritual practice.

Walking the Way Together. Kathleen E. Jenkins, Oxford University Press (2021). © Oxford University Press.
DOI: 10.1093/oso/9780197553046.003.0006

No matter how long these families walked or how difficult they found their journey, it was clear that they understood their Camino together as a spiritual practice that could bring new knowledge, discovery, and even relational healing. For those who told narratives of connective ritual memory, meeting other pilgrims and walking for hours through farmland, cities, mountains, and shore brought a kind of radical intimate presence where parent and adult child came to know and experience spiritualities together. The positive ritual energy implied in these stories was far from the accounts some told me of distancing Camino memories that dampened shared identity. However, both connecting and disconnecting narratives of pilgrim experiences touch on larger questions about how sacred practice, relationships, and identity are individually constructed and co-constructed through contexts that support multiple understandings and approaches to religion and spirituality. They are stories that reveal how people work to develop ideas about what is good in themselves and their relationship with family and the world at large. These narratives also affirm the weight of digital worlds, the marketing of religious/spiritual goods, and the importance of being reflective about such forces, especially regarding the pursuit of sacred practice. Their experiences, then, are reflective of the concerns of not just pilgrims who travel the road to Santiago but of all those who aspire to engage in transformative journeys across the globe.

The memories family members shared with me speak to the ongoing potential of spiritual practices like the Camino to ignite these individual, relational, and social goods; at the same time, they highlight disparities in access. Most of the family members with whom I spoke acknowledged their privilege and expressed how fortunate they were to travel to Spain and walk together. Charlie, reflecting on his Camino with his father, Bart, told me: "I just remember the scenery and thinking about how lucky I was. . . . I was just thinking like, wow, this is amazing. I'm so fortunate to have this experience." Rick stressed the benefit of extended time on pilgrimage and how he and his son David came to rely on each other: "How many people get the opportunity to spend five, six, seven, eight weeks with their young adults—their adult child in a situation like that, where you are dependent on each other to a certain degree? I understand just how priceless that was." Many also considered how their fortunate family pilgrimage might lead them to make a larger social impact, a concern prompted in part by the various forms of spirituality at work in their memories of Camino encounters.

The extent to which spiritual practices might bring recognition of privilege, increased consideration of others, and efforts to address social inequity is a question that contemporary religious individuals, sociologists, and theologians have given much attention.[1] For the majority of the people I interviewed, their pilgrimage was about acquiring a practice for individual and family growth; at the same time, their stories were about families experiencing together *engaged spirituality*: an ethical spirituality motivated by a sense of commitment to building relationships with, helping, and caring for others and the natural world.[2] They were, after all, individuals attracted to a Camino discourse that upheld such values, as well as people shaped by a political climate where environmentalism, eco-justice, and recognition of global stratification are central concerns for many. The taken-for-granted nature of these values gave moral weight to their investment in, and memories of, building communitas on the Camino. At the same time, these values stood in stark contrast to distancing ritual memories of alienation from fellow pilgrims shaped by competition for Camino resources and the omnipresence of digital technology. Taken together, the ritual memories I have interpreted in this book call attention to the potential of travel for transformation practices to both generate and impair engaged spiritual awareness and human connection. They also prompt consideration of inclusion and accessibility regarding practices like the Camino, as well as an awareness of the importance of self-reflexivity and purposive action related to digital habits and sacred practice.

Shared Spiritual Sensibilities

Most families recounted connective memories tied to acts of what many pilgrims refer to as "Camino kindness." In chapter 1, for example, I described Maia's father, Kyle, an executive for a large company in the United States, being overcome with thankfulness while walking one day with his daughter. It was their quiet memory of a shared revelatory moment. Kyle told me that as they paused to take in the landscape, he had been overcome with thankfulness for his family and his life, and regretted his treatment of others. Maia described this same moment to me, stressing how her father was "taken aback by the kindness of people on the Camino." Her father, she said, "was blown away by these people who would probably never see us again but were helping us. They worked hard to get my mother to a doctor, and the woman at the pension called her son to take my mom to the hospital." Maia remembered looking out at the field in front of them as her father became emotional and told her that he could have been kinder in his life in his relationships and wanted to help people more. She saw her father as a generous man, always there to help friends and employees, but at that moment she found him tearful about not doing enough. "He was comparing," she said, "the selfless actions of these hotel owners" to his actions. Maia said they took time together to "sit, and cry, and talk." I cannot answer whether Kyle followed through with changing how he interacted with others when he returned home, but, as I stressed in chapter 5, such quiet spiritual memories likely have potential to carry heightened emotional energy into everyday lives in large part because the memory is attached to what it means to be in relation with each other contemplating ethical spirituality.

In some families, people talked of intentional efforts to teach and consider caring for others through shared Camino practice. Recall that in chapter 3, for example, Danielle, a mother from the Netherlands who walked a week with her daughter Sophie, hoped to share the "calming life" of the Camino with her daughter. She wanted her to experience pilgrims caring for each other. The Camino was Danielle's repeat rejuvenation ritual to gain the energy she needed to go back to her daily job as a social worker taking care of families who had suffered what she described as "tragic circumstances." Her job was "high stress," and she wanted to share with Sophie her ritual of "filling up" with new energy to go back into the world and do care work for others. Several parents and children believed that sharing communitas and caring for others on the Camino might instigate new understanding and ethical sensibilities. Lindsey, for example, thought that perhaps a "miracle" could happen and that her mother, Margie, would learn to care for and treat others in the way Lindsey thought she should. While she realized on the Camino that she could not change her mother, Lindsey did speak of the Camino experience provoking Margie to apologize, and of having seen, for the first time, some indication that her mother might treat strangers with a new level of respect and dignity. In chapter 3, I relate Ariel's description of confronting her father, Allan, about his prejudice and rude treatment of the young women on their phones. The next day, as they were walking in the early morning hours, Ariel talked with him about how all pilgrims were walking to make their "lives work somehow," and that "the most powerful things in life are "understanding, kindness, and giving love." Like Lindsey, Ariel doubted Allan's ability to care and love in this ideal way but had hoped that the Camino would make some difference, in part by presenting the opportunity to have deep conversations with each other about such issues. Recall as well that Julie wanted her father to walk the Camino with her to remove him from his hectic world of work, and ultimately spoke of the spiritual revelations they experienced together that brought realizations of what was important in life. Her father, Ed, saw the walk with Julie as a "cleansing," a "reboot," and as prompting him to change his life upon their return home by spending more time with his family and working in the future at an animal shelter. Together, they told a story of being present with each other as new engaged spiritual sensibilities were born.

A handful of family members also spoke of their Camino bringing a shared desire to spread knowledge about Camino family intimacy as a spiritual approach to relational conflict and/or helping young adults face difficult issues. Charlie's father, Bart, impressed by the degree of knowledge and connection he shared with his son on the Camino, told a story of wanting to help other families at home. He described a recent effort to try to convince a father he knew from his workplace to take his son on the Camino: "This is powerful, I told him. His son is eighteen or seventeen . . . failing, busted for drugs all the time. They are super wealthy. . . . I said to the dad, 'Forget therapy and Prozac. What you do is, right now, go book two round-trip tickets, get your son to Madrid, take a train, and you hike this for twenty days, just you and him.'" Bart said he advised: "You meditate that it is going to be his trip and you are not going to be lecturing him, you know. Just you and him. Just go. If he can't do drugs and he's with you every day, you are walking and talking every day, just you and him." He told the father to "use it as an opportunity. I'm not saying it's going to work. But you will connect to your son like you have never before." Rather than supporting therapy for the son, Bart promoted a Camino approach that was about "connectiveness to people and planet and the world around you." At the end of our interview I asked Bart's son, Charlie, if there was anything important that we had not yet covered. His answer echoed his father's beliefs: "The biggest thing I would say is just encouraging people to do it—just do it! I would just say that it is such a good way for a parent and child to get connected. . . . If I could encourage any parents to do it with their kids, that could afford it, I would say just do it. Even if their kid isn't super into it, I would say just do it because they will appreciate it."

Some of the Camino stories I interpret in this book tell of a challenging physical experience that brought individuals and families to realize how little they needed in life and cultivated a renewed commitment to recognize and care for the environment. Carrying the weight of your belongings on your back and walking respectfully through nature emerged in stories that venerated the natural world. In chapter 3 Ann, a yoga teacher for many years who identifies as a "spiritual" person, describes the thunder and rain pouring down around her and Hannah as like "nature pouring itself into us." Nature as a power to be respected was also reflected in Kyle's story earlier in this chapter—both his interaction with "Camino kindness" and the beauty of the physical landscape prompted his revelatory moment. It is not surprising that families stressed the preeminence of nature given that, as I noted in chapter 1, most had read Brierley's popular guidebook that suggests pilgrims take on an environmentally conscious approach as they purchase and prepare for their Camino. His concern reflects a larger discussion in the literature on religious tourism, the effects of travelers on local and global environments, and the potential for spiritual tourism to bring a new awareness of institutional injustices and peace-building.[3] Brierley notes his efforts to defend the social value of pilgrims' carbon footprint: "I am often asked why I endorse 'cheap' air travel to and from Santiago when it is so costly for the environment." He legitimates the Camino by providing details on "how to offset damaging greenhouse emissions and travel *carbon-neutral*, whether this be by air, rail or bus." His "conscience is also clear," he writes, "because I know that walking the caminos can be a powerful catalyst for positive change so that the means (of getting there) fully justifies the end (expanded awareness). A central tenet of these guides is that pilgrimage starts the moment we become conscious that life itself is a sacred journey, carrying with it the responsibility to act accordingly" (6).

Family members' stories of engaged spirituality together were multidimensional, shaped by previous life experiences, religious/spiritual orientations and practices, and their shared Camino spiritual encounters. For example, in Lindsey's narrative, her recent conversion to Christianity drove her desire to not just walk the Camino but work to have her mother embrace a new practice regarding caring for others. Recall as well that Julie talked about being drawn to the Camino after spending time in the Taizé Community, an ecumenical monastic community in France. Taizé was her first experience of pilgrimage, where she removed herself from everyday life, met people from around the world, and recommitted to embracing diversity and social change. It was the spiritual study with others in that community and the peace awakened there that she named as bringing her hope that her father, whom she saw as controlled by an anxiety-ridden work environment, could be rejuvenated in his Catholic faith and connection to others and the natural world through pilgrimage. Jan, the woman from the Philippines who walked with her husband, Marcus, and their daughter Sue, identified as a Catholic woman grounded in her faith who made life decisions based on "God's will." Her particular approach to Catholicism was shaped by feminist theology, which helped frame her musings about the popular nature and purpose of the contemporary Camino. She stressed that it is not surprising that people return to the Camino, and wondered what the world would look like if the peace, the guidance, the brotherliness, and the spirituality experienced on the Camino was part of our daily life. In addition, several family members I interviewed, formally and informally, were folks already deeply engaged in various types of outreach ministries at home. Mary Ann came to the Camino carrying the prayers of people in her parish community, dedicating her walking on specific days to their personal or social concerns. No doubt, people came to the Camino with an individual spiritual constitution and left with new and renewed insights. When they returned home, their quiet, digital, and material Camino memories, as well as fresh social experiences, continued to shape their spiritual sensibilities.

I cannot say to what extent the pilgrims I encountered acted on the engaged spiritual sensibilities born from connective Camino experiences, or the relational consequences born from their disjunctive ones. Religious ethics and the extent to which a particular system of morality becomes part of a person's life habits and cultural world are forged through accumulated life experiences. An awareness of and commitment to ethical and engaged spiritualities is dynamic, constantly changing as ritual practices are remembered, repeated, abandoned, or altered. The nature and potency of any renewed sense of mystical connection, belief, or ethical responsibility shift with different environments, ritual encounters, and life challenges.[4] Several families with whom I spent time in Santiago talked of wanting to bring a walking practice back into their everyday lives, as they believed it would put them back in touch with each other and with nature on a routine basis. A handful of family members I interviewed identified regretfully that after they returned home the responsibilities of everyday life got in the way of making shared walking a practice. For example, Lauren, the mother from Canada who walked with her daughters McKenzie and Victoria, spoke about how work and educational goals had pulled her family in separate directions post-Camino, leaving little time for walking or reflecting together as they had hoped. Mary Ann contacted me months after our interview to tell me that her husband had passed away suddenly, a devastating loss and experience of grief that likely further impacted her engaged spiritual life in her parish and the spiritual intimacy she shared with her son George. To even begin to tease out the salience of Camino experiences for the composition of spiritual sensibilities, sociologists would need to conduct in-depth interviews with pilgrims over time, adopting a life history narrative approach that focused on developing spiritualities.

Camino ritual can be a force that brings consideration of actions that could foster a more equitable, environmentally conscious and caring world; at the same time, as I note in chapter 5, distancing memories fueled by technology and consumption have the power to bring a profound sense of alienation from others and encourage self-focused pursuits. The habitual nature of engagement with digital technology, as I suggest in chapters 1 and 4, brought online space and everyday practices into the daily ritual world of families' shared Caminos. Some families chose to discipline and use technology in ways that built connective memories, while others struggled to break digital ties that they saw as undermining their desire for relational connection. Robin and her daughter Ellen, from Australia, left the Camino with a memory of technology destroying their imagined Camino promise. They traveled home wondering if it was impossible for Ellen to escape social media, and were disappointed in those who shared fellow pilgrims' challenges and injuries without permission on Facebook blogs. In chapter 5, I stress as well how such ritual memories of competition and digital privacy transgressions can carry a destructive, negative sort of emotional energy that fails to create connection with groups and moral communities.[5] These were recollections of failed communitas that could separate one from ethical spirituality and Camino ideals, raising up in its place the single identity of a savvy consumer/tourist and the practices associated with that identity. To varying extents, the majority of my respondents left the Camino with memories of competing for lodging, especially on the crowded last 100 kilometers of the Camino Francés, and a growing awareness of social media and digital spaces pulling pilgrims away from each other. Such experiences ate away at their imagined Camino promise of communitas and caring for others. As I write, I still hold a distancing memory: an encounter with two women drinking wine and enjoying their dinner at a pension who chastised me for not making a reservation and frowned disapprovingly as I got into a cab to take me to the nearest lodging outside of town. After that embarrassing pilgrim sanction, and fear that I would not have a place to sleep at night, I became caught up in the ritual of grabbing reservations through my tablet or phone a day ahead, feeling afterward like I had been the smart Camino pilgrim. In my adoption of this practice of booking ahead, I could sense my deeper connection to other pilgrims fading, and my connection with a Camino community that put self above others becoming stronger.

I hope that the stories I interpret in this book push scholars and all those who may be interested in the effectiveness of pilgrimage practices at having an impact on spirituality and promoting social good to acknowledge the consequences of rote digital interaction on ritual. Use of digital devices to locate walking routes and hotels, to reach out to pilgrim friends on nearby paths, and to post images on social media platforms have become taken for granted, the routine that threatens to make pilgrimage ritual the everyday, to render the sacred mundane. Ariel's and Lina's stories in chapter 4 offer examples of how the use of therapeutic others from everyday lives followed them into their Camino ritual worlds—sacred players who were familiar daily shoulders in their digital routines. Engagement with these known advisors while on the Camino likely resulted in missed occasions to reach beyond for comfort and engagement with an as yet unknown confidant and advisor. Habitual therapeutic digital contacts helped Lina and Ariel avoid the uncomfortable and unknown in liminal space—emotional positions that other pilgrims talked about as bringing new ideas and visions of their future. Future research might explore the various ways and the extent to which explicit spiritual/religious ritual purpose is weakened by being constantly pulled into everyday time and relationships during practice. While scholars have taken up the importance of digital media for religious worlds and identity, and made clear how such technologies have become a taken-for-granted part of worship and practice, we still have much to learn about how, in a mediatized world, habitual media interaction impacts ritual intent. Such a focus is especially important when we consider what it means today for ritual practitioners who strive to embrace the unpredictable and mysterious for transformative purpose.

Sensing Spiritual Inequalities

Most of the pilgrims with whom I spoke had the time and money to routinely engage in spiritual marketplaces that offered a range of postures with regard to self-work and caring for others. In congregations, yoga studios, temples, or online spaces in their daily lives, they had access to strategies for building spiritual intimacy and awareness with family members. As the stories in this book suggest, this shared pilgrimage practice worked to strengthen relationships and foster a larger sense of caring for family, community, and distant others. Even pilgrims who spoke to me of challenging and contentious trips perceived some relational growth born from their shared Camino. We hear this in the narrative from Allan, who, several months after his emotionally draining Camino with his daughter Ariel, talked about the experience as bringing "trust" to their relationship, and in the narrative of Thomas and his daughter Marie, from Germany, repeat pilgrims who had built a walking practice at home that Marie credited with encouraging her to routinely open up emotionally with her father. Kristin, the mother from the Netherlands whose daughter, Maud, had a disabling condition that made it difficult for her to speak, told a story of how Maud took videos of natural landscapes during their Camino and during the walking practice they developed back at home. In sharing these videos, Kristen described gaining a window into her daughter's spiritual self—in particular, her sense of gratitude and appreciation of nature. In several cases, parents described experiencing reversed caretaking and relational growth as children cared physically and emotionally for them. My evidence of pilgrimage building stronger family relationships is based on participants' memories and aspirations of shared Camino experience. I cannot speak to the intensity of relational impact or how long these perceived family benefits and spiritual intimacy may have been effective. However, the passion with which people talked about their Camino-born spiritual sensibilities improving family relationships suggests positive relational outcomes. Furthermore, scholars have argued that there is such value in families sharing spiritual practices.[6] From an engaged sociological and spiritual perspective, recognizing this potential means paying careful attention to who has access to similar kinds of ritual and working to discern the institutional forces that might inhibit or encourage the pursuit of such practice.

Paid work, lack of financial resources, and care work are inevitable hurdles for families and individuals who wish to engage in travel for transformation. Parents in low-wage jobs likely face enormous challenges in securing the funds and time for family travel over an extended period of time. Most of my respondents, except for Allie, the single mother from the United States who walked with her two daughters and had to save for two years, had the cash on hand to pay for their Camino trip. Some research participants had physical issues that would have kept them from walking, but they were able to eliminate these obstacles by purchasing Camino packages with luggage services. Given statistics across nations that continue to show the burden of childcare on women, mothers of young children likely face additional obstacles if they wish to engage in time-consuming spiritual practices like the Camino at home or abroad.

The social factors shaping opportunities to engage in extended walking pilgrimage vary across geographic contexts. The Camino, for example, is accessible to a wider socioeconomic group in Western Europe. Carlos, whose mother, Maria, walked with him for his final week on the Camino Francés, had been living in Madrid with his family and came to the Camino for inspiration regarding employment and career in an economy that he said offered few opportunities for youth. The Camino, he said, was a "cheap way" to find direction in his life. I met several other young adults from Spain who saw their Camino as an affordable strategy for engaging in self-searching.

There is a strong expectation in North America and Western Europe that emerging adulthood is a time to find oneself before settling into work and long-term family partnerships. In the United States, the ability to take such time to search for a life path regarding relationships and career is shaped by class, and inevitably by race. Most of the stories in this book are about white families from North America with resources and time who are invested in a dominant therapeutic culture that rewards spending serious time working on the self. Such cultural logic is salient as well in the lives of young adults from families without resources and who work in low-wage jobs. Sociologists Stefanie Deluca, Susan Clampet-Lundquist, and Kathryn Edin (2016, 11), in their study of young men and women in inner-city Baltimore, illustrate an " 'expedited' path to adulthood," where opportunities to seek "inner purpose" or engage in self-searching travel rarely exist. Instead, the desire to begin work and family life to escape families of origin impaired by poverty and disruption weighs heavy. They identify a path of escape for a few through "identity projects," such as working with special-needs children or creative endeavors like writing poetry—practices introduced by religious communities, other institutional spaces, or "picked up from friends or family" (8–9). For the most part, though, young adults on "expedited paths" to adulthood have few opportunities to engage in such identity projects, are more likely to have jobs with little opportunity for advancement, and may suffer from debts amassed from for-profit trade schools and colleges.

Travel for transformation and pilgrimage could provide structures that function in some of the same ways as identity projects through their potential to promote practices that bring meaning, purpose, and connection to others. Despite the Camino's contemporary welcoming of all races and backgrounds, it is an expensive option for young adults and families in North America and represents a European Catholic tradition that may not appeal to the spiritual concerns of individuals from various other life positions and backgrounds. Those in the United States concerned with investing in opportunities for young adults and families from diverse backgrounds to engage in travel for transformation and the pursuit of spiritual intimacy could take serious note of a growing global pilgrimage marketplace, and the opening up of new structures and accessible local paths that promote contemplation of social justice.[7]

Expansion and Inclusivity

North America has seen an increase in opportunity for structured journeys to sacred sites, with more inclusivity and diversity related to racial/ethnic groups, goals, and purpose of travel for transformation. Daniel Olsen (2016, 35) points to the case of the Martyrs' Shrine in Midland, Ontario, Canada, promoted in its official online site as an eighty-nine- kilometer "off-road Pilgrim Route." Olsen writes that its original "mandate" was "preserving the memory of Jesuit martyrs," but that more recently it has become "more inclusive . . . preserving the memory of martyrs from immigrant homelands around the world" (35).[8] Pilgrimage efforts can be explicitly religious or spiritual, like the Martyrs' Shrine, or they may represent sacred civil sites such as (in the United States) the Trail of Tears National Historic Trail, the Underground Railroad, the National Museum of African American History and Culture in Washington, D.C., and the National Civil Rights Museum in Memphis, Tennessee. Some may combine cultural historical, religious, and political purpose. A yearly pilgrimage to Alabama organized by the Faith and Politics Institute marks the day that troopers attacked protestors marching from Selma to Montgomery. The horseback midwinter pilgrimage by the Lakota Nation youth of the American Great Plains marks the 300-mile trek to the site of the massacre at Wounded Knee. In Canada, a new pilgrimage route along the old North West Mounted Police Trail attempts to promote healing between indigenous and settler communities.[9] Each of these practices involves some element of moving through space with others that differs from the everyday, traveling with an aim to recognize how one sees one's position in relation to others and historical events that have shaped social injustices.[10]

Like the Camino de Santiago, these sacred journeys hold potential for the creation of engaged spirituality through the shared development of a social consciousness. Of particular interest is the rise of civil rights pilgrimages that mark a history of racism and political protest in the United States; for example, the recently launched United States Civil Rights Trail draws attention to more than 100 charged political sites. The trail's website helps visitors plan journeys "from Topeka, Kansas, to Memphis, Tennessee, from Atlanta, Georgia, to Selma and Birmingham, all the way to Washington D.C." Civil rights pilgrimages are especially powerful examples of using movement through sacred space and destination in an effort to awaken, strengthen, and affirm the historical and ongoing implications of structural racism in the United States. While their intent may be educational, cultural historical, or political in focus, many websites related to these trips associated with educational institutions and/or faith communities promote them as transformative travel, and some use the word "pilgrimage" in their descriptions—for example, trips offered by the University of Wisconsin, Eau Claire, and by the Howard Thurman Center for Common Ground at Boston University.[11]

The construction of urban pilgrimages that mark social justice is significant with regard to opening up transformative walking practice for working individuals and families with time and resource concerns and promoting social change. I live in Richmond, Virginia, a city that in 2011 unveiled a walking trail chronicling the history of the slave trade "from Africa to Virginia until 1775, and away from Virginia, especially Richmond, to other locations in the Americas until 1865."[12] The maintenance, promotion, and social justice potentials of urban pilgrimage structures such as the Richmond Slave Trail, and the development of new points of historical memory across this city and others, should be realized. In Richmond this might include focal points of recent Black Lives Matter protests where Confederate monuments have fallen, as well as the rising of new symbols such as the bronze sculpture at the Virginia Museum of Fine Arts, *Rumors of War*, by Kehinde Wiley, "commemorating African American youth lost to the social and political battles being waged throughout our nation."[13] Such urban pilgrimages can serve as resources for families, educational institutions, and congregational ministries that wish to engage new avenues for spiritual endeavor that call attention to social inequities and shared moral purpose. They provide ritual points of connection with a potential for high emotional energy and accessible practice that can bring families and other social groups together in solidarity.

The stories I convey in this book suggest that the desire for family pilgrimage can be born from individual exposure to travel for transformation practices. Julie, the young woman from the United States, found the inspiration to ask her father to walk the Camino through her individual engagement with the Taizé Community. Family pilgrimage was also instigated in several cases by a young adult's experience in educational study abroad on the Camino. There has been growth in educational efforts to take students on pilgrimage and attempts to make these experiences more accessible, affordable, and inclusive. But programs are still expensive, especially those like the Camino that involve international travel. Institutions could put more effort into funding networks for students and youth who would find the cost of travel and time lost at work prohibitive. People might also consider donations to a range of educational institutions to fund young adults with financial need who would like to engage in pilgrimage programs.

Pastoral and congregation promotion and development of pilgrimage can also fuel family intimacy through spiritual journey. Congregations, denominations, and religious community centers are spaces that have promoted pilgrimage trips with a range of religious, racial, ethnic, and political transformative goals in mind. For example, faith communities have sponsored cultural heritage, truth and reconciliation, and religious pilgrimage to Ghana, Senegal, the Gambia, and Holocaust sites of memory.[14] Given the potential for family spiritual intimacy implied in my analysis, engaged scholars and religious leaders and groups could look more deeply into how programs that encourage and financially support pilgrimage in various institutions are created, sustained, and made available to those without financial resources.

Moving Ahead

As the stories in this book make clear, Camino discourse, in its spiritual and therapeutic force, is made real in our contemporary setting through and alongside rituals of consumption and digital structures. All those concerned with the social and relational good that pilgrimage practices can bring should consider the dangers inevitable in these social forces and how they can impact the creation of connective rituals. But we must also recognize that the marketing and digital worlds associated with transformative practices can enhance spiritual attachments. The essence of keeping pilgrimage routes alive and relatable lies in efforts to build and expand markets.[15] Structures like the Camino are stronger and more accessible in many ways today because of the cultivation of consumers through information and communication technologies. As I suggest in chapter 1, it is this growth in religious/spiritual tourism and the accompanying discourse found online, in print, in documentaries, and in movies that shaped many of my research participants' experiences of their Camino from its inception as an idea, during their travel through Spain, and upon return home. My research participants represent a small segment of those who have walked the Camino de Santiago, yet their experiences speak to the tensions between purchasing spiritual therapeutic endeavors and the development of an engaged spiritual social consciousness. Scholars have articulated how self-focused purchasing power and emphasis on individual transformation in therapeutic practices like the Camino can reify the very structures of injustices that practitioners hope to question and desire to dismantle.[16] At the same time, as I have suggested, the families with whom I spoke engaged in reflective practices related to building alternative ways of encountering and understanding relationships between people, the natural world, and the myriad social injustices and environmental devastations that plague our fragile early twenty-first-century world.

Growing engagement with digital connections is a taken-for-granted part of everyday lives, an assumption that impacts both those who can afford devices and online access and those who cannot. Digital expectations in 2020 infuse almost every component of pilgrimage practice: the planning, people's expectations, the rituals themselves, the structures that support practice, and the mechanisms for remembering sacred experience. Pilgrims, researchers, congregations, clergy, and educational institutions concerned with constructing and supporting structures and opportunities for transformative travel should pay careful attention to digital habits in a society where smartphones, computers, and other components of information and communications technology deeply shape intimate and institutional relationships. As chapter 4 in this book suggests, digital worlds and the taken-for-granted nature of our online relational connections can be disciplined in ways that maximize intended ritual goals of connection. Individuals and those who conceive of and shape opportunities for transformative travel must be self-reflexive and critical of the role of digital forces. The builders of travel for transformation structures should ask how contemporary pilgrimage discourse itself might embrace such ongoing critical reflection. Such reflexivity demands a sociological imagination that contemplates how technology is active in institutional structures and individual experiences. To what extent can contemporary pilgrims find tech-free sacred spaces? How might such places exist as a choice, settings that pilgrims can consider as they plan their pilgrimage paths? Who has access to smartphones and contemporary digital devices?

Pilgrim structures are marked with spiritual guideposts, symbols, or words that point a direction for physical movement—a shell or yellow arrow on the Camino, contemplative words, prayers, invitations to story one's own experience. As I pass a sign on the Slave Trail in my home city, it invites me, a white woman born in Virginia in the 1960s, to absorb and awaken historical points of racism with each step: "The trail follows the path of a heritage that has been challenged and broken by the chains of supreme degradation and yet still found inspiration within itself. . . . Please, walk upon this trail. Continue this journey and accept the history revealed, for it is our history. May every step lead us to a brighter future." The sign implies to me that all those who engage the path with sacred intention are part of each other; we must contemplate the meaning of "our history" together to bring social justice. At the Hospital of the Soul, Katy experienced an allied spiritual device: "The fundamental mistake of humanity is to suppose that I am here, and you are there." She felt "the presence of God" in her first visit alone to this meditation room along the Camino Francés, a sacred space that invited her to exist for a fragment of time without digital connection, to contemplate the dangers of assuming, as the quote implies, that one does not exist wholly with humankind.

Katy's experience was so powerful that she feared its loss because of the lure of digital ties in her everyday life: "I wish I could feel that again. I don't know. I don't know how to stay away from it [social media] and worrying about what people say. Do you know how to? What do you think?"

I did not have any answers. I told her that I too was trying to manage it and that a lot of the pilgrims I had talked to were making concentrated efforts to construct tech-free time. I said that I tried to make such space in my own life and had advised my three young adult children and my students at William & Mary to do the same.

"It is okay," she assured me, "not to know the answer . . . the Camino teaches you—over time."

I hope that my efforts over six years to understand and interpret the spiritual goals and social forces at work in the experiences of Katie, José, and the many others who shared their Camino stories with me have provided some insight about family, spirituality, and transformative practices in a world fraught with contradictions and uncertainties born of social inequalities and the pervasive and monumental shifts in relationships that digital technologies have engendered. As I work on this concluding chapter in the spring of 2020, families across the globe are feeling a range of effects from the COVID-19 pandemic, and the Camino de Santiago has been shut down. In the media discord in the United States, I hear voices suffering loss, illness, hunger, and fear shaped by economic position, racism, and domestic violence. These voices exist alongside a chorus of those who describe walking the now hushed streets of their neighborhoods, awed by their discovery of the simple goodness of a long walk together. My hope is that this book brings pilgrims, engaged researchers, spiritual leaders, and builders of pilgrimage structures renewed energy for thinking deeply about how pilgrimage and transformative walking practices might build engaged spiritual sensibilities. Rather than envisioning travel for transformation as an extraordinary practice found in a distant place associated with exceptional time, we could aspire for connections and engaged sensibilities to be born, routinely, through common practice.

Methods Appendix

Research Design and Approach

My research question and approach developed over time as I talked with pilgrims in Santiago and on Camino routes. I progressively grew interested in how the parents and young adult children I met came to their experience of walking together, how they told their family stories, and what their Camino experiences and memories meant to them and their relationships with each other. At the same time, I became immersed in a burgeoning scholarship from across disciplinary perspectives on the Camino de Santiago and popular and expanding pilgrimage/cultural tourism structures. My sociological imagination led me to want to explore this growth through experiences of family pilgrimage, a research focus that could shed light on the institutional forces at work shaping contemporary meanings and processes related to travel for transformation.

My ethnographic research design had multiple data points. I conducted semi-structured interviews with parents and their young adult children (eighteen to twenty-eight) who had walked Camino routes for at least a week. I was a participant observer on Camino paths and in Santiago, walking and engaging in other ritual practices like attending Mass, sharing parts of my own life narrative with other pilgrims, and talking and listening to the Camino stories and concerns of family members. Walking on Camino paths and talking with pilgrims informally in Santiago offered perspective on how families moved through this pilgrimage structure, bringing to light the material and social forces that shaped their journeys. The formal interviews I conducted offered a window into how pilgrims understood their experiences and the consequences of their shared Camino. In addition, analysis of family blogs, the online Camino Forum, Camino guidebooks, published pilgrims' narratives, and Camino films and documentaries provided a window into the larger discourse of the Camino and the sources through which family members came to understand a set of expectations about Camino practice and how they should approach the journey. In particular, I made sure to get access, if possible, to the online journals and Facebook postings of the families I interviewed and the books and films they told me were influential in their decision-making and planning.

My formal interview sample was obtained through advertisements on Camino Forum sites and through nine months (across four years) interacting with pilgrims on the Camino and in Santiago. In the end, I had over one hundred informal field interviews, seventy-eight structured interviews from forty-one family cases, and ten Camino blogs and private family travel photo journals. All of the people I interviewed gave written or verbal informed consent. I have changed research participants' names. In a few cases I have also altered details of Camino interactions or family background in an effort to address confidentiality. I was careful when walking Camino routes to introduce myself and my project to those with whom I spoke informally. Given that I am primarily English-speaking and from the United States, the majority of my in-depth encounters and interviews with pilgrims were in English. During several summer months, a graduate student in the School of Education at William & Mary who is fluent in Spanish, Ben Boone, served as my research assistant and gathered field notes and made contacts with pilgrims in Santiago.

I gathered a purposive sample reflecting diversity in medium, length of trip, timing of narrative construction, and family composition. The family members I interviewed had walked anywhere from one to five weeks. I talked with parents and their adult children in the field as they finished their Camino and up to one year afterward via Skype or phone. I limited the sample to those with more recent Camino practice, in order to capture family narratives at a similar point in time regarding Camino structure and discourse and in order to work with fairly fresh memories and narrative constructions. Interviews ranged from an hour to three hours, depending on venue and case. In-person formal interviews in Santiago were longer encounters over coffee or a meal where I took handwritten interview notes that I then expanded in my field log. I did not digitally record interviews in Santiago given the culture of the Camino, where people regularly tell their stories to each other through extended informal conversation. In early exploratory interviews, I found that a recording device was suspect to many pilgrims. Given that I was often interviewing people in the middle of their Camino experience/practice, a digital recording device felt intrusive. However, I routinely recorded and transcribed phone and Skype interviews with the permission of respondents.

I interviewed some parents and their children together as they were celebrating with new friends in Santiago at the completion of their walking journey. This was at first out of necessity, as they were not in the city long enough for me to schedule separate interviews, but as theoretical relationships related to the social value of these family stories began to emerge and I started to see how co-authored family stories reflected the shaping of a spiritual intimacy between family members, I purposely gathered more parent/child narratives. These conversations enabled me to examine various points of narrative construction and performance. Such an ethnographic sample and approach are ideal for uncovering cultural expectations at work in family members' motivation, experience, and construction of shared memories. Co-authored verbal narratives offered a unique perspective for listening to how family members imagined their pilgrimage impacting their relationship in the future, and how they approached contradictory understandings as they told stories. In many cases, individual family members and co-authored Camino blogs provided an additional format for presentation of family narrative. These digital frontstage performances of family spiritual intimacy became theoretically significant as my analysis of practices and the emotional energy carried in ritual memory took shape. Overall, the narrative data I collected reflect diversity in how stories were told (as individuals or families recounting), the length of trip (anywhere from approximately one to five weeks), the Camino path they walked (e.g., French Way, English Way, Portuguese Way), when they told their story (on arrival in Santiago or after return home), how they told their stories (e.g., verbal recounting, digital platforms), and family composition. This sample diversity offered distinct vantage points for understanding the types of spiritual practices that families saw as impactful and the dynamics of ritual memory.

Parents and their adult children were not always on the same page regarding how they understood family goals and spirituality, nor did they agree to share their stories with me with the same level of detail or intensity. A few offered to only answer questions via email; some declined to speak with me at all; others agreed at first but never contacted me after our first encounter. While some social scientists might view this as problematic, as an ethnographer, I welcome the task of exploring and making sense of the multitude of ways people talk about, or do not want to talk about, their most intimate encounters with spirituality.

Parents and young adults walking together were not the most common pilgrim or group of pilgrims I came across on the Camino. I more frequently encountered older individuals, married couples, and younger adults on their own. Thus, I used multiple approaches to find research participants. My summer research assistant, Ben Boone, helped pass my contact information to a number of family cases he encountered in Santiago and on Camino paths. I met pilgrims through walking on official Camino routes, hanging out in cafés in Santiago, volunteering in the Pilgrim's Office in Santiago, and walking around the city. For example, one summer afternoon walking in Santiago I heard a mother and daughter speaking English and saw them enjoying an ice cream. I introduced myself and asked if they had walked the Camino together and if they were a mother and daughter. They said yes, and I told them where I was from and that I was conducting research about parents who walk with their young adult children on the Camino. They were from the United States and familiar with William & Mary, and quickly agreed to sit down with me and talk about their trip. I offered to buy them some food at the restaurant where I was headed for lunch. We walked together to a garden restaurant where we sat outside at a table and spent a couple of hours talking about their Camino. Respondents also answered my call for interviewees posted on the Camino Forum, and I always asked people I interviewed if they knew any other families who had traveled together. If they said yes, I asked them to forward my email and contact information.

My respondents' narratives generally began with a purpose for walking and included difficulties encountered as they traveled, people befriended along the way, lessons learned, and ultimately, for most, the creation of a stronger relationship or more intimate understanding of one's family member. Parents and young adult children voiced various reasons for walking: marking graduations and/or helping children make decisions about future goals, disconnecting self or son/daughter from social media, or working through physical or psychological issues. I presented open-ended questions to elicit narratives—for example, asking them about how they came to walk together and if a particular day or encounter stood out in their memory of the trip. I also used a broad approach to photo elicitation, asking research participants to share or refer to photographs that they felt stood out to them from their Camino experiences. Referring to photographs to talk about Camino experience was not always introduced by me: respondents often talked about how a story or moment they had described to me was captured in a digital image, and they showed it to me as we spoke. During one interview, a respondent began talking about a 100-page scrapbook she had assembled. As we spoke on the phone she said: "I actually have it in my hands right now." I asked her, "Are you looking through it or are you holding it?" She replied, "I am looking through it as I talk to you."

Family cases for the formal semi-structured interviews included seven father/daughter pairs, fourteen mother/daughter pairs, eight father/son pairs, and four mother/son pairs. The remaining cases involved larger family groups: three cases of a mother and two daughters; one case of a mother, daughter, and son; and one case of a mother with two sons. Three cases involved two parents walking with two or more emerging adult children. Twenty-two of these formal cases were from the United States, and nineteen from other countries: three from Australia, three from Canada, two from Spain, three from the Netherlands, three from Ireland, and single cases from the United Kingdom, Germany, Sweden, South Africa, and the Philippines. The majority of these parents were professionals and/or had the resources and time to travel; one parent worked in a low-wage job.

I asked individuals if they identified with a particular faith tradition and if they considered themselves to be a religious or spiritual person. Twenty-two identified as Catholics and as both religious and spiritual, sixteen as Protestants, one as Anglican, one as Pagan, one as Buddhist, thirty-four as spiritual, and three as not religious or spiritual. As I note in the book, regardless of their religious/spiritual identification, almost all of the people I interviewed saw potential in the Camino to bring what they named as a spiritual experience. Given the racialized nature of American society and the history of the Camino as a Catholic European pilgrimage, it is not surprising that the majority of pilgrims I encountered in Santiago from North America were white.

The strength of my qualitative approach is its ability to uncover how these family members made sense of and represented their Caminos, the sacred weight they gave to them, and what they understood as supporting and inhibiting shared spiritualities. My study is somewhat limited to a particular perspective, in that my formal interviews are largely with those pilgrims who agreed to tell me their story, a group that likely consisted of people who felt they had stories about family experiences that they thought I wanted to hear. However, through participant observation walking Camino routes, spending time in Santiago, and working two summers as a volunteer at the Pilgrim's Office, I found pilgrims who agreed to participate in the research and who were willing to tell me stories of unsuccessful attempts to connect with family members through Camino practice.

I cannot say whether or not everything people told me actually happened to them on their pilgrimage, nor can I make any concrete assessment of the extent to which their family Camino family experiences carried over into their everyday lives, but that is not my purpose. My ethnographic goal is to capture how they understood their journeys—where they saw meaning, experienced frustrations, envisioned success and failure related to the Camino promise—and to capture the dynamics of the memories they held of their experiences of walking with their family member. We can learn much from the stories that people want to tell: their values and spiritual understandings, how they see the world and each other, and the obstacles they encounter as they work to form what they see as good family relationships and selves.[1]

My method of analysis was a systematic creative process most closely associated with grounded theory, an inductive method that involves repeated review of unstructured data to reveal new empirically based theory.[2] In the grounded theory tradition, I analyzed data through open, focused, and axial coding processes of field journals, interview transcripts, and media documents. More specifically, I see my approach resembling an "abductive analysis" that promotes cultivating "anomalous and surprising empirical findings against a backdrop of multiple existing sociological theories" through "systematic methodological analysis" (Timmermans and Tavory 2012: 169). In my coding of data, I worked in an inductive way that asked what codes, categories, and themes were most prevalent or theoretically relevant in interviews, field logs, and documents. At the same time, I turned to previously developed theoretical frames from multiple fields of study including psychology, sociology, and ritual theory, building on existing concepts to make sense of the data. For example, spiritual intimacy is an existing concept that was useful for theorizing many of the experiences my respondents described.[3] In addition, to make sense of the variation in level and type of connective experience I was sensing in the data, I turned to Randall Collins's (2004) work on ritual and emotional energy.

My connections with researchers I met through the Institute for Pilgrimage Studies at William & Mary and other institutions helped to broaden my theoretical toolkit as I approached analysis. My colleague at Villanova University, Ken Chih-Yan Sun, introduced important ideas from the literature on intimacies and families that furthered my analysis both in chapter 4 here and in our co-authored 2019 article in *Qualitative Sociology*, "Digital Strategies for Building Spiritual Intimacy: Families on a 'Wired' Camino," where we develop concepts related to disciplining technology. Extended conversations with anthropologist and pilgrim Nancy Frey also shaped my theorizing about codes related to technology and liminal space and the setting aside of tech-free time for contemporary pilgrims. Engaging literature from multiple disciplines and conversations with these colleagues helped me think about how my respondents' family stories shed light on other social contexts related to spirituality and intimate relationships. Thus, as in most forms of sociological analysis, my work involved a constant moving back and forth from theory to data, and the collection of additional data. Axial coding in later stages of analysis shaped theoretical relationships between dominant conceptual codes; for example, the connections between spiritual intimacy and distancing memories together informed developing conceptual codes such as disciplining technology. Focused and axial coding guided theoretical sampling choices toward the end of the ethnographic data gathering process; for example, working to gather more interviews with family members through spending time on the Camino and in Santiago to capture more negative cases of spiritual intimacy, individuals who might not otherwise have answered my interview calls out of a concern that they did not have a positive family story to tell. Coded data, theme folders, and analytical memos were organized in Microsoft Word.

Research Ethics and Relationship to the Field

I was careful to obtain informed consent from all those I interviewed and made sure that the families and other pilgrims I spent time with when walking the Camino knew who I was and that I was writing a book. I assured them that I would do all that I could to protect their identity and maintain external confidentiality. When interviewing families, researchers must also consider issues related to internal confidentiality.[4] When I interviewed family members together, this concern was minimal, as they were well aware of their co-constructed narrative. However, before interviewing those family members with whom I talked separately, I explained that there might be details that their parent or adult child might recognize in publications, and I reinforced to them that they should not feel like they had to answer all my questions. Still, in several cases I have changed some information to disguise research participants from other family members. I believe that I have done so in ways that do not compromise the analysis. When I was concerned that a family member might recognize a particular event and that the description of the event might cause family conflict, I sent the parent or child excerpts from the book to gain permission a second time to print particular details of their stories.

I consider my presentation of the stories in this book my interpretation of family members' narratives, and I imagine my research participants as co-creators. Many of the people I interviewed were excited to tell their stories because they felt that they might help other families who were considering walking together. As other researchers have noted, interviewees often think of the interview process as therapeutic. This was especially true for those pilgrims with whom I spoke in the city of Santiago who were just completing their Camino. In most cases the pilgrims I interviewed appreciated what I often felt was an intrusion into their sacred practice. They commented that our conversations provided a space for them to voice, discover, or revisit what their shared family Camino had meant to them. Pilgrims were used to telling their stories to other pilgrims on the Camino, and many were, in fact, expecting that this walking pilgrimage would bring multiple opportunities to share their lives and feelings with new acquaintances and friends.

Ethnographers who study religious or spiritual practices inevitably become ritual practitioners to a certain degree. Doing so requires consideration of how much one is a part of the community and sincerity in approaching religious/spiritual practice. Over the years, as I have studied communities of faith and spirituality, I have been clear about how I came to be interested in respondents' ritual life and my own religious/spiritual background. I identify as a religious and spiritual person. I was raised a Presbyterian and converted over twenty years ago to Judaism. At the end of interviews, after I had heard respondents' stories, I shared my faith background with some pilgrims and told them that I did not come to the Camino in search of healing or spiritual purpose. I stressed that I had first approached the Camino as a professor hoping to explore with my students how people found meaning in this contemporary revival of medieval Catholic routes. At the end of interviews, I would share, if appropriate and in conversation with respondents, that I did find some religious/spiritual meaning in the practice myself. There were many times while walking, helping pilgrims in Santiago, and interviewing pilgrims where I made discoveries about my own life and how I move through and approach time in my daily activities. For example, after walking the first time on the Camino, I returned to my everyday routine with a newfound urge to get rid of "stuff" that I had accumulated over the years, and I developed a practice of traveling light. I came to appreciate walking more and longer distances. And I slowly grew to understand, as I tried to figure out ways to walk with my own young adult children, the disappointment that comes from knowing that education and work schedules and responsibilities were going to present constant challenges to engaging in extended pilgrimage with them.

Even though I identify as Jewish, in spending time in Santiago, like other pilgrims, I found friendships, connection, and worship spaces beyond my own faith community where I could connect spiritually. I also inevitably became a part of families' Camino practice when I interviewed them in Santiago. This was true with José and Katy, whose story I tell at the beginning of the book, and it was true as well with Ed and Julie, who asked, at the end of our long discussion, for a café patron to take a picture of the three of us together to mark our meeting. That request seemed natural in the context of the Camino, but looking back, in the wake of my analysis, I feel the weight of the part I played. In that family's digital memories somewhere lives a photo of the three of us, previously strangers, pilgrims made friends through the practice of sharing stories, with our arms around each other, smiling.

Many of the pilgrims that I spent time with gathered with their "Camino families" in Santiago for a celebratory dinner after they had recovered a bit and, for most, after they had received their documents of completion from the Pilgrim's Office. They would sit together over drinks or dinner and reminisce about their Caminos, telling stories, laughing, and at times crying. During the busy season in Santiago in the summer such Camino family/friend groups were not hard to find in restaurants and cafés around the city. There were times when I declined to join a family who invited me to the dinner marking the end of their Camino; if I had just met them and they were gathering with their Camino family, it felt too intrusive. On occasion, however, I seemed to naturally end up at such a celebration, and so I tried to be a part of their gathering while gently letting people know who I was and what my research goals were. I found those instances emotionally exhausting and at times felt guilty for inserting myself into their practice.

I knew early on during that first summer in Santiago that it would be impossible to study families walking the Camino without engaging in the practice myself free from the burden of caring for and teaching students. Given the focus of my research, it would have been ideal to walk with my children, but they were in school, busy with jobs, and/or had no interest in walking the Camino, and so I asked my husband to join me on the French Way for several weeks. In part, I wanted to experience the responsibility of walking with a family member while maintaining communication with others back home, a concern that many of my research respondents had voiced. And so in 2016 my husband, Mark Lerman, and I set off with our backpacks from St.-Jean-Pied-de-Port in France and told our children and my mother that we would send emails and photos as often as we could detailing where we were and what we had seen and experienced.

I understand self-reflexivity as critical to representing and understanding complex social and individual practices. An ethnographer must be aware of how her emotions and relational memories might help in analyzing experiences, and at the same time work to separate her feelings and emotions from respondents' stories. This is the task of balancing and naming subjectivity and objectivity as a social scientist. I consider myself lucky at this point in my life to have close relationships with my children (ages thirty, twenty-two, and twenty); even so, I came to long for the prospect of sharing with them the various manifestations of spirituality that my respondents described. I was aware of my place of class and economic privilege in even being able to think about spending such extended time with my children, and I was doubtful that, if given the chance to walk, we could ever discipline technology the way that some families had done. Being constantly immersed in Camino discourse and pilgrims' stories of family intimacy continually brought to mind memories of my father, who died as I was working on this research. I came to regret that, for various reasons, we had never had such experiences. I came to appreciate even more the shared spiritualities that I have with my mother. Qualitative researchers often name the emotional costs that result from exhaustive immersion, careful field log construction, attachment to our research participants, our individual relatedness to the research topic, and the melancholy of leaving the field to spend time alone in later stages of writing. Throughout the writing process I found solace and inspiration in long walks closer to home with family and reading novels and memoirs. My son recommended a book written by his professor at Bard College, Daniel Mendelsohn, *An Odyssey: A Father, A Son, and an Epic* (2017), an incredible read related to themes of family intimacy, and a memoir that, when I would tire of writing, renewed my zeal to return to analysis and to tell these stories of walking the way together.

Notes

Introduction: Seeking Connection

1. Scholars have addressed the relational consequences, both positive and negative, of shared religious and spiritual practices and beliefs (Kusner et al. 2014: 604–614; Mahoney 2010: 805–827).
2. Few sociologists of religion have analyzed how parents may turn to spiritual spaces outside of congregations and faith traditions to shape parental identity and strengthen family intimacy (Nelson 2014: 59–75). We know that contemporary emerging adults, like their parents, claim spiritual identities that embrace ritual practices and beliefs outside of organized religious institutions (Barry and Abo-Zena 2014; Heelas and Woodhead 2005; Smith 2009). Christian Smith, for example, drawing from the National Study of Youth and Religion in the United States, explores the religious and spiritual lives of teenagers as they move into "emerging adulthood" (2009). *Walking the Way Together* offers a voice in this sociological and engaged religious conversation by illustrating how ritual structures outside of congregational walls are impacted by numerous social forces and how young adults encounter these social dynamics as they engage in spiritual practice with their parents.
3. Nick Couldry and Andreas Hepp, in their book *The Mediated Construction of Reality*, suggest that in our "mediatized" social world, digital technologies play a continuous role in how meaningful relationships are constructed (2017: 170). A number of empirical studies have explored how information and communications technologies play a role in mediating intergenerational family relationships. See, for example, Rice and Haythornthwaite 2010: 92–113; Nelson 2010; Clark 2013.
4. Regarding the force of therapeutic culture in family relationships, see, for example, Furedi 2004; Blum 2015. How intimacy is achieved in relationships is shaped by changing cultural and institutional forces, but these changes are complex and can be fast or slow-moving; see Goodwin 2009. Precarious work environments and insecurities in the new economy shape family relationships in positive and/or negative ways and must be understood in context. See, for example, contributions to Allison Pugh's edited volume *Beyond the Cubicle: Job Insecurity, Intimacy, and the Flexible Self* (2017).
5. See Bowman 2013: 8–23; Amato et al. 2007.
6. Pilgrimage scholars agree that the pursuit of spiritual connection is a primary motivation for contemporary pilgrimage (Loveland 2008: 317–334; Oviedo, Courcier, and Farias 2014: 433–442; Reader 2007: 210–229). Pilgrims, whether they identify as religious or non-religious, are many times in search of transcendence through spiritual

forms of encounters that involve reflexive experience with nature, self, and others (Farias et al. 2019: 28–44).

7. See Pilgrim's Office 2019.
8. See Talbot 2016: 36–56.
9. See Frey 1998 for a historical description of the significance of Finisterre for pilgrims. Also see Lopez, Perez, and González 2017: 186–212.
10. See, for example, Kurrat 2019: 11–18; Farias et al. 2019: 28–44.
11. Here I am referring to Clifford Geertz's articulation of the concept in "Thick Description: Toward an Interpretive Theory of Culture" (1973).
12. See Timmermans and Tavory 2012: 169; Charmaz 2014.
13. Elements of this argument in Chapter 4 can be found in my co-authored work with Ken Sun, "Digital Strategies for Building Spiritual Intimacy: Families on a 'Wired Camino'" (2019: 567–585).
14. Collins's work, an extension of Erving Goffman's writings on interaction rituals and the Durkheimian tradition, stresses the function of ritual forces for carrying sacred beliefs and collective energies (Collins 2004; Goffman 1967; Durkheim 1912).

Chapter 1

1. Sociologists of religion point to religious pluralism in the United States historically and in contemporary context and the need for religions to market their religious "products" (Warner 1993: 1044–1093; Berger 1967). Scholars have also referred to a global religious/spiritual marketplace that focuses more directly on individual choice and spiritual pursuits. See, for example, Van Hove 1999: 161–172.
2. The marketing of meaningful, mystical family experiences can be found in various types of popular tourist destinations. Disneyland is a prime example regarding contemporary family travel, with such lure reflected in advertisements that promise to make "magic happen" and photographs of families dancing, smiling, and being adventurous together. For an investigation of the nature of the sacred/religious in such space, see Lyon 2000. I do not mean to reduce the Camino to Disneyland; rather, I wish to stress the pervasive cultural belief that a utopic ideal of family intimacy can be purchased in enchanted places.
3. See Ian Reader's work *Pilgrimage in the Marketplace* (2014) for a careful consideration of the growth of choice in contemporary pilgrimage across the globe, how markets construct and sustain pilgrimage routes, and the relationship between pilgrimage identity and consumption. Regarding the growing commercialization of the Camino de Santiago via online website efforts, see González 2018: 969–999; Fernández-Poyatos et al. 2011: 23–46. See as well research concerned with the quality of services during hajj and pilgrims' expectations of these services and range of for-profit and not-for-profit efforts (Alsharief and El-Gohary 2017). For larger scholarly debate regarding the relationship between religion and tourism, see Butler and Suntikul 2018. Also see Olsen and Timothy 2006: 1–21; Olsen 2011: 17–30; Badone and Roseman 2004.

4. See Turner 1969.
5. See Marly Camino 2019.
6. See Caminoways.com 2019.
7. See Pilgrims' Office n.d. ("Spiritual Preparation").

Chapter 2

1. The film's redemption narrative revolves around the central character's experience of loss and of walking and communitas as a therapeutic practice for overcoming grief. For analysis of media depictions of the therapeutic/transformative role in travel see, for example, Frost and Laing 2017: 46–54.
2. In using the term *interaction ritual* I am referring to Erving Goffman's book *Interaction Ritual: Essays on Face-to-Face Behavior* (1967). Randall Collins, as I note in chapter 5, builds on Goffman's work on interaction rituals in his text *Interaction Ritual Chains* (2004). My use of the terms *props* and *costume* is grounded in Goffman's text *The Presentation of Self in Everyday Life* (1959).
3. See Pilgrim's Office n.d. ("Pilgrims").
4. Ammerman notes that whereas in a Theistic package understandings involve connection to God or a Divine source, in pulling from an Extra-Theistic package people locate spirituality "in the core of the self, in connection to community, in the sense of awe engendered by the natural world and various forms of beauty, and in the life philosophies crafted by an individual seeking life's meaning" (2013: 268). This Extra-Theistic package reflects a belief in the spiritual interconnectedness and essential oneness of all phenomena. In "Ethical Spirituality," "living a virtuous life" is "characterized by helping others" and "transcending one's own selfish interests to seek what is right" (272). Theistic understandings relate to what Streib and Hood (2013: 143) would call more "vertical" forms of transcendence, characterized by experience of "otherworldly symbols" and the supernatural. When individuals pull from an Extra-Theistic package, their understandings represent what Streib and Hood would note as more "this-worldly," "horizontal" forms of transcendence, where people are concerned with the "creative potential of life, including the individual person, humanity, or nature."
5. Van Gennep's (1960 [1902]) *Les Rites de Passage* addresses rituals of change in individuals' lives, such as marriage, birth, death, etc. Such rites were, as Van Gennep noted, *liminal*, representative of a kind of in-between stage. Communitas is tied to such rites of passage. See Turner 1969 and Turner 2012. The individuals I interviewed expected that some would occur in the Camino as a liminal space, they understood, influenced by a strong Camino discursive message of potential transformation that liminal spaces, as they believed the Camino could be, becomes itself a kind of way of life, a *compressed life*. See Turner 1969; Turner 2012; Myerhoff 1982: 109–135.
6. Scholarly literature of an engaged nature often contributes and strengthens existing discourse. For example, see Havard 2018: 89–97. As stated in the article's

abstract, Havard's research intends to offer recommendation for the "cultivation of communitas, including mindfulness practices and maintenance of behaviors" (89).

7. See Taizé Community 2019.

Chapter 3

1. See Bowman 2013: 8–23; Amato et al. 2007.
2. See Streib and Hood 2013:143; Ammerman 2013: 258–278.
3. I am referring here to intensive parenting approaches that involve heightened monitoring and cultivation of children's educational skills, self-esteem, emotional competence, and relationship to professional therapeutic "experts" (Bowman 2013: 8–23; Hays 1996; Lareau 2003; Nelson 2010; Rutherford 2011: 407–412).
4. See Townsend 2002.
5. See Garey 1999.
6. See Bengston 2013.

Chapter 4

1. See Jenkins and Sun 2019: 567–585.
2. See Walking to Presence 2020.
3. See Couldry and Hepp 2017 for a social constructionist perspective regarding how information and communication technologies have created a mediatized society. Researchers have also illustrated how ICTs play a role in mediating intergenerational family relationships (Rice and Haythornthwaite 2010: 92–113; Nelson 2010; Clark 2013). Scholars have found increased use of media and technology in individual religious practice, congregational settings, and online religious spaces (Campbell 2013; Sisler 2011: 1136–1159; Meyer 2011: 123–139).
4. See, for example, Frey 2017; Ogden 2016: 81–89; Nickerson 2015.
5. See Frey 2018: 151–167.
6. For more detailed analysis of creative engagement with technology, see Jenkins and Sun 2019: 567–585.
7. Concerns regarding self-reflection and control of digital devices have been a focus of journalistic work regarding intimate relationships and family dynamics. For example, an article in the *New York Times* was titled "Step Away from the Phone!" (Tell 2013), and an article on the newspaper's Learning Network entitled "Are You Distracted by Your Phone?" (Gonchar 2015) begins with these questions: "Do you think you pay full attention to the people you are with? Are you engaged in what's happening around you? Or are you distracted by your phone?" A number of scholarly books and articles have addressed impact of ICTs on social relationships. See, for example, Rice and Haythornthwaite 2010: 92–113. Regarding family relationships in particular, see Clark 2013.
8. For social constructionist theory regarding the impact of mediatized society, see Couldry and Hepp 2017. In naming these stories moral family performances, I am

drawing from social interactionist Erving Goffman's theory (1959, 1967, 1974) that emphasizes how social norms and roles impact the ways individuals and groups/organizations present and understand themselves in relation to others. Social performances are dictated by the stages people inhabit. The interview itself is a stage, as I discuss in my methods appendix, where family members presented to me their stories of self-searching and emotion-work.

9. See, for example, Gagalis-Hoffman et al. 2016: 392–412. Through a qualitative interview study on recreational family storytelling, the authors suggest that storytelling created space for family bonding. Family storytelling builds intimacy through its ability to focus on difficult issues, transfer values, and offer the chance to learn emotional skill sets related to relationality. Each of these functions is related to characteristics of spiritualities that I address in this text.

Chapter 5

1. See Bowman 2013: 8–23; Amato et al. 2007.
2. Scholars have noted the centrality and importance of ritual memory in the construction and transmission of shared family memories and identity. See Smit 2011: 355–367; Shore 2009: 95–103.
3. Hillary Kaell explores "how (pre-trip) intent relates to (post-trip) outcomes" in experiences of evangelical pilgrimage to the Holy Land, and calls attention to the rarity of narratives of failed pilgrimage (2016: 394). The few distancing memories that pilgrims related to me, and the tendency for most pilgrims to describe their Camino as successful, speak to Kaell's argument regarding perceptions of ritual efficacy; pilgrimage practices are "incremental, in flux, and unbounded," pushing us to "recognize pilgrimage as a process that unfolds over time" (404). How memories of Camino ritual carried low emotional energy over time is significant and could be explored through longitudinal approaches to studying family narratives of spiritual intimacy and their impact over time.
4. Edith Turner suggests that memories of communitas are best conveyed through stories (2012). Connective memories are similar in this regard.
5. For further reading on concept of digital memories, see Garde-Hansen, Hoskins, and Reading 2009.
6. For an explanation of the creation of pilgrimage/religious identity through photos, see Caidi, Beazley, and Colomer Marquez 2018: 8–31.
7. Annie Hesp has spoken of these permanent sellos (2018). Social scientists are also at work studying the meaning of Camino tattoos—for example, German sociologists Christian Kurrat and Patrick Heiser 2020.

Conclusion

1. See critical theological concerns, in particular liberation theologies and prophetic activism (Slessarev-Jamir 2011). See as well sociological conversations related to the

relationship between religious/spiritual belief and practice and civic engagement and/or moral behavior (e.g. Putnam and Campbell 2010; Baker 2013: 343–369). Regarding religion and environmental action, see Vaidyanathan, Simranijit, and Ecklund 2018: 472–494.

2. My use of the term "engaged spirituality" is shaped by Gregorary C. Stanczak's work in his book *Engaged Spirituality: Social Change and American Religion* (2006). In this text Stanczak suggests that if we consider "spirituality as a social resource," we might explore various "contemporary contexts" that provide "a rich backdrop for accumulating these resources." The Camino, like other spiritual "products" that have emerged in an active religious/spiritual marketplace, offers an opportunity for exploring how "spiritual connections are ultized in everyday life." Nancy Ammerman's more recent work on lived religion provides theory for analyzing how engaged spirituality is understood and talked about by individuals in U.S. and European culture and how it may be activated in everyday life (2013: 258–278). Stanczak gives a working definition for engaged spirituality: in its "most literal sense, engaged spirituality is the social juncture between the transcendent, active and ongoing, multidimensional, unlimited, emotional, and pragmatic aspects of spirituality that motivate actions for social change." Unlike a "solely personal spiritual quest of self-exploration, engaged spirituality is always directed outward with the intention of making a discernable difference in the social world" (2006: 20). See also literature on altruism and spiritual transformation (e.g., Koss-Chioino 2006: 869–876).
3. See, for example, Stewart-Kroeker 2017. For an example of a social scientific approach to understanding the relationship between discourses about environmental change, environmental behavior, and pilgrimage, see Shinde 2011: 448–463. For conversations on the relationship between religious tourism, pilgrimage, and local/global impacts, see El-Gohary, Edwards, and Eid 2018; Álvarez-García, del Río Rama, and Gómez-Ullate 2018; Trombino and Trono 2018; Fitzgerald 2015. For conversations on religious tourism, awakening social consciousness, and peace-building, see Sharma 2020. See McIntosh, Haddad, and Munro 2020 for an edited volume that speaks to pilgrimage, religious tourism, and peace-making, and calls for a "paradigm shift in pilgrimage and religious tourism research through the development of new definitions that recognize that pilgrims and pilgrimages are embedded not just within religions and economies, but in ever-changing cultures, societies, and political systems" (viii).
4. See Hillary Kaell's work for discussion of the dynamic nature of efficacy in pilgrimage practice and the importance of belief in individual understandings of ritual success or failure (2016: 393–408). Stanczak notes spirituality as an "*active and ongoing* process that not only seeks out the sacred, but also maintains and even changes it in one's life" (2006: 20). Spirituality is also "*multidimensional*—traditional and/or creative, individual and/or collective." In addition, an understanding of spirituality recognizes that it is "*unlimited* in its experience," and "bound neither to time nor place nor objects, but rather is accessible in all aspects of life." Spirituality can be understood as "*pragmatic*," meaning "both a resource" and as being "resourceful, and as such it can be

honed and utilized through active practice by individuals throughout their lives." Finally, and highly significant in my analysis here, Stanczak notes spirituality as "*emotional*, connecting individuals to their lived environments in deeply affective ways" (2006: 5).

5. This is Randall Collins's concept of emotional energy (EE), where low ritual EE can lead to disconnection (2004). By moral communities I mean, in a Durkheimian sense, the norms and ideals of a particular community, not any one set of moral beliefs or practices (1912).
6. For example, some scholars have addressed relational consequences, both positive and negative, of shared religious and spiritual practices and beliefs, including Kusner et al. 2014: 604–614; Mahoney 2010: 805–827.
7. See McIntosh, Quinn, and Keely 2018. See also Timothy and Olsen 2018: 220–235. In addition, see Routledge's Studies in Pilgrimage, Religious Travel and Tourism book series (https://www.routledge.com/Routledge-Studies-in-Pilgrimage-Religious-Travel-and-Tourism/book-series/RSRTT). See as well McIntosh 2020.
8. Olsen 2016: 34–48. See Martyrs' Shrine 2020.
9. See Faith and Politics Institute 2020; United States Civil Rights Trail 2020; Armada 2010: 897–914. For more detail on the Lakota horseback pilgrimage, see Greenia 2018: 137–147. Information about the new Canadian route can be found in the same volume in a chapter by Matthew R. Anderson (2018: 148–174). For discussion of national parks as sacred/religious space, see Ross-Bryant 2013; Campo 1998: 40–56. For recent promotion of the National Park Service in the United States as more inclusive space, see National Park Service 2019. The opening of national parks and walking trails in the United States to the public historically took on a civil religious fervor associated with America as a "promised land" and representing a love of nature as sacred space where people can reflect and think about the meaning of life. However, such opportunity and experience stand against a history of exclusion in promotion and accessibility of national parks and open public outdoor spaces in general. See, for example Finney 2014.
10. See McIntosh 2017 for further examples.
11. Examples of civil rights pilgrimage and other social justice pilgrimage in educational settings: Wright State University 2020; Boston University Howard Thurman Center for Common Ground 2020.
12. See Richmond Slave Trail Commission 2020.
13. Virginia Museum of Fine Arts 2020.
14. See Olsen 2016: 34–48. For a truth and reconciliation example, see The Episcopal Church 2020. For an example of a travel company that promotes Jewish pilgrimage/genealogy, see Polin Travel Guide and Geneaology 2020. For Catholic parish efforts to reunite children with kin in Guatemala and engage in Mayan and Catholic rituals, see Argueta 2014.
15. See Reader 2014.
16. For a review of scholarly debate regarding therapeutics and politics, see Salmenniemi 2019: 408–424.

Methods Appendix

1. See Yamane 2000: 171–189.
2. See Corbin and Strauss 2015; Glaser and Strauss 1967.
3. See Mahoney 2010: 805–827; Kusner et al. 2014: 604–614.
4. Tolich 2004: 101–106.

References

Alsharief, Raja, and Hatem El-Gohary. 2017. *Service Quality and Religious Tourism: The Context of Hajj (Islamic Pilgrimage)*. Riga: Noor Publishing.

Álvarez-García, José, María de la Cruz del Río Rama, and Martin Gómez-Ullate. 2018. *Handbook of Research on Socio-Economic Impacts of Religious Tourism and Pilgrimage*. Hershey, PA: IGI Global.

Amato, Paul R., Alan Booth, David R. Johnson, and Stacy J. Rogers. 2007. *Alone Together: How Marriage Is Changing in America*. Cambridge, MA: Harvard University Press.

Ammerman, Nancy. 2013. "Spiritual but Not Religious? Beyond Binary Choices in the Study of Religion." *Journal for the Scientific Study of Religion* 52 (2): 258–278.

Anderson, Matthew. R. 2018. "Pilgrimage and the Challenging of a Canadian Foundational Myth." In *Pilgrimage in Practice: Narration, Reclamation and Healing*, edited by Ian S. McIntosh, E. Moore Quinn and Vivienne Keely, 148–174. Boston: CAB International.

Argueta, Luis. 2014. *Abrazos*. DVD. Directed by Luis Argueta. Newburgh, NY: New Day Films.

Armada, Bernard. 2010. "Material Transformation and Community Identity at the National Civil Rights Museum." *Journal of Black Studies* 40 (5): 897–914.

Badone, Ellen, and Sharon R. Roseman. 2004. *Intersecting Journeys: The Anthropology of Pilgrimage and Tourism*. Chicago: University of Chicago Press.

Baker, Christopher. 2013. "Moral Freighting and Civic Engagement: A UK Perspective on Putnam and Campbell's Theory of Religious-Based Social Action." *Sociology of Religion* 74 (3): 343–369.

Barry, Carolyn M., and Mona M. Abo-Zena. 2014. *Emerging Adults' Religiousness and Spirituality: Meaning-Making in an Age of Transition*. New York: Oxford University Press.

Bellah, Robert N. 1967. "Civil Religion in America." *Journal of the American Academy of Arts and Sciences* 96 (1): 1–21.

Bengston, Vern L. 2013. *Families and Faith: How Religion Is Passed Down Across Generations*. New York: Oxford University Press.

Berger, Peter. 1967. *The Sacred Canopy: Elements of a Sociological Theory of Religion*. New York: Doubleday.

Blum, Linda. 2015. *Raising Generation Rx: Mothering Kids with Invisible Disabilities in an Age of Inequality*. New York: NYU Press.

Boston University Howard Thurman Center for Common Ground. n.d. "Civil Rights Pilgrimage." Accessed March 25, 2020. https://www.bu.edu/thurman/programs/civil-rights-pilgrimage/.

Bowman, Carl D. 2013. "Holding Them Closer." *Hedgehog Review* 15 (3): 8–23.

Brierley, John. 2018. *A Pilgrim's Guide to the Camino de Santiago: Camino Francés*. Glasgow: Kaminn Media Limited.

Butler, Richard, and Wantanee Suntikul, eds. 2018. *Tourism and Religion: Issues and Implications*. Blue Ridge Summit, PA: Channel View Publications.

Caidi, Nadia, Susan Beazley, and Laia Colomer Marquez. 2018. "Holy Selfies: Experiencing Pilgrimage in the Age of Social Media." *International Journal of Information, Diversity and Inclusion* 2: 8–31.

CaminoWays.com. n.d. "All Camino Ways." Accessed May 3, 2019. http://caminoways.com.

Campbell, Heidi A. 2013. *Digital Religion: Understanding Religious Practice in New Media Worlds*. London: Routledge.

Campo, Juan Eduardo. 1998. "American Pilgrimage Landscapes." *Annals of the American Academy of Political and Social Science* 558: 40–56.

Charmaz, Kathy. 2014. *Constructing Grounded Theory*. 2nd edition. Thousand Oaks, CA: Sage Publications.

Clark, Lynn Schofield. 2013. *The Parent App: Understanding Families in the Digital Age*. New York: Oxford University Press.

Codd, Kevin. 2008. *To the Field of Stars: A Pilgrim's Journey to Santiago de Compostela*. Grand Rapids, MI: Eerdmans Publishing Company.

Coelho, Paul. [1987] 1995. *The Pilgrimage: A Contemporary Quest for Ancient Wisdom*. New York: Harper Collins. Orig. O Diário de um Mago. Rio de Janeiro: Rocco.

Collins, Randall. 2004. *Interaction Ritual Chains*. Princeton, NJ: Princeton University Press.

Corbin, Juliet, and Anselm L. Strauss. 2015. *Basics of Qualitative Research*, 4th edition. Thousand Oaks, CA: Sage Publications.

Couldry, Nick, and Andreas Hepp. 2017. *The Mediated Construction of Reality*. Cambridge: Polity Press.

Deluca, Stefanie, Susan Clampet-Lundquist, and Kathryn Edin. 2016. *Coming of Age in the Other America*. New York: Russell Sage Foundation.

Durkheim, Emile. 1912. *The Elementary Forms of the Religious Life*. Translated by Karen E. Fields. New York: Free Press.

El-Gohary, Hatem, David John Edwards, and Riyad Eid. 2018. *Global Perspectives on Religious Tourism and Pilgrimage*. Hershey, PA: IGI Global.

Episcopal Church. 2020. "Truth and Reconciliation Pilgrimage to Ghana." https://episcopalchurch.org/reconciliation-pilgrimage. Accessed June 1, 2020.

Estevez, Emilio. 2010. *The Way*. DVD. Directed by Emilio Estevez. Santa Monica, CA: ARC Entertainment, LLC.

Faith and Politics Institute. n.d. "Programs." Accessed March 25, 2020. https://www.faithandpolitics.org/programs#.

Farias, Miguel et al. 2019. "Atheists on the Santiago Way: Examining Motivations to Go on Pilgrimage." *Sociology of Religion* 80 (1): 28–44.

Fernández-Poyatos, María-Dolores, et al. 2011. "The Way of Saint James and the Xacobeo 2010 in the Tourism Websites of the Spanish Autonomous Communities." In *Revista Latina de Comunicación Social* 67: 23–46. http://www.revistalatinacs.org/067/art/946_Alicante/02_LolaEN.html___.

Finney, Carolyn. 2014. *Black Faces, White Spaces: Reimagining the Relationship of African Americans to the Great Outdoors*. Chapel Hill: University of North Carolina Press.

Fitzgerald, Janine. 2015. "Marx on the Camino de Santiago: Meaning, Work, and Crisis." *Monthly Review* 67 (1): 52–61.

Frey, Nancy. 1998. *Pilgrim Stories: On and Off the Road to Santiago*. Berkeley: University of California Press.

Frey, Nancy. 2017. "The Smart Camino: Pilgrimage in the Internet Age." Keynote address, Annual General Meeting of the London Confraternity of St. James, St. Alban's Centre, London, United Kingdom, January 28, 2017.

Frey, Nancy. 2018. "Leaving Home and Coming Back." In *My Camino Walk 2: 18 Pilgrims Share Their Stories, Their Insights and Their Camino Journey*, edited by Andrew Priestley, 151–167. N.p.: Writing on Demand.

Frost, Warwick, and Jennifer Laing. 2017. "Long-Distance Walking in Films." In *Routledge International Handbook of Walking*, edited by C. Michael Hall, Yael Ram, and Noam Shoval, 46–54. Abingdon, UK: Routledge.

Furedi, Frank. 2004. *Therapy Culture: Cultivating Vulnerability in an Uncertain Age*. New York: Routledge.

Gagalis-Hoffman, Kelly, et al. 2016. "A Retrospective Consideration of Recreational Family Storytelling Among Parents and Their Adult Children." *Marriage and Family Review* 52 (4): 392–412.

Garde-Hansen, Joanne, Andrew Hoskins, and Anna Reading, eds. 2009. *Save As . . . Digital Memories*. New York: Palgrave Macmillan.

Garey, Anita I. 1999. *Weaving Work and Motherhood*. Philadelphia: Temple University Press.

Geertz, Clifford. 1973. *The Interpretation of Cultures: Selected Essays*. New York: Basic Books; 3–30.

Gennep, Arnold van, Monika B. Vizedon, and Gabrielle L. Caffee. 1960 [1902]. *The Rites of Passage*. Chicago: University of Chicago Press.

Glaser, Barney G., and Anselm L. Strauss. 1967. *The Discovery of Grounded Theory: Strategies for Qualitative Research*. Chicago: Aldine.

Goffman, Erving. 1959. *The Presentation of Self in Everyday Life*. New York: Doubleday.

Goffman, Erving. 1967. *Interaction Ritual: Essays on Face-to-Face Behavior*. Garden City, NY: Doubleday.

Goffman, Erving. 1974. *Frame Analysis: An Essay on the Organization of Experience*. New York: Harper & Row.

Gonchar, Michael. 2015. "Are You Distracted by Your Phone?" *The Learning Network: Teaching and Learn with the New York Times*, September 29, 2015. Accessed March 25, 2020. https://learning.blogs.nytimes.com/2015/09/29/are-you-distracted-by-your-phone/.

González, Pablo Alonso. 2018. "The Camino Is Alive: Minor Logics and Commodification in the Camino de Santiago." *Anthropological Quarterly* 91 (3): 969–999.

Goodwin, Robert. 2009. *Changing Relations: Achieving Intimacy in a Time of Social Transition*. New York: Cambridge University Press.

Greenia, George. 2018. "The Future Generations Ride of the Lakota Sioux." In *Pilgrimage in Practice: Narration, Reclamation and Healing*, edited by Ian S. McIntosh, E. Moore Quinn, and Vivienne Keely, 137–147. Boston: CAB International.

Havard, Megan E. 2018. "When Brother Becomes Other: Communitas and Conflict Along the Camino de Santiago." *International Journal of Religious Tourism and Pilgrimage* 6 (2): 89–97.

Hays, Sharon. 1996. *The Cultural Contradictions of Motherhood*. New Haven, CT: Yale University Press.

Heelas, Paul, and Linda Woodhead. 2005. *The Spiritual Revolution: Why Religion is Giving Way to Spirituality*. Malden, MA: Blackwell.

Hesp, Annie. 2018. "Indelible Memories: Peregrina Tattoos." Presentation at the 21st Annual National Gathering of American Pilgrims on the Camino.

Jacobs, Janet. 2016. *The Holocaust Across Generations: Trauma and Its Inheritance Among Descendants of Survivors*. New York: New York University Press.

Jenkins, Kathleen E., and Ken Chih-Yan Sun. 2019. "Digital Strategies for Building Spiritual Intimacy: Families on a 'Wired' Camino." *Qualitative Sociology* 42 (4): 567–585.

Kaell, Hillary. 2016. "Can Pilgrimage Fail? Intent, Efficacy, and Evangelical Trips to the Holy Land." *Journal of Contemporary Religion* 31 (3): 393–408.

Kerkeling, Hape. 2009. *Losing and Finding Myself on the Camino de Santiago*. New York: Free Press.

Kirkpatrick, Julie. 2010. *The Camino Letters: 26 Tasks on the Way to Finisterre*. Milbrook, ON: Pyxis Press.

Koss-Chioino, Joan D. . 2006. "Spiritual Transformation, Healing, and Altruism: Introduction to the Symposium." *Zgyon* 41 (4): 869–876.

Kurrat, Christian. 2019. "Biographical Motivations of Pilgrims on the Camino de Santiago." *International Journal of Religious Tourism and Pilgrimage* 7 (2): 11–18.

Kurrat, Christian, and Patrick Heiser. 2020. "'This Trip Is Very Meaningful to Me, So I Want to Remember It Forever': Pilgrim Tattoos in Santiago de Compostela." *International Journal of Religious Tourism and Pilgrimage*. 8 (5): 12–24.

Kusner, Katherine G., Annette Mahoney, Kenneth I. Pargament, and Alfred DeMaris. 2014. "Sanctification of Marriage and Spiritual Intimacy: Predicting Observed Marital Interactions Across the Transition to Parenthood." *Journal of Family Psychology* 28 (5): 604–614.

Lareau, Annette. 2003. *Unequal Childhoods: Class, Race, and Family Life*. Berkeley: University of California Press.

Lopez, Lucrezia, Yamilé Perez Guilarte, and Rubén Camilo Lois González. 2017. "The Way to the Western European Land's End: The Case of Finisterre (Galicia, Spain)." *Italian Journal of Planning Practice* 7 (1): 186–212.

Loveland, Matthew. 2008. "Pilgrimage, Religious Institutions, and the Construction of Orthodoxy." *Sociology of Religion* 69 (3): 317–334.

Lyon, David. 2000. *Jesus in Disneyland: Religion in Postmodern Times*. Malden, MA: Polity Press.

Mahoney, Annette. 2010. "Religion in Families, 1999–2009: A Relational Spirituality Framework." *Journal of Marriage and Family* 72 (4): 805–827.

Marly Camino. n.d. "The Best Camino de Santiago Tours." Accessed May 3, 2019. https://marlycamino.com.

Martyrs' Shrine. n.d. "Home." Accessed May 19, 2020. https://martyrs-shrine.com/pilgrim-route-to-martyrs-shrine/.

McIntosh, Ian S. 2017. "Pilgrimages and Peace-building on the Global Stage." In *The Many Voices of Pilgrimage and Reconciliation*, edited by Ian S. McIntosh and Lesley D. Harman. Boston: CAB International.

McIntosh, Ian. 2020. *Pilgrimage: Walking to Peace, Walking for Change*. N.p.: Xlibris.

McIntosh, Ian S., Nour Farra Haddad, and Dane Munro, eds. 2020. *Peace Journeys: A New Direction in Religious Tourism and Pilgrimage Research*. Newcastle upon Tyne: Cambridge Scholars Publishing.

McIntosh, Ian S., E. Moore Quinn, and Vivienne Keely, eds. 2018. *Pilgrimage in Practice: Narration, Reclamation and Healing*. Wallingford, CT: CABI Press. http://oficinadelperegrino.com/en/preparation/spiritual-preparation/.

Mendelsohn, Daniel. 2017. *An Odyssey: A Father, a Son and an Epic*. New York: Knopf.

Meyer, Brigit. 2011. "Meditation and Immediacy: Sensational Forms, Semiotic Ideologies and the Question of the Medium." *Social Anthropology* 19: 123–139.

Myerhoff, Barbara. 1982. "Rites of Passage: Process and Paradox." In *Celebration: Studies in Festivity and Ritual*, edited by Victor Turner, 109–135. Washington, DC: Smithsonian Institution Press.

National Park Service. n.d. "Office of Relevancy, Diversity, and Inclusion." Accessed April 26, 2019. https://www.nps.gov/orgs/1244/index.htm.

Nelson, Larry J. 2014. "The Role of Parents in the Religious and Spiritual Development of Emerging Adults." In *Emerging Adults' Religiousness and Spirituality: Meaning-making in an Age of Transition*, edited by C. M. Barry and M. M. Abo-Zena, 59–75. New York: Oxford University Press.

Nelson, Margaret. 2010. *Parenting out of Control: Anxious Parents in Uncertain Times.* New York: NYU Press.

Nickerson, Robert. "Mobile Technology and Smartphone Apps on the Camino de Santiago: The View from Beyond the U.S." Symposium on Pilgrimage Studies, William & Mary, October 16-18, 2015.

Ogden, Cristina. 2016. "Picturing the Camino in Pilgrimage Blogs." In *The Camino de Santiago in the 21st Century: Interdisciplinary Perspectives and Global Views*, edited by Samuel Sánchez y Sánchez and Annie Hesp, 81–89. New York: Routledge.

Olsen, Daniel H. 2011. "Towards a Religious View of Tourism: Negotiating Faith Perspectives on Tourism." *Journal of Tourism, Culture and Communication* 11 (1): 17–30.

Olsen, Daniel H. 2016. "Ritual Journeys in North America: Opening Religious and Ritual Landscapes and Spaces." *International Journal of Religious Tourism and Pilgrimage* 4 (1): 34–48.

Olsen, Daniel H. and Dallen Timothy. 2006. "Tourism and Religious Journeys." In *Tourism, Religion and Spiritual Journeys*, edited by Dallen Timothy and Daniel H. Olsen, 1–21. New York: Routledge.

Oviedo, Lluis, Scarlett de Courcier, and Miguel Farias. 2014. "Rise of Pilgrims on the Camino to Santiago: Sign of Change or Religious Revival." *Review of Religious Research* 56: 433–442.

Pilgrim's Office. n.d. "Pilgrims." Accessed September 15, 2018. https://oficinadelperegrino.com/en/pilgrimage/pilgrims/.

Pilgrim's Office. n.d. "Spiritual Preparation." Accessed March 25, 2020. https://oficinadelperegrino.com/en/preparation/spiritual-preparation/.

Pilgrim's Office. n.d. "Statistics." Accessed January 27, 2019. https://oficinadelperegrino.com/en/statistics/.

Polin Travel Guide and Geneaology. n.d. "Private Guiding and Genealogy Research Services in Central Europe. Auschwitz-Birkeneau, Cracow, Warsaw, and Holocaust Sites Expert Tours." Accessed March 25, 2020. http://www.jewish-guide.pl/.

Pugh, Allison, ed. 2017. *Beyond the Cubicle: Job Insecurity, Intimacy, and the Flexible Self.* New York: Oxford University Press.

Putnam, Robert D., and David E. Campbell. 2010. *American Grace: How Religion Divides and Unites Us.* New York: Simon and Schuster.

Reader, Ian. 2007. "Pilgrimage Growth in the Modern World: Meanings and Implications." *Religion* 37: 210–229.

Reader, Ian. 2014. *Pilgrimage in the Marketplace.* Abingdon, UK: Routledge Press.

Rice, Ronald E., and Caroline Haythornthwaite. 2010. "Perspectives on Internet Use: Access, Involvement and Interaction." In *Handbook of New Media: Social Shaping and Social Consequences of ICTs, Updated Student Edition*, edited by Leah A. Lievrouw and Sonia Livingstone, 92–113. London: Sage.

Richmond Slave Trail Commission. n.d. "Richmond Slave Trail." Accessed March 25, 2020. http://www.richmondgov.com/CommissionSlaveTrail/documents/brochureRichmondCityCouncilSlaveTrailCommission.pdf.

Ross-Bryant, Lynn. 2013. *Pilgrimage to the National Parks: Religion and Nature in the United States.* New York: Routledge.

Rutherford, Markella. 2011. "The Social Value of Self-Esteem." *Social Science and Public Policy* 48: 407–412.

Salmenniemi, Suvi. 2019. "Therapeutic Politics: Critique and Contestation in the Post-Political Conjecture." *Social Movement Studies* 18 (4): 408–424.

Sharma, Veena. 2020. "Building a More Sensitive World Through Religious Tourism." In *Peace Journeys: A New Direction in Religious Tourism and Pilgrimage Research*, edited by Ian S. McIntosh, Nour Farra Haddad, and Dane Munro, 176–191. Newcastle upon Tyne: Cambridge Scholars Publishing.

Shinde, Kiran A. 2011. "This Is Religious Environment: Sacred Space, Environmental Discourses, and Environmental Behavior at a Hindu Pilgrimage Site in India." *Space and Culture* 14 (4): 448–463.

Shore, Bradd 2009. "Making Time for Family: Schemas for Long-Term Family Memory." *Social Indicators Research* 93 (1): 95–103.

Sisler, Vit. 2011. "Cyber Counsellors: Online Fatwas, Arbitration Tribunals and the Construction of Muslim Identity in the UK." *Information, Communication and Society* 14 (8): 1136–1159.

Slessarev-Jamir, Helene. 2011. *Prophetic Activism: Progressive Religious Justice Movements in Contemporary America.* New York: NYU Press.

Smit, Ria. 2011. "Maintaining Family Memories Through Symbolic Action: Young Adults' Perceptions of Family Rituals in Their Families of Origin." *Journal of Comparative Family Studies* 42 (3): 355–367.

Smith, Christian, with Patricia Snell. 2009. *Souls in Transition: The Religious and Spiritual Lives of Emerging Adults.* New York: Oxford University Press.

Smith, Lydia B., Sally Bentley, Theresa Tollini-Coleman, Kyra Thompson and Jacoba "Coby" Atlas. 2014. *Walking the Camino: Six Ways to Santiago.* DVD. Directed by Lydia B. Smith. Newtown, PA: Virgil Films & Entertainment.

Stanczak, Gregory. 2006. *Engaged Spirituality: Social Change and American Religion.* New Brunswick, NJ: Rutgers University Press.

Stewart-Kroeker, Sara. 2017. *Pilgrimage as Moral and Aesthetic Formation in Augustine's Thought.* New York: Oxford University Press.

Streib, Heinz and Ralph W. Hood. 2013. "Modeling the Religious Field: Religion, Spirituality, Mysticism and Related World Views." *Implicit Religion* 16 (2): 137–155.

Taizé Community. n.d. "Community." Accessed March 25, 2020. https://www.taize.fr/en_rubrique8.html.

Taizé Community. n.d. "Home." Accessed September 25, 2019. http://www.taize.fr/en.

Talbot, Lynn. 2016. "Revival of the Medieval Past: Francisco Franco and the Camino de Santiago." In *The Camino de Santiago in the 21st Century: Interdisciplinary Perspectives and Global Views,* edited by Samuel Sánchez y Sánchez and Annie Hesp. 36–56. New York: Routledge.

Tell, Caroline. 2013. "Step Away from the Phone." *New York Times*, September 20, 2013. Accessed March 25, 2020. https://www.nytimes.com/2013/09/22/fashion/step-away-from-the-phone.html.

Terreault, Sara, and Matthew Anderson. 2015. "De Vieux-Montréal à Kahnawa:ké: The Story of an Urban Pilgrimage Between Settler and Aboriginal Cultures." *Room One Thousand* 3 (3). Accessed March 25, 2020. https://escholarship.org/uc/item/3j47g590.

Timmermans, Stefan, and Iddo Tavory. 2012. "Theory Construction in Qualitative Research: From Grounded Theory to Abductive Analysis." *Sociological Theory* (30) 3: 167–186.

Timothy, Dallen J., and Daniel H. Olsen. 2018. "Religious Routes, Pilgrim Trails: Spiritual Pathwaya as Tourism Resources." In *Tourism and Religion: Issues and Implications*, edited by Richard Butler and Wantanee Suntikul, 220–235. Blue Ridge Summit, PA: Channel View Publications.

Tolich, Martin. 2004. "Internal Confidentiality: When Confidentiality Assurances Fail Relational Informants." *Qualitative Sociology* 27 (1): 101–106.

Townshend, Nicholas. 2002. *The Package Deal: Marriage, Work, and Fatherhood in Men's Lives*. Philadelphia: Temple University Press.

Trombino, Gabriella and Anna Trono. 2018. "Environment and Sustainability as Related to Religious Pilgrimage Routes and Trails." In *Religious Pilgrimage Routes and Trails: Sustainable Development and Management*, edited by Daniel H. Olsen and Anna Trono, 49–61. Boston: CAB International.

Turner, Edith. 2012. *Communitas: The Anthropology of Collective Joy*. New York: Palgrave Macmillan.

Turner, Victor. 1969. *The Ritual Process: Structure and Anti-structure*. Ithaca, NY: Cornell University Press.

United States Civil Rights Trail. n.d. "Home." Accessed May 19, 2020. http://civilrightstrail.com.

University of Wisconsin–Eau Claire. n.d. "Civil Rights Pilgrimage." Accessed March 25, 2020. https://www.uwec.edu/diversity/civil-rights-pilgrimage/.

Vaidyanathan, Brandon, Khalsa Simranjit, and Elaine H. Ecklund. 2018. "Naturally Ambivalent: Religion's Role in Shaping Environmental Action." *Sociology of Religion* 79 (4): 472–494.

Van Hove, Hildegard. 1999. "The Emergence of a 'Spiritual Market.'" *Social Compass* 46 (2): 161–172.

Virginia Museum of Fine Arts. 2020. "Sculpture Created by Kehinde Wiley for VMFA." https://www.vmfa.museum/about/rumors-of-war/. Accessed May 27, 2020.

Walker, Bill. 2011. *The Best Way: El Camino de Santiago*. N.p.: CreateSpace Independent Publishing Platform.

Walking to Presence. n.d. "Home." Accessed March 25, 2020. https://www.walkingtopresence.com/home/.

Warner, R. Stephen. 1993. "Work in Progress Toward a New Paradigm for the Sociological Study of Religion in the United States." *American Journal of Sociology* 98 (5): 1044–1093.

Winchester, Simon. 1994. "The Long, Sweet Road to Santiago de Compostela." *Smithsonian* 24 (11): 64–75.

Wright State University: Diversity and Inclusion. n.d. "Civil Rights Pilgrimage: The Children's Crusade and the Civil Rights Movement: Living the Dream, Ensuring the Legacy." Accessed March 25, 2020. https://www.wright.edu/diversity-and-inclusion/culture-and-identity-centers/bolinga-black-cultural-resources-center/civil-rights-pilgrimage.

Yamane, David. 2000. "Narrative and Religious Experience." *Sociology of Religion* 61 (2): 171–189.

Index

For the benefit of digital users, indexed terms that span two pages (e.g., 52–53) may, on occasion, appear on only one of those pages.